W9-CNU-089

# From Caesar to the Mafia

*By the same Author*
THE ITALIANS

# LUIGI BARZINI

# From Caesar
# to the Mafia

*SKETCHES OF ITALIAN LIFE*

HAMISH HAMILTON
LONDON

*First published in Great Britain*
*by Hamish Hamilton Ltd 1971*
*90 Great Russell Street London WC1*

© 1971 by Luigi Barzini
All rights reserved. No part of this publication may be reproduced, stored in a
retrieval system, or transmitted, in any
form or by any means, electronic, mechanical, photocopying, recording or otherwise, without prior permission of the
Copyright owner.

SBN 241 01946 X

*"Dangerous Acquaintances"* (*ch. 5*), *"A Founding
Father"* (*ch. 7*) and *"The Society of Friends"* (*ch. 21*),
*reprinted with permission from* The New York Review
of Books, *copyright © 1969, 1967, 1966 The New York
Review; "Grand Hotel Montecitorio"* (*ch. 17*) *reprinted
with permission from* Atlas Magazine (*December 1963*),
*translated from* L'Europeo, Milan; *"The Fine Italian
Hand"* (*ch. 16*) *reprinted by permission from* Lithopinion
#15, *the graphic arts and public affairs journal, Local 1,
Amalgamated Lithographers of America, New York,
N.Y.; "Curzio Malaparte"* (*ch. 4*), *"The Italian Aristocrats"* (*ch. 6*), *"On the Isle of Capri"* (*ch. 10*), *"Letter
from Italy"* (*ch. 18*), *"On the Locomotive"* (*ch. 19*) and
*"The Anatomy of Expertise"* (*ch. 20*) *reprinted with
permission from* Encounter, *copyright © 1960, 1956,
1959, 1970, 1969 and 1968 by Encounter Ltd.*

*Printed in Great Britain by*
*W. & J. Mackay & Co Ltd, Chatham*

TO PAOLA

# CONTENTS

# ACKNOWLEDGMENTS

Much of the material in this book (roughly a half) has not been previously published in English. Some of it I have written, as was the case in my previous book on *The Italians*, directly in English; some of it I have translated from the Italian, and for the assembling and preparation of these articles and manuscripts for publication I am grateful for the help of Miss Isabel Quigly. I also gratefully acknowledge the permission of the editors of the following journals to re-publish material which originally appeared, in somewhat altered form, in their pages: *Life* (ch. 1, now much expanded and re-written); *New York Review of Books* (chs. 5, 7, 21); *Lithopinion* (ch. 16); *Atlas* (ch. 17); and *Encounter* (chs. 4, 6, 10, 18, 19, 20).                L.B.

*Part One*

# PERSONS

# JULIUS CAESAR

<hr>

T HE IDEA that there was something contradictory, inexplicable, and elusive about Gaius Julius Caesar's
behavior on the last morning of his life haunts us still as it
haunted his contemporaries. Surely the most powerful and
feared man in Rome had been fully informed of the conspirators' plans to kill him. We know the secret had not been kept and
many people were aware that something was afoot. Why then
had he gone to the Senate meeting? Why did he expose himself
so recklessly? Had he gone because he had wanted to die that
day? Did the Republic, to which he had given so many victories,
owe him this last benefit too, his own death, the death of the
tyrant who had extinguished the ancient liberties? Had he tried
to rob the conspirators of their glory?

And, if his secret decision was to die, how had he come to it?
Like many others in Rome at the time, he knew that all problems were tied up in one inextricable knot; there was no solution,
peace was maintained only by the threat of his invincible armies
camping outside the walls, and pressure was mounting daily.
"He could not see a way out," Cicero wrote after his death,
"and if a man of his intelligence could not see a way out, who
could?" Disenchanted and embittered, was Caesar also too
tired to fend off his own death when it seemed inevitable—even
necessary? "Some of his friends", Suetonius relates, "suspected
that, having no wish to live longer, he had not desired to take
any precautions."

Surely no murder in history was more clearly and more in-
sistently predicted by supernatural and natural signs. No murder
of a great man could have been more easily prevented. The

presages were so many and so evident that Plutarch, listing some of them, felt insecure without the backing of an authoritative contemporary witness: he quoted Strabo. The Greek Strabo was an 11-year-old schoolboy in Rome when Caesar died; presumably what details he related in his *History* (which has been lost) he had seen with his own eyes or learned first-hand and were indelibly etched in his memory like all dramatic events in children's lives. These are some of them: "On the day preceding the death of Caesar, men were seen looking as if they were heated through by fire, contending with each other; a quantity of flames issued from the hands of a soldier's servant, so that who saw it thought he must be burned . . ." Plutarch, who knew that similar prodigies had also appeared in the past to warn the public at large of indeterminate catastrophes, advised the reader to ignore most of them. "As to the lights in heaven," he says warily, "the noises in the night, and the wild birds perched in the Forum, these are perhaps not worth noticing . . ." Only the omens clearly concerning one man, Caesar, and pointing to one possible event, his death, were to be considered.

The meaning of some was unmistakable. A few months before, the veterans who had been sent to settle on land near Capua were breaking up ancient tombs to gather stones to build their farmhouses. One tomb turned out to be that of Capys, the legendary founder of the city, and there the men found a bronze tablet with a Greek inscription to this effect: "Disturb the tomb of Capys and a man of Trojan stock will be murdered by his kindred, and later avenged at great cost to Italy." (Caesar believed he was the descendant of Aeneas, the fugitive Trojan prince who found refuge in Italy.) A few days before his death, news reached him about a herd of horses which he had freed, after fording the river Rubicon—they were beginning to show a repugnance for the pasture and were shedding bucketsful of tears. On the very day before the Ides of March a little bird called a "king wren" flew into the hall of Pompey's theater (which the Senate used at the time for their meeting) with a sprig of laurel in its beak. Pursued by a swarm of hostile different birds it was torn to pieces there and then.

All these signs were obviously aimed at Caesar, as direct as arrows from a bow. The veterans looking for stones were his own soldiers; they wanted to build farmhouses on land granted to them by the "Julian Law", the law he himself had proposed to reward them. The weeping horses were his own, sacred to the fateful river he had to cross to start the civil war. The bird had been killed where the Senate met and not anywhere else, and was called "king".

Other omens were, if possible, even more personal and specific. When Caesar was at a sacrifice a few days before his death, the animal's heart could not be found. The night before his death, as he was in bed with his wife, all the doors and windows of the house suddenly flew open at once. He was startled at the noise and the light that broke into the room; he sat up in his bed; by the moonlight he saw Calpurnia asleep, and heard her utter indistinct words and inarticulate groans. She had dreamed she was weeping over Caesar, holding his body, harried with wounds, in her arms. Suetonius adds this most explicit omen of all: "During a sacrifice, the augur Spurinna warned him that the danger threatening him would not pass until the Ides of March. 'Beware of the Ides of March!' he said. . . ."

\*     \*     \*

IT IS IMPORTANT to describe these portents, obviously not because we believe that future events can be read in the entrails of slaughtered animals, lights in the sky, or nightmares, but because such omens were considered at the time clear and awe-inspiring warnings which the bravest man could not easily bring himself to disregard. That Caesar himself knew what they meant is suggested by something he said the night before his murder. He was dining at the camp of Marcus Aemilius Lepidus, outside Rome, where an army was being outfitted and trained for an expedition. He signed a few letters, reclined on his triclinium, and chatted with his old comrades during the long meal. Somebody asked idly what kind of death was the best. Before anyone else could speak, as if the thought had been in his mind for days, Caesar said: "A sudden one."

He was certainly also warned of his fate by more down-to-earth means. Like all dictators, he too had a network of spies in important households and government offices in Rome and the provinces. He too must have received anonymous letters and informers' tips. (Anonymous letters have always been a curse of Roman life: even today they descend like autumn leaves on the desk of every high official.) An ordinary tip was probably concealed in Spurinna's words, "Beware of the Ides of March!" Information had surely come from at least one of the many conspirators: how irresistible must have been, for the weakest of them, the temptation to assure himself a future of immense power and wealth by betraying his friends and saving the life of Caesar! Surely slaves had noticed and gossiped about their masters' mysterious meetings in strange places at night, the masked-ball disguises they wore, the preposterous orders they gave to ensure secrecy. Wives probably complained about the behavior of their husbands, so similar to their behavior when falling in love with other women, their abrupt replies to civil questions, the anxious expression always on their pale faces.

We know that there were leaks. Only minutes before the assassination, one senator, Popilius Laenas, approached Brutus and Cassius and said: "My wishes are with you, that you may accomplish what you design, and I advise you to make no delay, for the thing is now no secret . . ." We also know that one man who had learned about the plot tried to warn Caesar at the last moment. He was the Greek scholar Artemidorous, a former tutor of Brutus who had remained his friend; he was also an old acquaintance of Caesar who had met him in Greece many years before. He reached the dictator's house just as the litter started, ran after it and caught up with it in front of Pompey's theater. He gave Caesar a written message, containing the list of conspirators and their plans, and besought him to read it immediately, for it was a matter of life and death. Caesar had no time to open it. Petitioners were crowding around him, giving him written requests, and these he did not read either and handed them to his followers.

*       *       *

NEVERTHELESS, Caesar disregarded everything: the supernatural omens, the prophecies, the informers' tips, his wife's entreaties, his own premonitions. He did even more. He walked alone into the meeting, having dismissed the armed Spanish bodyguard who usually escorted him, as if he had taken at its face value the Senators' recent oath of loyalty and granted their request henceforth to entrust his safety to them when in their midst. This he did on a morning when gladiatorial contests were scheduled in Pompey's theater, and the place was teeming with unknown armed ruffians. He carried no weapons. He did not keep a short poignard (or *pugio*) concealed under the elegant folds of his crimson bordered toga, as he had often done; did not even wear a breastplate or a coat of mail, as the conspirators immediately discovered when they pressed close to him, before striking.

And yet he knew (even if he had known nothing more) that he was walking into a partly hostile assembly, to be surrounded by men who had fought valiantly against him in open battles during the Civil War and had been forgiven. Some he had even elevated to the highest positions: Brutus became governor of Gaul and Cassius one of his legates. Caesar was too wise not to know that, if forgiveness makes of many defeated opponents irreconcilable enemies, magnanimity and generosity make some of them ruthless and full of hatred. Can there be any doubt, then, when all this is considered, that Caesar contributed to his own death, and even collaborated with his murderers? Without his help they would not have succeeded.

He might, to be sure, have been unaware of doing so. He was never the kind of man who would be awed by omens or prophecies. "No regard for religion," Suetonius wrote, "ever turned him from any undertaking." Once, in Africa, he had even made irreverent use of a hallowed prediction. He was facing the remnants of Pompey's army commanded by Metellus Scipio, and (according to Plutarch) "was informed that his enemies relied much upon an ancient oracle, that the family of the Scipios should always be victorious in Africa. There was in his army a man, otherwise mean and contemptible but of the house of

Africanus, and his name was Scipio Sallutio. This man Caesar put at the head of his troops as if he were the general." Caesar won, of course.

He had been too much pursued by bad omens all his life to pay much attention to them. Not many months before, as he was riding through the Velabrum on the day of his Gallic triumph, one of the four he celebrated after he had become the sole master of the Roman world, the axle of his chariot broke and he was almost flung out. He calmly straightened the crown on his head, rearranged his clothes, and went on with the show. The very last omens of his life, drawn from the innards of the chickens sacrificed on the very steps of Pompey's theater a few minutes before his death, were appalling. Yet they did not stop him from walking on.

\*     \*     \*

WE KNOW, on the other hand, that he had habitually disregarded warnings, friends' pleas and informers' tips many times in the past. He had a low opinion of ordinary men's fortitude and determination to undertake dangerous projects. He often said he doubted there was anybody in Rome great enough to kill Caesar. It was not only a practically impossible undertaking— and a sacrilegious one, now that he had been proclaimed Divus Julius, a god among the gods—but also, above all, a pointless one. Who would gain by his death? He had come to think of himself as an immovable pivot of the world's equilibrium, the keystone without which everything would crumble, an indispensable tool of history.

This delusion sometimes overtakes old and tired leaders who mingle with dangerous crowds, shake off their escorts, and announce their itineraries beforehand, as if everybody was as aware as they were that their death would solve no problem but only create new ones. A few days before the Ides of March Caesar had said disdainfully: "It is more important for Rome than for myself that I should survive. I have long been sated with power and glory. But should anything happen to me, Rome will enjoy no peace. A new civil war will break out under far worse conditions than the last . . ." He, of course, should have known that some men at least, irresponsible fools or great heroes, start civil wars lightly and plunge the world into chaos without knowing how it will end or who will win. Had he himself not done just that only a few years before?

Perhaps it was simply impossible for Caesar not to take risks. He had never lived prudently, even as a disreputable debt-ridden young playboy dabbling in rabble-rousing oratory and dubious politics, sleeping with the bored wives of powerful men. His nature irresistibly drove him to face the greatest dangers. They attracted him like a magnet. In his military campaigns, he rarely played for safety except when he faced an inferior and weaker enemy: he did not want to waste his own men's lives to achieve a practically certain victory. But when he found himself on unfavorable ground—with a small army worn out by marches, without supplies and far from their base, facing a superior, confident and well-entrenched enemy—he had always attacked. He attacked also because, at such times, the enemy least expected him to do so. "He joined battle," Suetonius records, "not only after planning his movements but on a sudden opportunity as well, often immediately at the end of a march, and sometimes in the foulest weather, when one would least imagine him to make a move."

He surely did so the day he crossed the Rubicon, his biggest gamble. On one side of the river he was a loyal and victorious general in command of legions whose mission was to pacify the Gauls. On the other side, he formally became a rebel, at the head of a seditious army which had to be destroyed by the forces of law and order. People who knew him well, as Pompey did (and Pompey was the general facing him, commander-in-chief of the armed forces of the Republic, his son-in-law and his partner for years), were certain that he could not resist the temptation to cross the river but thought he would have to wait at Ravenna for the arrival of his full army. With only one legion at hand Caesar spurred his horse over the little bridge, explaining: "If I do not cross this river my holding back will be the source of my misfortunes. If I cross it, it will bring misfortunes to the whole of the human race. The die is cast . . ." He was not a man who would prefer his own to the world's ruin.

A few months later, trying to pursue Pompey and his army across the Adriatic Sea, he arrived in Brindisi with a handful of men. Even as a youth he loved to rush ahead practically alone at great speed, without stopping for rest and food; he was pleased to be able to arrive somewhere even before the news of his departure from Rome had gotten through. His army would not be in Brindisi for days or weeks. The winter weather was forbidding, the sea was rough, he had few ships and no supplies. He said to his staff: "I consider rapidity of movement the best substitute for all the things I want . . . The most potent thing in war is the unexpected." And so he crossed the Adriatic.

Above all he believed in himself. He believed that his very presence would dominate men's wills, still passions, and deflect history. He had fully employed his mesmeric charm in both politics and war, and he owed his rise largely to it. Centuries before Clausewitz, Caesar had understood that politics and war were closely connected—almost inseparable—and governed roughly by the same rules. He could arouse or persuade the common people of Rome, the senators, enemy sovereigns, or his legionaries at will, with a well-studied and ornate speech, a few angry sentences, or his silent presence. He once quelled a mutiny of his best men, the veterans of the Tenth Legion, with a single word. He addressed them contemptuously as "Citizens". "We are your soldiers, Caesar," they shouted, "not citizens." And, being his soldiers, they suddenly realized they had to obey him.

He also overawed men who did not know who he was, and this even before he had become great and famous. Once, in his youth, while on his way to Rhodes to study literature and oratory, he was captured by pirates. He treated them disdainfully as his servants; when he wanted to sleep he sent orders to them to keep quiet; and for the best part of six weeks joined in their games, practiced his rhetoric on them, called them illiterate barbarians to their faces, and in raillery threatened to have them crucified. Somehow sensing the leader in him, they admired and obeyed him meekly. Six weeks later, when his ransom arrived and he was freed, he hired several galleys, returned to surprise the pirates in their lair, and crucified the lot as he had promised.

Men were eager to die for him for no other apparent reason than that he was he. "Those who in ordinary expeditions were but ordinary men displayed a courage past defeating . . . where Caesar's glory was concerned," wrote Plutarch, who goes on to cite examples of his gift to inspire in others an unnatural contempt for life. "One time in Africa, Scipio, having taken a ship of Caesar's in which Granius Petro, lately appointed quaestor, was sailing, gave the other passengers as free prizes to his soldiers, but thought fit to offer the quaestor his life. Granius Petro said it was not for Caesar's soldiers to take but give mercy, and, having said so, fell upon his sword and killed himself."

Many times, in one of those desperately uneven battles in which Caesar liked to stake his luck, he saved the day by rushing where his men were being beaten back. During one of his early campaigns in Gaul, his troops were surprised, while they were busy building trenches, by an overwhelming army of Nervii. Caesar says in his *Commentaries* that "he himself had everything to do at one moment": raise the red battle-ensign, sound the alarm, bring in the men who were digging trenches and felling timber, and give orders. He then rushed over to the Twelfth Legion, which was being massacred and was falling back in disorder. He seized a shield from one of the soldiers in the rear ranks, pushed his way to the front, called upon the centurions by name, then sounded the charge. The mere gesture revived his men and made them surge forward. At the end of the day the Nervii were hacked to pieces. "This engagement," Caesar drily noted in his memoirs, "brought the name and nation of the Nervii almost to utter destruction."

Caesar's presence had saved the last battle he ever fought, near Munda, in 45 B.C. in Spain, against Pompey's son Gnaeus. Caesar's men were frightened and had started to run away. When he saw the confusion and panic in their ranks, he felt helpless for the first time in his life and cried out against Fortune "who had reserved him so unworthy an end". "The thought of death could be read in his face," writes Florus. He was so desperate he even tried to appeal to the gods: he raised his hands to heaven and implored them "not to make him lose the fruits of so many victories in one single battle." Then he rallied. He sent away his horse, dropped his shield, removed his helmet and sword which hindered him, and ran "like a madman" to the front line, where he insulted, exhorted and threatened his men.

As this did not check their panic, he once again seized a shield from a soldier, and, running forward, cried: "It is here that I am going to die, killed by the enemy, and that you see the end of your military service . . ." (Defeated soldiers could scarcely enjoy slaves and estates in their retirement.) "With these words," Appian relates, "he dashed from the ranks and advanced toward the enemy until he was no more than ten feet away. A hailstorm of two hundred arrows descended upon him; some passed without touching him, his shield protected him from the others. Then each of the tribunes came running towards him and fought at his side. This movement led the entire army to turn with vehemence against the enemy."

The fighting ended in the evening. "Never had Caesar waged a more bloody and more perilous battle," says Velleius Paterculus. As he entered his tent he told his men: "I have often fought for victory, but today, for the first time, I have fought for my life."

\*            \*            \*

IN TROUBLED TIMES, things look infinitely simple to young men in a hurry at the bottom of the ladder. The problem of reaching the next rung and the rung after that absorbs them almost completely. Their preference in political abstractions (if they think about them at all) is for the most drastic and radical; whether of the right or the left matters little as long as they promise to get them to the top fast enough. They have a natural liking for revolution: there is nothing like a revolution to liberate the top echelons quickly and thoroughly. At 16 years of age, Julius Caesar, the penniless patrician, was just the type: ambitious, impatient, immensely gifted, proud, restless, dissolute and angry—as angry as the sons of an hereditary élite can be who grow up to see themselves dispossessed by *nouveaux riches* with crass, cynical and dull ideas.

Power in Rome clearly no longer depended on birth, a respected name, a well-ramified family, as it had done when the Republic was small, virtuous, and poor. Power now came from wealth. Well-managed wealth gave a man friends, allies, *dignitas* (which meant status, prestige and honor); it could give him power to increase his wealth and, thus, to acquire more power. Ordinarily only men of noble birth sat in the Senate, but, without wealth and power of their own, they had become bit players without importance. A man with wealth and power no longer needed to sit in the Senate: he got others to do that for him. If power came from wealth, wealth itself (when not inherited) had to come from power. And the wealthiest, most powerful men in Rome were the generals. A commander-in-chief at the head of loyal legions could always threaten the Senate with civil war. Plunder and army contracts enriched many people, but Rome's commanders most of all.

This was a relatively recent development, and the cause of many of Rome's misfortunes. In the old days, when wars had been simple and short, fought not far from home against primitive tribes or effete Greek colonies, temporary armies were formed by Roman citizens, mostly farmers in the infantry and a few richer men in the cavalry. These men fought hard to defeat the enemy as quickly as possible and to get back to their fields and plows. Political responsibility was in the hands of the Senate, as it had always been. After the Punic wars, when vast domains across the seas were conquered—Africa, Sicily, Sardinia, and Spain—waging wars became the most profitable industry of Rome. Tributes, plunder and the sale of slaves enriched the treasury, the army commanders, and the soldiers; contracts enriched a new business class. The soldiers, however, had to fight far from home and for indefinite periods, sometimes for many years. Obviously, the Latin farmers were no longer suited for these campaigns. Who could take their place?

It was Marius, the plebeian dictator and leader of the popular

party (and the husband of Caesar's aunt) who solved the problem.
For the first time, he made use of volunteer professional soldiers,
men belonging to all classes, landless city rabble, dispossessed
farmers, freed slaves, foreigners who enrolled only for the hope of
getting rich. Naturally these men preferred long wars against
affluent and defenseless enemies and, as soon as one war had
ended, they enrolled for the next one. Their loyalty no longer
went to the Republic but to their paymaster whose fortune was
their fortune. Political power gradually passed to the generals in
the fields, and it was they who became the protagonists of life
in Rome: they had the wealth, the power, the legions to threaten
the Senate. When two or more of them were simultaneously in
the field, civil war was an irresistible temptation and indeed
became endemic.

How could a relatively obscure young man become a general?
It took time, luck and pertinacity. He had to climb the political
ladder, one election after another, to always more important
posts, without ever making a mistake. Finally, if everything
went well, the people would elect him consul and the Senate
would give him a key province to govern and the command of
the legions garrisoned there. But to win even minor offices, a
man needed both a large popular backing and plenty of money
with which to campaign and to bribe the electorate. The two
things went together. A strong popular backing brought in the
money: but money was needed in the first place to win popular
backing. As in other lands and other times, in Rome during the
last years of the Republic, it took wealth to amass wealth, money
went where money was, and the first hundred million sesterces
were the hardest to make. This was the vicious circle that young
Caesar, without wealth or power, had to break. It was a formidable obstacle.

He developed a plan (or perhaps his homing instinct took him
in the right direction). First, a short spell of military service
(every man had to have a grounding of that, just in case, in a
State in which generals were chosen among the leading politicians) and it was easier to learn the first elements in subordinate
positions when one was young. Then he concentrated on the

study of jurisprudence and Greek rhetoric. Caesar's native capacity to talk convincingly and his incredibly persuasive presence were his best assets. He later became one of the best orators of his age. He could charm his most obstinate opponents with words. Cicero, no mean judge, wrote: "He is the master of an eloquence which is brilliant and without a suggestion of routine ... Which orator is more pointed and terse in his periods, or employs more polished and elegant language?" He was also a witty private conversationalist: "His talk showed good taste and exquisite savor," Cicero noted after he had entertained Caesar at dinner, three months before the Ides of March.

Rhetoric, young Caesar rightly assumed, was an inexpensive way to acquire a reputation in the Forum, an initial popular following, and to make a few important people notice him as a promising young man. Friends, he reckoned, would help him get elected to the lower and easier posts. With the money he could make or borrow and the more important friends he could gather, he would then climb on, a rung at a time. How high depended on the help of Venus (the goddess of love who was one of his "ancestors"), depended on luck and on himself.

Caesar was also physically well suited for such a career. He was tall—tall, that is, for a Roman of his day. He had black, piercing eyes, and an ironic expression hovering over his face. He was subject to fits of epilepsy, but otherwise enjoyed excellent health and an abnormal capacity to endure hardships. He was an excellent swimmer and a fine horseman, he could travel at great speed, like a courier, work or fight day and night without rest. In his mature age he used to dictate literary works and military reports to two or three secretaries simultaneously. He was always extremely elegant, although he had the slovenly habit of keeping his belt loosely tied, an affectation which was later copied by everybody. To disguise his premature baldness, he combed his hair forward and, in later years, frequently wore a laurel wreath. His gallantries were notorious. He started early in his youth sleeping with the wives of some of the most important gentlemen in Rome and the famous beauties of his time. Rumor whispered that he often also slept with their husbands as well. As with many ambitious men, beds were stepping-stones in his career.

Caesar did not have to choose political sides: although an aristocrat, he was born a member of the proletarian party. He was 14 when his uncle-in-law Marius triumphed over the patricians' party, conquered Rome for a time, and had the leading men in the Senate massacred by his soldiers. Caesar was 16 when Marius died in 86 B.C.; 20 when Sulla, the champion of the conservatives, defeated the *populares*, and proceeded to slaughter all his opponents. Caesar had to flee. A party of Sulla's soldiers found his refuge in the Samnium, but he saved his life by promptly bribing their commander. There were no other serious attempts to persecute him: he was, it was said, too dissolute and wild to be taken seriously. And by heritage at least, he had many aristocratic relatives among the winners.

He thought it prudent nevertheless to go to the farthest war he could find and start his training. In 81 B.C. he was in Asia, on the staff of the praetor Minucius Thermus, where he distinguished himself in various ways. He was given an award for bravery and entrusted with delicate diplomatic tasks at the court of the King of Bythinia. "There," says Suetonius, "he wasted so much time that a homosexual relationship between him and the King was suspected." Perhaps he was shrewdly using the royal bed as a conference table. He later campaigned in Cilicia with another army, all the while keeping carefully away from Rome.

When news of Sulla's death reached him, he gave up soldiering for a time and proceeded to the next stage in the education of the future "conqueror of the world". He went to school in Rhodes, studying literature, philosophy, and the arts of persuasive eloquence under the most famous master of his days, Apollonius Molon, who had also taught Cicero. He tried his new abilities as soon as he returned to Rome, dabbling for a time in law practice. For one of his first legal cases, he chose a powerful opponent, a former consul, Dolabella, and prosecuted him for extortion while in power. He lost the case, but obviously Caesar was more interested in notoriety than in justice or righteousness. Dolabella, he should have known, was too big to be convicted. But the young lawyer's eloquence won many admirers; people talked about him, and he began to gather a small following.

To make friends he kept an open house and (according to Plutarch) "the general splendor of his life increased his political influence." His opponents did not suspect his aims. They thought he was one more frivolous young man who frittered away ill-gotten gains on entertainment, and that his growing influence would vanish when his credit gave out. Only Cicero, a provincial who had made good in Rome and knew how hard it was, detected in him the first signs of an unquenchable thirst for absolute power. "But," he said, "when I see his hair so carefully arranged, and observe him adjusting it with one finger, I cannot imagine it should enter into such a man's head to subvert the Roman state."

The borrowed money soon did give out and Caesar quickly plunged into further debts which soon reached such an unheard of magnitude that his creditors, men of considerable power, began to worry. Caesar must have figured that some of them would be obliged to help him get an army command in hopes of being paid back. This, of course, was his great gamble—the way he had devised to break the vicious circle.

"Even before he had any public employment", Plutarch explains, "he was in debt thirteen hundred talents, and many thought that by incurring such expense to be popular he changed a solid good for what would prove but a short and uncertain return; but in truth he was purchasing what was of the greatest value at an inconsiderable price. When he was *aedile* he spent great sums out of his private purse; he provided such a number of gladiators that he entertained the people with 300 single combats, besides offering theatrical shows, processions, public feastings . . . Everyone was eager to find new offices and new honors for him in return for his munificence."

He ran for election to minor positions, climbing steadily. In 61 B.C., fourteen years after his return from Rhodes, when his debts were on the point of overwhelming him, he managed to reach his first substantial and profitable post: he was appointed *praetor* in charge of quelling rebellious Spanish tribes. This was the chance he had been working for. At the last minute an apparently insurmountable obstacle threatened to prevent his voyage and defeat his plans to find power and wealth in Spain. Some of his creditors insisted he pay a large part of the money owed them before he left, and had his baggage, carriages, and horses seized. His great gamble looked like a failure. He could not get to Spain if he did not pay his debts; he could not pay his debts (and prepare himself to conquer greater power) unless he went to Spain.

Caesar turned to the only man who could save him—Crassus. Crassus was the richest man in Rome, known as "*Dives*", The Wealth, and, like many very rich men in times of anarchy and chaos, was almost paralyzed with fear. He was so nervous he had been playing every side, "being", as Plutarch deplores, "neither a trusted friend nor an implacable enemy, and he easily abandoned both his attachments and his animosities, so that in a short space of time the same men and the same measures had him both as their supporter and their opponent . . ." Crassus knew that the men then in power (an oligarchy of conservative patricians feebly controlling the Senate) could have been overturned by almost anybody with enough strength and determination.

What would happen, for instance, when the great Pompey—the most glorious general of his time, with his huge seasoned army, immense fleet, and all the treasures of the East he had plundered—came back from war? Crassus knew: his own father and brother had been killed for opposing Marius, although they had not been his active or outspoken opponents. Rich men, even those who paid no attention to politics or who were on both sides of every dispute, somehow had a much better chance of being murdered than anybody else, and of having their property seized and distributed among the winners. Crassus knew he needed as many strong friends as he could find: ruthless, ambitious, clever, bold men, possibly in need of money but with a strong popular backing. Caesar was everything Crassus could wish for.

So Crassus paid off most of Caesar's debts and pledged himself to finance the rest of the expedition. On Caesar's arrival in Spain "he took money from the proconsul who was his predecessor . . . and from the Roman allies, for the discharge of his debt" (according to Suetonius) and proceeded to subdue the Lusitanians and the Calaici in a quick campaign. "Advancing as far as the Ocean he conquered new tribes which had never been subject to the Romans," Suetonius continues, and which, therefore, had never been thoroughly plundered before. Caesar sent some of the booty home to the Roman treasury, distributed more than a fair share among his soldiers, and, for the first time in his life, became a wealthy man. He was finally ready to try for bigger stakes.

*        *        *

THE SITUATION in Rome in 60 B.C. was extremely precarious. The conservative oligarchy had been in command since the death of Sulla. Sporadic revolts and uprisings showed the angry mood of the people. The *populares*, after Marius' defeat, were broken, disheartened, impotent. Caesar was sympathetic—it was the party of his youth—but there was little he could do immediately. He encouraged popular agitations, whenever possible, even tried his hand at promoting a revolution (on a trip back from Spain, the uprising of the Transpadanes demanding full political rights), but with only modest results. He played a careful game. Democratic enough to be considered the moral head of the *populares*, their champion, he fanned the people's discontent with his speeches, whenever it looked convenient and safe. He was a demagogue just sufficiently to alarm the oligarchy and to force them to try to win his favor, but not enough to provoke their fear and serious enmity.

Once again time was ripe for a great leader, with the means and the will to reach for supreme power, as Marius and Sulla had in their days. But who? There was no single obvious leader. There were three men, each one of whom could have tried it:

Crassus, Pompey, and Caesar. Crassus had his immense wealth, the backing of a large section of the population and of a fair share of the Senate, and could easily find military commanders who would lease him their legions for a price. Pompey was the great military conqueror, who had destroyed the pirates infesting the Mediterranean, had defeated Mithridates, and had amassed money and men. There was enmity between the two leaders which might have broken out into a new civil war at any time.

Caesar was clearly the weakest of the three: he had neither the money of one nor the armies of the other. What should he do? The obvious course was to encourage the enmity between Crassus and Pompey, play his hand very prudently, and hope to come out as sole survivor of the struggle. When one of them seemed to be winning, he could rush to his aid. But it was a risky plan. Would the winner tolerate a minor rival for long? Would he not destroy Caesar, too, in the end?

Caesar's final decision shows the magnitude of his versatile political genius. It took immense diplomatic ability and exceptional persuasive power. It would have probably been impossible to any other man. Afterwards, the main developments of his whole life inevitably fell into place, one after another, as predictably as the moves of a chess game played by a champion after the opening gambit. He simply convinced Pompey and Crassus to make peace and secretly join with him in a partnership to dominate Rome. What each one of them could not hope to achieve without an exhausting and hazardous war, the three of them could do overnight by merely sealing a pact.

"Everybody was astounded," wrote Guglielmo Ferrero, the Italian historian who is recognized as an authority on this period. "The rivalry between Crassus and Pompey had been the principal reason why the reactionary clique had preserved power for so long; it was such an old rivalry that everybody considered it permanent. Then, overnight, as if by magic, the two enemies were seen to agree and to join forces with the very popular leader of the Roman populace . . . It was obvious that the alliance of the three men could dispose of the people's assemblies, all public officers, the banks; they were, as the Americans would say, the bosses of an all-powerful political machine. From then on it would be impossible to obtain a post, a command, or a loan without their consent. The majority of Senators without party, who always sided with the strongest, tumultuously deserted the little faction of intransigent conservatives which had held power until then; and, if they did not immediately pay obeisance to the three, they certainly avoided coming into open conflict with them."

With the help of his partners, Caesar in 59 B.C. easily became consul and, within a year, governor of the two Gauls (Northern Italy and France). His military achievements are too famous to be recounted here. He spent ten years in Gaul (always coming back to North Italy, but not to Rome, to mend political fences and direct the work of his agents in the city). He consolidated the Roman domination, pacified the inhabitants simply by killing one million of them out of a total of three, defended the Rhine frontier against the encroaching Germans, and made two expeditions into Britain. Meantime, he amassed one of the greatest fortunes of his times, possibly larger than that of Crassus, acquired unsurpassed military experience and became one of the most successful generals of all ages, with a brilliant and tested staff of officers and a number of practically invincible legions, all loyal to him to the death.

He also collected statues, mosaics, paintings, cameos, engraved precious stones, rare jewels (the invasion of Britain was prompted also by the hope of finding fresh-water pearls which he loved). He bought the most expensive slaves, the best specialists in all fields; entertained imperially (one dining room in camp was reserved for his officers and Greek friends, another for mere Roman citizens and provincials). He himself ate and drank little. (Cato said of him: "He is the only sober man who tried to wreck the Constitution.") He spent fortunes for his household but kept a strict account of every penny and condemned to death negligent or wasteful servants.

He dressed like a dandy. His affairs with women continued

being described as numerous and extravagant. He perfected his skills as a horseman, swimmer and swordsman; and he went bareheaded in the sun or rain. In the midst of his campaigns he carried on several intricate political intrigues at once, mostly at a distance, like a chess champion playing many games by mail. He wrote poems, dialogues, orations, the history of his campaigns, and many other works (most of them lost to us) which were considered masterpieces. Cicero observed: "Caesar wrote admirably; his memoirs are cleanly, directly and gracefully composed, and divested of all superfluous ornaments."

In all this time the day was approaching when the triumvirate would be reduced to two partners, and make civil war inevitable. It was Crassus who disappeared first: he went off in 53 B.C. to fight a private war of his own, leading an army financed by him, and was defeated and killed by the Parthians. Caesar had no fear of Pompey. He judged himself to be a better general, with superior troops, a larger political following in Rome and the Senate, and adequate financial reserves. He knew he would triumph in the end. And yet he delayed the outbreak of hostilities for as long as possible.

Pompey had drifted from the original political inspiration of the triumvirate and sided more and more with the old patrician minority. He thought he could intimidate his remaining partner more easily if he had the national gods, the sacred institutions and the historic families of the Republic on his side, as well as the new financiers. Caesar preferred the plebeians in the Forum. The showdown came when the Senate ordered the governor of Gaul to give up the command of his loyal legions and to come to Rome as a private citizen to be tried for his actions; Pompey was asked to defend the city at all costs, at the head of his own army, if it became necessary. Caesar reluctantly and only after some indecision crossed the line between his territory and that of the Republic: the Rubicon. It was January 10, 49 B.C., four years after the death of Crassus and five years before Caesar's assassination.

So swift and unexpected was his advance into Italy that Pompey was forced to flee to Greece to gain time. Everybody recognized that the war was not what it pretended to be, a conflict between the Republic and a seditious general, but between two candidates for the supreme power. Whoever was going to win, the Republic would lose. "I cannot endure the sight of what is happening," Cicero wrote, "or of what is going to happen."

Caesar entered Rome (where he emptied the treasury), and went on to Spain (which had been Pompey's fief) to remove the threat of hostile armies moving behind his back while he campaigned in the East. In January of 48 B.C. he finally crossed the Adriatic, pursued Pompey, defeated him first at Dyrrachium in Albania, and finally destroyed his army at Pharsalus, in Thessaly, on August 9. Pompey got away together with his sons and most of his generals. Caesar looked at the many dead enemies on the battlefield and bitterly commented: "This they forced me to do, because if I had relinquished command of my armies, even after my many victories, I would have been lost."

Pompey found refuge in Egypt, but the Egyptians did not want other people's wars brought to their own lands and promptly had the great Roman general murdered. They offered his embalmed head as a gift to Caesar, when he finally arrived in Alexandria. Victorious Caesar refused it and wept. But he went on to wage wars against Pompey's sons and successors in command. Among them were patrician lovers of the ancient liberties, the men who in the end murdered him. They were all defeated. Julius Caesar (now 57) returned to Rome, absolute master of the State.

\*       \*       \*

HISTORY usually presents one great problem for each epoch to solve. Only later historians know the answer and gauge the comparative capacity of the players by how close each one gets to the hidden solution. The actors themselves are rarely aware of what is required of them, and of what they are actually doing. Many revolutions are notoriously stirred by the wrong hopes: the killers of Julius Caesar thought they were re-establishing the authority of the Senate and the rule of law. Most revolutions end up marching backwards, in the opposite direction from that intended by the early chiefs and aggravate the very ills they tried to abolish.[1]

The problem presented to Roman society at the turn of the first century before Christ was definitely not that of deciding the future with one more civil war. That was the old notorious system: expensive, dangerous, wasteful and ineffectual. The victorious leader marched on the capital with his loyal army, packed the Senate with his partisans, hurriedly passed a jumble of laws in the interest of the winning party, put his friends for a short time in marble halls, proscribed or killed his rivals, and finally ran away as fast as possible when the next victorious army marched on Rome. The real problem of Caesar's generation was to find a simple and bloodless method to pick supreme leaders, to govern far-flung domains with stability and establish a reasonably durable peace. The alternative was ruin: if civil wars did not cease, economic activities would come to a standstill, all wealth would be dissipated, provinces would rise in revolt, barbarian hordes would swarm across the borders, and civilized life would gradually become extinct.

Obviously something was fundamentally wrong. The constitution which had been good enough for the small city, for the short and necessary wars and for a few subjected people, was obsolete. The Senate was no longer able to start or stop wars, curb the generals' ambitions, discipline the rich, keep order in the city, or defend the Roman world from invasions.

The venerable virtues which had made the simple and sturdy Latin farmers invincible and allowed them to conquer vast possessions and immense wealth were clearly inadequate to govern those very possessions and to administer their new

---

[1] Most leaders seem to us, in retrospect, to have floundered on blindfolded most of the time. How many of them were aware of their historic roles? It is difficult to tell. In the old days we have little to go on; we can only guess. In the last two centuries, however, they have left an ample documentation. If you consult these sources—Napoleon's memoirs, Lenin's pamphlets, Hitler's *Mein Kampf*, Mussolini's exegesis of Fascism, to mention a few examples —you realize they knew they were great historical characters all right but had only vague and inaccurate ideas of what history was using them for.

wealth. They had to transform themselves and reform the State. Yet their very greatness was rooted in their obsolete virtues. They had to cling to their old traditions, ideas, institutions, beliefs—without them they would have lost their identity. They would have become decadent, effete, corrupt, and impotent. This, of course, is the problem of many successful republics, whose simple virtues make them strong enough, at one point, to conquer other people and assume imperial responsibilities. How can men, who are dedicated to liberty and the defense of their own independence, efficiently dominate subject peoples, without damning their own soul?

There was not much time in which to devise new ways of Roman government, capable of coping with the new problems, yet preserving at least the forms of the old institutions and providing a smoother way to transfer power from one leader to the next. It was with this dilemma that Caesar grappled and which he almost solved: the creation of what was to be called the Imperium. It was solved finally, years later, by his grand nephew, the grandson of his sister Julia, Octavian Augustus, his heir and a much better politician. But without Caesar to defeat all his rivals, to demonstrate *per absurdum* that civil wars were useless by winning them all, to establish a precarious peace in Rome, to consolidate and placate overseas possessions and frighten the barbarians, Augustus probably would not have had his chance. Augustus himself recognized this when he consecrated his dead grand-uncle's position among the gods and assumed the name of Caesar for himself and his successors. This was also recognized by all peoples in the following centuries. "Render unto Caesar the things which are Caesar's," said Jesus Christ, when he really meant Tiberius. The heads of all Germans once called themselves "Holy Roman Emperors" and Caesar, or *Kaiser*, until 1918. The Grand Dukes of Muscovy adopted the title of Caesar, Czar, when they pretended to be the heirs of the Emperors of Constantinople, the "Second Rome", and called Moscow the "Third Rome".

It is doubtful whether Caesar himself fully appreciated what he was doing. He was a clever opportunist, who followed his immediate ambitions with ruthless energy, who allied himself with, bought, seduced, cajoled, fought and destroyed other men, who adopted or rejected ideas and projects according to convenience. At times, however, he vaguely realized there was a greater significance to his achievements than his own elevation to absolute power. He tried to guess and guessed wrong.

He sometimes believed that he had been forced by circumstances to restore the legendary Roman monarchy. In the end he had suspected that he had introduced something new: despotic and absolute one-man rule over slave-like subjects, based on the divine worship of the ruler as God, after the example of Asiatic autocracies. His contemporaries thought so too. The opposition to his rule, which culminated in his assassination, was the first resistance of freedom-loving western Europe to the importation of despotic Eastern ways—the sign of an instinctive revulsion which has lasted the centuries till our very days, when its last form became the reluctance of many Europeans to be dominated by Eastern Communism.

Shortly before his death, Caesar had assumed some of the outward forms of sovereignty: he not only installed a gilded throne in the Senate but kept his seat in the presence of standing Senators, his supposed peers. He had his image stamped on coins; his birthday was celebrated by public sacrifices; the month of Quintilis was renamed July after him. Senators addressed him outright as Jupiter Julius and ordered a temple to be consecrated to him and his clemency—an Asiatic novelty. Caesar was delighted. Yet he had publicly and ostentatiously refused a royal diadem, saying loudly "Caesar is not a king"; and at another feast, when the crowds started hailing him as their king, he cried: "My name is Caesar not Rex."

The basic problem escaped him. How could a lasting peace be assured unless the control of the army, upon which Caesar's authority was based, was surrendered to the Senate and the people? And if it was surrendered, how could the Senate and the people guarantee durable stability when the loyalties of the soldiers went to their generals and not to the Republic? Caesar realized he could not contemplate the surrender of power without becoming a party to his own destruction, without benefit to the Republic. He could not have prevented new and ambitious men, proconsuls in charge of wealthy provinces or rabble-rousing demagogues, from waging new wars, which would have doomed Rome to ruin and oblivion within a generation or two. What was he to do?

\*    \*    \*

FORCED by logic to follow one move with another in his game, he had never clearly known what he would do in the end, after the final victory. He tackled legislative problems, packed the Senate with his friends (some of whom were trousered Gauls who did not know their way about the city), and carried out some reforms, but more to consolidate his power and repress possible revolutions than to reorganize the government of the Republic. His most famous contribution to civilization, the reform of the calendar, seems insignificant compared to the number of battles fought, the men killed, the countries ravaged in order to bring it about (as insignificant perhaps as one of Napoleon's most lasting achievements, the development of beet sugar).

That Caesar had no clear ideas about the future is proved by the project he was working on just before his death. He did not want to stay in Rome. He was planning the biggest war ever seen—more of the same thing he had done all his mature life. He would lead a vast army to Persia, destroy the Parthians and avenge the defeat of Crassus; then he would penetrate Hyrcania, the northern region of Persia, and, following the shore of the Caspian Sea, reach the Caucasus and conquer the Scythians inhabiting what is now Russia. From Russia he would attack the Germans from the rear, cross Germany, and return to Gaul. He reckoned that all this would take him three years. But should he have accomplished all this without a setback—by the conquest of immense territories, the subjugation of more millions of barbarians, the acquisition of other incalculable wealth— would he finally have tackled the real problem at home? Could he ever have pacified parties and factions, erected a new

government which would preserve the ancient liberties, and
created at the same time the efficient machinery necessary to
rule the world? Could he make new civil wars impossible?

The task was tremendous, even for a man of Caesar's genius.
He was always in a hurry. He had no longer the patience to
conciliate opponents. He preferred to defeat them and then to
forgive them magnanimously. He did not really like to live in
Rome. We know he was toying with the idea of transferring the
capital to Alexandria. He could see no way out of the present
difficulties. And he was too tired and sick. "Almost all authorities
believe," Suetonius concluded, "that he welcomed the manner
of his death."

*       *       *

ON THE DAY of his assassination, he walked into the Senate, as
we saw, alone, unarmed, unescorted, apparently unperturbed.
He joked with the soothsayer: "You see," he said to him, "the
Ides of March have come." "Yes," replied Spurinna, "but they
are not yet over." Senators pressed close to him, all talking at
the same time, each pleading his own little cause before the
start of the meeting. As he approached his gilded throne, the
defiant symbol of monarchy, he silenced most of them with a
gesture meaning, "Later, later."[2] He was obviously impatient
to get on with the business on hand. Did he know the agenda
concerned one thing only, the suppression of the tyrant?

Closest to Caesar was Tullius Cimber, one of the conspirators.
He appeared not to take Caesar's annoyed gesture for an answer,
and grabbed his toga as if to hold his attention by force. It was
the signal for the attack. Caesar was astonished and cried: "But
this is violence!"

Did he not expect violence that morning? Was he not resigned
to it? Was his resentment feigned?

At that moment one of the Casca brothers, who was behind

[2] The present-day Roman gesture is made by moving a hand forward in a
circular motion, as if symbolizing the jump over a fence or brook, the fence
or brook of time. It means "later" but also "eventually" and, sometimes,
"Don't bother me now."

him, tried to cut his throat with a sweep of the dagger. Caesar caught Casca's arm and ran it through with the only weapon he had, his stylus. If Caesar had wanted to defend himself, why was he carrying only the pointed instrument of a writer? Another dagger practically pierced Caesar's breast. Like a boar encircled at the finish by the pig-stickers' spears, the bleeding dictator was surrounded by naked steel swords. The conspirators had sworn each would plunge his blade into Caesar's body, so that all would be held equally responsible for his death. They were so awed by what they were doing that their hands trembled and, in the confusion, wounded each other at the same time.

After the first blow had drawn a groan from him, Caesar did not utter another sound. But finally, when he saw Brutus—the son of his old mistress, the woman he had cherished all his life— about to deliver his blow, he said in Greek (as a Russian aristocrat would speak in French): "You, too, my son?" Was that really a surprise? Did he not know that the name of Brutus was indispensable to the conspirators, that the homonymous descendant of the legendary hero who had rid Rome of its last king was necessary to give the conspiracy a legitimate, patriotic, traditional, respectable face, that without him the plot would have merely seemed a sordid struggle for power among the Roman élite? The dictator then drew himself up against the statue of Pompey, his old friend, ally, son-in-law, and defeated enemy—the statue he himself had generously ordered to the memory of the defender of law and order against Caesar's revolt—pulled his gown over his face and allowed himself to be butchered in silence.

# 2

# CASANOVA

THE Italians' art of living has been called duplicity by severe and unsympathetic observers. Italians are said to excel in such disreputable and dubious fields as diplomacy, the conduct of intrigues, and all kinds of shady business from fraudulent speculations to the organization of swindles. Foreigners point out that the arts of political deception were codified, once and for all, by the Italians. Also some of the most famous adventurers were Italian; names like Giacomo Casanova or the Count of Cagliostro are often cited to prove the point. These accusations are old, so old that some go back to the Middle Ages and some probably to earlier times, rooted as they are in deep racial and religious prejudices and misunderstandings. But there is some truth in some of them.

It must be admitted, first of all, that the virtues of the Italians, like those of other peoples, may at times degenerate into their corresponding vices. The parsimony of the French easily turns into avarice; the reserve of the English into deaf and dumb isolation; the animated activity of the Americans into senseless agitation. It is not surprising, therefore, that the possession of a knack to correct and embellish the appearance of life may at times tempt some Italians to utilize it to mystify their neighbors for their own private advantage. But something always prevents an Italian from achieving a lasting, world-wide, stupendous swindle. He is usually the victim of his own machinations. Italian adventurers, founders of counterfeit religions, and dishonest large-scale financiers are few and insignificant when compared to those born in other countries. None of the internationally famous scandals of the past is connected with an

Italian name. John Law was a Scotsman; no Italian was involved in the South Sea Bubble, the speculation in tulip bulbs
in the Netherlands, the scandal of the Panama Canal company
shares in Paris at the end of the last century, the Stavisky case
in France between the two World Wars, or the growth and
collapse of the empire of Kreuger, the Swedish match king. The
Italian arts are not sufficient for truly historic achievement.

There is no doubt that Casanova had the qualities for a career
as an international adventurer and swindler comparable to the
best foreign examples, but it can be proved that what prevented
him from reaching ultimate success, was, curiously enough, his
most typical Italian characteristics. He was tall, handsome, with
a spacious forehead and a Roman nose, the looks of a gentleman,
and an air of authority about him. He was untiringly vigorous
and healthy. He was also clever, wrote well and fluently,
played several musical instruments, spoke and wrote several
foreign languages with ease, Italian and French with elegance.
He had read a great deal, quoted glibly from the Latin and
Greek classics and contemporary authors; he could converse as
an equal with philosophers, poets, and novelists. He visited
Voltaire to dispute with him on some minor point. He pleased
women at first sight, women of all ages and conditions, and
usually succeeded in rendering them helpless and defenseless in
front of his pressing entreaties. His physical capacity to satisfy
the most exacting mistress by renewing his homages to her a
practically unlimited number of times through the night and the
following day, with only short *entr'actes* between the exertions,
is not as surprising as the feat of psychological endurance: he
was never bored, never embittered by experience, sincerely
admired one woman after another, and slipped into bed at a
moment's notice with the fat, the lean, the young, the old, the
dirty, the *soignée*, the lady, the chambermaid, the strumpet,
the nun, always admirably animated, till very late in life, by the
same school-boyish eagerness.

He often impersonated any character he chose, and spoke in
a very persuasive manner. "My secret is simple; I always tell
the truth, and people naturally believe me," he lied in his

memoirs. His truths were, to say the least, improbable and, at times, blatantly absurd; yet most people trusted him for a time. He had no scruples of any kind, in any field, to embarrass him. Other men with half his gifts, managed to reach safe positions of power and renown. He died penniless, alone, far from his native land. He was saved from destitution by a charitable friend, Graf Waldstein, a relation of the Prince de Ligne, who gave him a dreary job as librarian in his castle at Dux, in Bohemia. The great adventurer's last years were saddened by humiliating squabbles with the Graf's servants, who played backstairs tricks and practical jokes on the defenseless old man.

\*          \*          \*

HE WAS BORN in Venice in 1725. His father and mother were actors, who, in the fashion of the day, toured Europe playing the famous comedies of the *Teatro italiano* in their native language. His mother, Zanetta Farusi, like other actresses of all times, was also the favorite bed companion of petty princes, powerful noblemen and wealthy merchants until a remarkably old age. There is no doubt that Giacomo inherited his good looks, aplomb, ability to create illusions, and appetite for an indiscriminate love life, from his parents, as well as the restlessness which drove him from nation to nation until his death. Zanetta wanted him to become a priest. He was soon expelled from the Padua seminary, after a brief stay, when he was discovered in bed with a companion. As a punishment, he was locked for a time in the fort of Sant'Andrea, at the Lido. This incident did not prevent him, a little later, while still wearing the robes of an apprentice priest, from becoming the secretary of the Spanish Cardinal d'Acquaviva, in Rome. The job lasted but a short time: he was dismissed for having engineered the scandalous abduction of a distinguished Roman young lady. The Venetian army then attracted him. He enlisted, was stationed in various Ionian and provincial garrisons, where he carried on several intrigues, seduced a number of women, and had many adventures. Back in Venice, without any means of support, he tried

at first to become an actor like his parents, failed, and accepted
the miserable job of fiddler in the theater of San Samuel. One
night, coming back from a ball where he had played the violin,
he was offered a lift in the gondola of an elderly gentleman who
was going his way. His host was stricken with paralysis a few
minutes later. Casanova stopped the boat, ran for the nearest
surgeon, dragged him out of bed, had the sick old man bled on
the spot, took him home, put him to bed, and stood by, day and
night, until he recovered.

The nobleman, Senator Bragadin, a bachelor of means who
dabbled in magic, attributed his unexpected recovery to supernatural powers. He asked Casanova if he had any special charms.
The young man, who had stayed behind merely to eat two square
meals a day, admitted without difficulty that he owned a table
of figures, given to him by a hermit on the mountains of Carpegna,
to which he proposed questions, turned into numbers, and from
which he got back answers, in numbers which he turned into
words. The senator was beside himself with joy. He knew what
the magic table was: it was the famous "Solomon's scapula", in
other words the veritable Cabala of the ancients. He also knew
it was impossible to extract answers from it without some supernatural powers, which Casanova obviously possessed. In order
to attach him, and the Cabala, to himself, Bragadin adopted the
young fiddler, gave him an ample allowance, and installed him
in his *palazzo*. This was the origin of Casanova's luck. Without
the help of the elderly senator he would probably be unknown
today. For years thereafter, he milked the credulous nobleman
of all the money he needed, by promising to get Solomon's
shoulder-blade to dictate instructions on the best way to turn
lead into gold and reveal other desirable secrets. It never did.
The senator, however, never tired of waiting.

Casanova caused his adopted father a lot of trouble by leading
a scandalous and expensive life of gambling and whoring, to
the point where it became necessary for him to travel abroad. He
left for France in 1750. In Lyons he was admitted to a Masonic
lodge. He lived in Paris for two years, then visited Dresden (where
his mother lived at the time), Prague, and Vienna. Back in

Venice he was soon denounced as a freemason, a spy, and a dabbler in black magic—three among the few activities forbidden its subjects by the Most Serene and indulgent Republic—and thrown without trial into the secret dungeon, the Leads. After fifteen months of incredible efforts and cunning plotting, he managed to do what had practically never been done before: he escaped. He went back to Paris, where he met his second benefactor, more noble, credulous, elderly and rich than the first the Duchess of Urfé. She also had an immoderate passion for the supernatural, wanted to turn lead into gold, wanted to go to the moon, but, above all, desired to discover the formula of a potion which would assure her eternal youth. Casanova had no trouble in convincing her that he was the right man to help. Somehow he never managed to bring together all the rare elements and persons necessary for the completion of the magic rites. Something was always lacking, the veritable blood of a salamander, a magic child fathered by him on a virgin of royal lineage or a youth born of an immortal mother. The duchess kept on hoping that the next experiment would finally succeed and paid him money until the end.

Before she died, Casanova reached the pinnacle of his career. He taught the French government to run lotteries, in the fashion of the Venetian Republic, and was appointed manager of the lottery bureau. His old friend, now Cardinal de Bernis, with whom he had shared the love of the beautiful nun in Murano, had now become a Cabinet minister. On his recommendation, Casanova was entrusted with a delicate official mission, to negotiate loans with Amsterdam bankers. Probably the cardinal believed that only an astute adventurer was an adequate match for the Dutch financiers. Casanova lived in splendor, like a great man, in a beautiful house, with servants, horses and carriages, and a merry-go-round of mistresses. He hobnobbed with the aristocracy, the intellectuals, the politicians, the poets. His only mischance came, naturally enough, when he tried investing money in a legitimate enterprise: he founded and ran for a while a factory producing printed cotton cloth and he was almost ruined by it.

At about this time he called himself the Chevalier de Seingalt (he arrived at the name by mixing cards bearing letters and drawing them, one after another, at random). He was in London where, having forgotten the old saying that *"les femmes suisses sont comme les edelweiss, c'est très difficile à prendre et ça ne vault pas la peine,"* he was defeated by a Swiss girl, the only woman who ever resisted him and practically drove him mad with frustrated vanity and incredulity; he was in Germany, where he discussed philosophical problems with Frederick the Great of Prussia; he was in Switzerland, where he revenged himself on the London girl by seducing the six daughters of the mayor of Geneva. Everywhere he gambled for high stakes, won, lost, got himself involved in scandals, extricated himself with the usual persuasive arguments, was imprisoned, escaped, disappeared without money and friends, reappeared somewhere else with a purse full of gold coins, a carriage and horses, powerful protectors, and a pretty woman at his side.

His luck lasted as long as the Venetian senator and the Parisian duchess lived. They were apparently the only two people he had managed to deceive permanently. In the end, he returned to Venice, a broken man. He eked out a living by selling his services as an informer to the secret police, but a scandal provoked by the incautious publication of a pamphlet written by him forced him to flee once again. Possibly he would still be remembered as a man of letters if he had not had such an adventurous life. He dabbled in poetry, theology, mathematics, philology and history. He translated Homer from the Greek, wrote a confutation to Amelot de la Houssaye's attack on the Republic of Venice and criticisms of Voltaire's philosophy. His most memorable book, after his memoirs, was a novel, written in French and published in Prague in 1788, called *Ycosameron, ou Histoire d'Edouard et d'Elizabeth qui passèrent quatre-vingt-un ans ches les Mégamicres, habitants aborigènes du Protocosme dans l'interieur de notre globe.* It is possibly one of the first science-fiction novels of modern times. He died at Dux, in 1795.

\*　　\*　　\*

THERE ARE many evident reasons why Casanova could hardly have been born elsewhere. It is not so much the fact that his adventurous life can be (and has been) interpreted as a ribald revenge *all'italiana* against a fate that had made his country and himself poor, corrupt, and contemptible, and his glorious city, *La Serenissima*, the brothel and gambling casino of Europe; much more important is the fact that he himself believed it true, believed, that is, he had no other chances in life, and that the lowest subterfuges were therefore justified. It was, of course, true that life in Italy during the eighteenth century seemed to a man haunted by an almost monstrous concept of his own worth and of his talents, an impatient, inventive man incapable of constant efforts, to offer few honorable fields in which to advance rapidly enough to the rank of the mighty, the rich, the well born.[1]

To many, including Casanova, the easiest thing was to turn to buffoonery, to schemes for exploiting the senile credulity of some imbecile, to trying alchemy or pandering or brazen impersonations, to try one's hand at swindling, or indiscriminate love making. Casanova was the best of all and the most successful. By the use of his abundant natural advantages he lived for years a life of splendor. But he also was Italian in this, that he never really exploited his natural advantages in a purposeful and stable way (as foreign, less brilliant swindlers managed to do). He did not make himself, in the end, one of the great men of his age, did not conquer durable honors, wealth, prestige, and security, and a name to hand down to his sons and grandsons. The reason is, of course, that he wanted to achieve none of these things but only to enjoy the life connected with them: he only wanted to play the part of a great man.

He was also Italian in this, that he had to look abroad for suitable theaters in which to stage his exploits. His victims (with the sole exception of Senator Bragadin) had to be foreigners;

[1] This was, of course, only partly so. In Venice alone the list of men who became famous, and some even rich, merely by cultivating artistic talents is impressive. It includes the Tiepolos, Cesare Vivaldi, Carlo Goldoni, and Gaspare Gozzi.

the milieus in which he dazzled everybody, from princes to coachmen and money-lenders, had to be beyond the Alps, because in his native country men like Casanova (even if seldom as gifted as he) were a well-known phenomenon and easily spotted. In point of fact, every time he returned to Venice he was pursued by the police and had to flee. In the end, impunity which he enjoyed among less suspecting foreigners made him over-confident. As the years went by, his impersonations became more and more incredible, the stories he told more and more dubious, the way he seduced women increasingly curt and offensive, the swindling schemes ever more daring, because he did not wait to accumulate concrete rewards but enjoyed the spectacle of his own dazzling audacity and his power over his victims. In this, above all, he was unmistakably Italian: he stage-managed his life as a work of art, acted a picaresque novel while living it, and was so conscious of so doing that, in the end, he was able to write it all down out of his memory, almost without the inevitable errors of old men's reminiscences, as a writer sometimes puts down on paper the masterpiece he had been composing in his mind for years. This confusion of the thing itself and its simulacrum—of military might and picturesque military parades, of words and emotions, of the saint and his statue—is perhaps the most constant Italian trait; it is at once the source and cause of both unique achievements and national misfortunes.

## 3

# CAVOUR, OR THE FOREIGNER AS NATIONAL HERO

ITALY was not made in 1848. The year of romantic revolutions and heroic barricades, of rhetoric and high hopes, was
also—not just in the marshy districts of Lombardy but
throughout Europe—the year of great mistakes and improvisations, of ineptitude and defeats. The surviving liberals, patriots,
democrats, revolutionaries and socialists crept back into their
hiding places, returned to exile and to obscure provincial life
and reconsidered their ideas, trying, in heated arguments and
endless discussions, to see where they had gone wrong. Why had
"the others" won?

In London Karl Marx put this question to Friedrich Engels.
Bakunin in the fortress of Königstein, Garibaldi making
candles on Staten Island, Mazzini in London, Herzen and
Orsini in Nice, Pisacane and Kossuth; they were all troubled
by the same problem. Camillo Benso, Count of Cavour, also
brooded over mistakes of the past and how to avoid them in the
future. To his banker and friend la Rue, in Geneva, he wrote:
"Our military and political disasters have dulled my wits. I no
longer have the strength to write a line. Dear God, how many
errors we have made! Impossible to imagine a drearier case of
ineptitude of every kind, in the army as in the government!..."

Italy was made in 1859 and 1860, in little more than a year!
from 26 April 1859, to be exact (the date of the ultimatum sent
by Franzis Josef to Victor Emmanuel, still "King of Sardinia"),
till 26 October 1860 (the date of Garibaldi's meeting with Victor
Emmanuel, virtually already "King of Italy", at Teano after the

conquest of the South). Many things about that year resembled 1848, above all the emotional wave that looked as if it would sweep away every obstacle and made everything seem possible. In that year, too, there were the romantic revolutionaries with their circular cloaks and their beards *all' italiana*, the soldiers of fortune in their strange uniform, the adventurers, the patriots, the poets, the students who had run away from home, the unknown heroes and the heroes with great and famous names. In that year, too, Garibaldi had taken command of a flying column, but this time he wore the uniform of a general in the Royal Army, with an embroidered collar, and his men wore the proper uniform of the *Cacciatori delle Alpi*.

In the spring of 1859, as it had done eleven years earlier, the Sardinian army advanced towards Lombardy in some confusion and with no precise plan, with the King at its head, the tricolor flags (with the arms of Savoy in the middle) streaming in the wind, and the most glorious regiments in the vanguard, commanded, as ever, by sprigs of the old aristocracy. Victor Emmanuel was no better general than his father, Charles Albert, had been in 1848. Neither was any sort of strategist. They were heroic leaders who kept marching against the enemy, swords unsheathed and careless of danger. (Bolton-King said that Victor Emmanuel was an excellent cavalry colonel and no more, just as he had shown he was at Novara in 1849.)

But in many other ways 1859 was unlike 1848. This time, the Emperor of the French stood beside the King of Sardinia, and the *Zouaves* beside the *bersaglieri*. Italy was no longer "on its own". The alliance was the result of political, diplomatic, and military moves over nearly ten years that had made the "Italian question" a European problem. The war was aided by an organisation of communications, supplies, finance, and industry that no one, ten years earlier, would have foreseen. Behind the two armies advancing to victorious battles were the telegraph, railway lines, canals, steamships, Italy's first commercial port at Genoa and first military port at La Spezia, a tunnel through the Alps, a healthy bank balance, plenty of international credit, vigorous international trade, and a prosperous agriculture.

Ten years—half a generation—had passed, and the whole of Europe had moved forward. Yet there is no doubt at all that the real, great difference between 1848 and 1859, between defeat and victory, between heroic, pointless sacrifice and a plan with good chances of success, lay in one man: Camillo Cavour. It was he who used all that was new in the century to forward his single plan, the "making of Italy"—inventions, industries, rapid communications, and all that history was bringing to maturity; traditional methods of diplomacy and intrigue as well as revolutionary methods involving conspiracy, sedition, and rebellion; strategy like street rioting, old loyalties and shady new commercial deals. It was he who had enticed Napoleon into an alliance. One man, and one alone.

What he had avoided above all was the most serious mistake made in 1848, a mistake always made and never noticed by revolutionaries, and one of the main causes of failure ten years earlier. In 1859 he had made sure that respectable people were not afraid of what was about to happen. He prepared a revolution that might seem desirable to patriots (who were few) but that also seemed acceptable or inevitable, or at any rate not harmful, to the rest—a revolution that could be achieved or accepted by obeying one's own sovereign (or, at least, a sovereign) and the law, as conscience demanded—a revolution made by shrewd, prudent folk who could be trusted. Alexander Herzen, the great Russian revolutionary, noticed the difference between the two years. "Italy," he wrote, "the most poetic country in the world, has abandoned her fanatical lover Mazzini, and betrayed her husband Ercole Garibaldi, as soon as the plump, bespectacled, clever and middle-class Cavour suggested making her his kept woman . . ."

A letter dated 27 May 1861 and signed by Victor Emmanuel, addressed to Napoleon III and asking for France to recognize the new Kingdom of Italy, was certainly dictated by Cavour. It was one of the last letters he wrote before his death and what he said in it sums up what he had done: "I (the King) have not concealed from myself the fact that the conduct of my government, being little in conformity with diplomatic traditions, would arouse many doubts over, and misunderstandings of, the motives that had inspired it . . . A great political transformation, which an irresistible force, the national sentiment, had been preparing for a very long time, took place without the principles of social order being in any way shaken."

Cavour, like many great characters who have ruthlessly intervened in their country's history and in the space of a few years forcibly transformed it, sometimes making it play a part that was not in fact its own, was a man from the frontiers, almost a foreigner. Foreign (or almost so) to the countries they transformed were, among others, Mazarin, Catherine the Great, Napoleon, Stalin, Hitler, and, more modestly, De Gasperi. They all spoke with an accent. The foreigner, or the man who is almost foreign, has perhaps the cold decisiveness of a surgeon operating on another's flesh, the convert's fanaticism and illusions, and a confused misunderstanding of the national character that distorts and simplifies faults and virtues, real and imaginary possibilities, and often helps him make ambitious plans for the country he lives in, and to envisage a great destiny for it which he would not dare if he saw things in sharp focus.

One of Cavour's grandmothers came from Savoy, which meant she was nearly French; she belonged to the de Sales family which gave St. Francis de Sales to the Church. His mother's name was de Sellon; she came from Geneva, of a Huguenot family that had emigrated there much earlier. From his Savoyard grandmother he acquired a taste for reading and philosophical speculation, tastes unknown in his own home. (His father, Michele, was, Massimo d'Azeglio said, "marquis, an officer in the police, and a fool.") Every year Cavour spent some time with his relations in one of the oldest of European republics, Geneva, whose motto is *"Patrie et Liberté"*. He began this practice as a boy, and continued it all his life. Three aunts in Geneva, many cousins, learned friends, and a pacifist uncle whose life was dedicated to campaigning against capital punishment and war, formed his circle. Camillo read, studied, attended some university lectures, and wrote articles on economic subjects for erudite local papers. All this helped to form his mind far

more than his modest, dusty Italian studies at the military
academy in Turin. What was Genevan about Cavour was his
love of freedom, which he believed in as the supreme method of
solving all problems; and a certain basic seriousness, which in
Italy is still rare today, and which meant he went deeply into
every technical problem, worked things out exactly, and made
cautious trials before launching out on any new enterprise.
Genevan, too, was his love of money. As a young man he left
Italy almost penniless, but before he went to the government he
had acquired one of the largest fortunes in Italy at the time.
(Before becoming minister he sold all his stocks and shares.) In a
discussion before the war of 1859, Victor Emmanuel said to him:
"It's all very well for you to talk. If things go wrong, you can go
and enjoy your income of 150,000 lire somewhere. But I'll end
up like my father . . ." (His father, Charles Albert, died poor
in Oporto, a voluntary exile after his defeat at Novara in
1848.)

To the Italians who met him, Cavour appeared a foreigner.
(He was only *un italiano nuovo*, a rare specimen at the time.) "He
spoke in a clipped, Frenchified way, and made so many howlers
that it would have seemed an impossible task to anyone to make
him agree with the Italian dictionary," maliciously wrote Brof-
ferio, one of his political opponents. Gioberti said he was "English
in his ideas, French in his language . . . Cavour is not rich in
the gift of Italianness . . . Indeed, his senses, instincts and
understanding are almost foreign to Italy." Guerrazzi described him at his first meeting:

Is this the man who must understand Italy?, I said to myself, Well,
maybe . . . I don't deny that count Cavour has brains. What I suspect
is that he has not the capacity to be an Italian minister. And although
he may not lack ability, in the long run it would be no use because he
has never asked the Graces to sprinkle him with their holy water . . .
a man without a feeling for art cannot understand Italy.

Cavour himself confessed (in one of his last great speeches in
which he showed that Rome would inevitably become the
capital and that the Papacy would achieve greater prestige
once it was freed of the burden and shame of its temporal power);

"I have little artistic bent, and I am sure that among the most splendid monuments of Rome, both ancient and modern, I should miss the severe and unpoetic streets of my birthplace." He never saw Rome or Venice. (He had been to Paris, where he felt at home, several times, and to London, where he had much-loved friends and admired English politics, industry, agriculture and club-life.) He reached Milan, Florence, and Pisa only in 1860, accompanying his King after the annexation. The sight of so many wonders set him dreaming for the first time. He was a younger son in a noble family from Piedmont, and he had the psychology of the younger son. Above all he was determined to succeed by every possible means, determined to make his way and show he was better than his brother Gustavo; determined to get honors, make his fortune, and achieve fame and success greater than his older brother had received by the accident of birth. (Gustavo became a Senator in the new Kingdom, and always voted against Camillo, among the Senators on the far right.) The British Empire was made at about the same time by men like him, the younger sons of great families flung about the world to make a new name for themselves by winning lands and fortunes. In the *palazzo* Cavour, Camillo lived on the second floor, in a low-ceilinged room where, when he was a child, his hard-up old bachelor uncles had lived, while his elder brother enjoyed the elegant apartments on the first floor. Camillo quarrelled with his whole family for years, of course, until his riches, power, and fame soothed them.

The Italian aristocracy has always been rustic, tight-fisted and family-minded. Servants, children, poor relations, important relations, all lived together in huge bare houses like the castle at Fratta. In Piedmont the aristocracy was poor, dignified, and dedicated to serving the King from generation to generation, sacrificing its money and its sons for him in lengthy wars.

Cavour had the zealousness of the new men but, at the same time, the social ease of *un homme du monde*, a gentleman used to great houses, to people of rank and an aristocratic life. As a young man in Paris he was received everywhere, was a member of the Jockey Club, and was considered an elegant dandy. In

London he knew the best clubs, noblemen's castles, aristocratic drawing rooms. With humble people he had the friendly, easy relations that perhaps only a man of patrician background, a country gentleman, manages to achieve. He treated important people without humility and small people without haughtiness, in a friendly courteous way. For years, every day, he read, understood, digested and judged mountains of documents, studies, reports, and balance-sheets, wrote dozens of letters, always in his own hand, every one of them loaded with responsibility, received dozens of people, colleagues, opponents like Guerrazzi, secret agents, revolutionaries, patriots who had come from a distance; went to the *Camera* where he dominated discussion on any problem for he had the facts at his finger-tips and his ideas were always clearer and more practical than anyone else's. He had been a professional soldier, and so had a good knowledge of military matters; in fact, he had been a sapper, specializing in mathematics, the sciences, and fortifications. He had been an agriculturalist, a speculator on the stock exchange, a financier, the founder and director of firms, an industrialist. In almost all these activities he had had some success. "That devil Cavour," wrote a French general during the war of 1859. "I ask him for 100,000 rations for such and such a day. Of course, what I really needed was 50,000 three weeks later. Before the day I had arranged he sent me 110,000."

In his last years, he brought together all or nearly all the important ministries—Finance, War, Internal Affairs—and ruled them with a sure touch and a perfect knowledge of every detail. He trusted only himself. Like all the great centralizers, he used mediocre men. His contacts with Italians of great ability and fame at the time were fleeting and superficial. The ineptness of many of his colleagues was shown by the failure of their policies in the months in which he gave up power after Villafranca, and in the disaster that followed his death. The only man of strong character with whom he collaborated was King Victor; he could not avoid it, and there was never any great love lost between the pair of them.

Cavour was above all an agriculturalist. He had a passion for transforming the land, improving stock, cutting canals, draining rough, watery country, trying out new crops, experimenting with new fertilizers and studying the new industrial or commercial techniques which his farming activities showed him were needed. All this was not merely a gentleman's whim; he did so for shrewd and strongly-held motivations of economic profit. Every undertaking must pay, otherwise it would be no use either to itself or to society. Ruffini said of Leri Cavour's estate:

In the centre of an estate of more than 3,000 *giornate*, intersected only by the symmetrical lines of canals and tree-lined borders, is a large, square, rough peasant farm-house. Everything here belongs to the master, no less than the surrounding land. His are the monumental white Piedmont oxen, the barns, the enormous granaries; his the peasants' houses, the carpenter's workshop, the smithy, the farrier's shop, the coachman's quarters; his the chemist's and the doctor's houses; his the parish church and the rectory; his even the cemetery. So the estate is a small world, entirely self-sufficient. But the master does not rule it from some hostile battlemented tower. He is not there for enjoyment and power, but to work and to produce, and so has no need to defend himself. He lives in a small house that is barely decent, whose windows and door all open on to the immense barn-yard, where men and oxen, chicken and children, all live, grow, multiply, shout and frolic together.

Cavour had the farmer's patience, prudence, tenacity and serenity in the face of bad luck that could ruin the most carefully laid plans. In politics he had the farmer's way of seeing to a hundred things at once, in various stages of development, each of them to be driven ahead cautiously, in its own time. He did not put too much pressure on the course of events. He followed nature, because men and plants do not obey like machines, but need to be encouraged to follow their own bent. Farming, like politics, is *l'arte del possibile*.

He was a gambler too. He loved cards, playing for high stakes at the green baize table, late at night, or speculating on the stock exchange. (He founded three societies, based on his three passions, the Agricultural Association, the Whist Club, and the National Society.) In Paris, when he was thirty, he used confidential information which he had been given by the mistress of the English chargé d'affaires, Bulwer, and made fifteen thousand francs on the bourse. Later he tried to do the same thing again and lost forty-five thousand. He wrote to his father, asking for help: "*Il faut payer ou se bruler la cervelle.*" His father paid. In April 1859, when it looked as if the war on which he had staked everything was not going to break out (it broke out only because Francis Joseph sent an ultimatum), Cavour kept a pistol on his desk, and had decided to use it if events made him ridiculous and impotent and ruined Piedmont and Italy.

He was not always lucky, as we have seen. When he was young, speculations that went wrong—a navigation company on the Rhone that never managed to work, another on Lake Maggiore, and other undertakings—cost him and his associates large sums. But he soon learned how to deal with luck, how not to rush in unless he could see good reason for it, how not to take risks that were too great. Only a gambler, however, could have continued to run the Piedmontese policy after Villafranca (the armistice between Franz Josef and Napoleon, which terminated the war of 1859 before the end Cavour had hoped and worked for) and to complete the by then desperate task of achieving national unity. Only a gambler could have staked himself on Garibaldi and the Thousand. Only a gambler could have asked Victor Emmanuel to invade the Papal States, leaving northern Italy undefended, and Lombardy under the Austrian cannon, to reach Naples at about the time the Red Shirts had reached it.

Providence sometimes makes a man the right tool at an historical moment; a man whose very faults are essential qualities for a particular task. Such a man was Camillo Cavour. On his moral legacy, on his experience and his teaching, Italy lived from 1861 to 1918, *l'Italia Liberale* that was transformed from a small agricultural country into one of the industrial nations of Europe, still respecting that liberty which he had considered its single beacon of light.

When, in 1860, the King was in southern Italy with the army, Austria was planning revenge, the powers were protesting, the Pope was urging all Catholics to join together against the new regime, and everything might have been lost within a few days, someone wrote to Cavour from Paris, advising him to dissolve Parliament and appoint himself dictator. It was a temptation to which others would later yield. He replied: "I could not betray my origins, and deny the principles of my whole life. I am the son of liberty: all that I am, I owe to her."

# 4

# CURZIO MALAPARTE

K URT ERICH SUCKERT, called Curzio Malaparte, was
only ten years older than "we" were. "We" were young
writers and journalists who, twenty-five or thirty years
ago in Italy, were hoping to make our way and were unknown to the general public. Did we choose each other knowing
we should later succeed, did we have some secret sign? Did we
really believe that one day we would be able to write what we
liked and what really interested us? Everything made us suppose
that we should live, like so many other obscure little groups, in
the shadows, known only to a few like-minded acquaintances.

We were tied to no program, and we had no name, like
the Futurists or the Nationalists before us. We were united by
indefinable links, read what our friends had written with
pleasure and occasionally with envy, and understood one another's allusions; there were few, in fact, apart from ourselves,
who managed to laugh at our mysterious jokes. We met, that
was all: lunched together in Rome or Milan; exchanged un-
topical irrelevant ideas. Above all, we were annoyed by the
same things, things we hated, despised, and ridiculed. The sense
of "our generation" was something that linked us, no doubt
about that; but this had nothing to do with the dull fact of birth
dates. It was a matter of being formed alike, of having the same
*sensibilité*, and in fact some of us were younger and some older
than the norm, among them the painter and caricaturist
Amerigo Bartoli and the writer Paolo Monelli, who were both
older than Malaparte.

We had all grown up and been formed in the years after the
first World War: Alberto Moravia, Indro Montanelli, Dino

Buzzati, Ercole Patti, Guido Piovene, Leo Longanesi, Mario Soldati, to name just a few. We were at school while others were fighting. We still wore short pants when there was the first street-fighting between Fascists and anti-Fascists. How irritated we were by Italian rhetoric, and how disgusted by the way of the official world around us! Malaparte, though, belonged to that world, had fought in the war with conviction, and was steeped in the fashionable ideologies of the day. For this reason he did not appear to us as a slightly older brother, but as a venerable—even if vigorous—example of another historical period, as an adversary.

He wasn't quite as old as his ideas, and how young he looked, with the faultless youthfulness of a wax statue. We attributed this remarkable fact to the miraculous diet which he followed with monastic discipline, to the regularity of his life, in which vice and women mattered little, and to the exercises which (he said) he performed diligently every morning. And Malaparte died before his "cheeks drooped", died with the untroubled face of a young man, with his straight hair thick and black, and still with his air of being a grown-up adolescent confused and worried by the ideas of a world to which he didn't really belong. One day, it was always said, he would write maturely, freed from acrobatic politics and literary trickery. But he never had time to write these last books of his; this he regretted, and even said so to a friend a few days before he died (in 1957). He was something of a poet, no doubt. His language was rare, he had a unique feeling for Italian prose and its rhythm, and was so skillful that he could change his style and flavor with each book, like an actor who changes with each play, almost parodying himself. His intuition was sometimes profound and illuminating, as when he wrote of the Tuscans and of Tuscany, where he was born and grew up, and especially of Prato, his home town. His last book, *Quei Maledetti Toscani* (*Those Cursed Tuscans*), which dealt with the subject he loved best, contains some magnificent passages among others ruined by arrogance and jumbled repetitiousness. Malaparte rarely failed to charm, even when he failed to ring true. He was basically so attractive that he became

annoying and suspect; he was too clever, and could never speak
for us. He had grown up too quickly, had matured too precoci-
ously, had made himself known to the generation that preceded
him while he was still at school, and was fatally linked to the
old, as indeed so often happens with *enfants prodiges*. The distance between him and us was short but impassable; it was like
the space between a rearguard withdrawing and a vanguard
advancing.

*           *           *

WHAT ANNOYED us most about him was the smell of d'Annunzio.
Not that Malaparte was a d'Annunzian and imitated his precious prose. Not at all. He obviously thought himself his successor,
and had things to dispute with him and his followers. All the
same, we felt he could not escape a profound resemblance, due
not so much to any conscious effort as to the age he had lived in
and the air he had breathed. All that was d'Annunzian about
his prose were a few unfortunate tricks and some bad habits—
the use of strange words, the assumption of superhuman airs, an
air of self-satisfaction—not from necessity but for effect, to get
applause and shouted bravos from the audience. What was
*really* d'Annunzian in Malaparte was his "heroic" life. At seven-
teen, in 1914 (the year in which d'Annunzio, then fifty, was
preaching from Arcachon the need to fight beside our "Latin
Sister"), he volunteered for the Garibaldians, and was among
the first irregular Italian troops at the front in France. When
Italy declared war on Austria the following year (d'Annunzio
had aroused in the young a wave of enthusiasm for Italian intervention in the war, in his speech at Quarto on the 5th of May,
1915), Malaparte joined the regular army.

He fought bravely and honorably right to the end, earning
decorations and promotion for his heroism in the war, and
severe reprimands for some unmilitary "artistic" oddities and
whims. Yet one can see in him too the longing to live through
an adventure of "blood and glory" in the Italian literary and
political taste of the day. He did not go to Fiume with d'Annunzio and I have never understood why. It would have suited him.

After the war, though, to make up for it, he was one of the first Fascists, in the "Disperata" troops in Florence. His Fascism was literary as well: the defense of the "barbarous" Italians against modern industrial Europe and America. At that time he wrote a famous anthem which rather complacently imitated various peasant songs:

> *Sorge il sole, canta il gallo,*
> *Mussolini monta a cavallo. . . .*
> (The sun rises, the cock crows,
> Mussolini mounts his horse. . . . )

He became one of the most brilliant journalists of the new régime, editor-in-chief of *La Stampa* in Turin—until his imprisonment in 1933 for various misdemeanors. Among other things he had written an insolent letter to the editor of a newspaper in Ferrara, the mouthpiece of Italo Balbo, accusing the Fascist chief of wanting to take over from Mussolini. Balbo at once asked for him to be punished; and Mussolini, for his own private reasons, wanted nothing better. Malaparte was arrested and sent to Lipari. All the same, no anti-Fascist considered the imprisoned writer a serious opponent of the régime. He was a man who had merely offended one of its minor bosses by defending Mussolini from an imaginary threat. He was obviously a faithful follower whose capricious, anarchical character made it impossible for him to keep calm and enjoy the advantages his past as a stormtrooper might have given him.

The truth was that Malaparte was not even a Fascist. He had a d'Annunzian longing to keep in the limelight, to warm himself in the glow of the powerful, to interpret the desires of the crowd with a word or a gesture. But he lacked d'Annunzio's genius, and was never famous or authoritative enough through his work to allow himself the older poet's eccentricities. The woman Curzio loved most of all, and at one time was going to marry, was born a Roman princess (like the girl d'Annunzio married), but became the widow of one of the most powerful industrialists in Europe, and was undoubtedly the richest woman in Italy: ideal for a climber, perhaps, but not for a poet. None of the other women in his life was as well known and romantic as d'Annunzio's Eleonora. No novelettish and fanciful great lady abandoned palaces and horses and income, husband, and children, to follow him. Although when I knew him Malaparte always had a girl with him, it was always some pale, gentle creature who hardly said a word. No one can compare the outcry which d'Annunzio's French works—his *Martyre de Saint Sebastian* and other plays—aroused in Paris with the failure of Malaparte's *Das Kapital*, when it opened there.

D'Annunzio was sincerely admired and loathed by his outstanding contemporaries. Malaparte managed to irritate mildly and to charm only obscure and unpretentious souls. With Mussolini he soon quarreled. Shortly after 1922 Curzio criticized his taste in ties and made an enemy of him for ever (Mussolini's ties were, in fact, hideous). His best friend was Galeazzo Ciano, who got him out of prison and defended him: a rather provincial creature, drunk with his position as the Dictator's son-in-law, an intimate friend of Princess Colonna's, but an important man in the régime. And, finally, Malaparte never had the opportunity to undertake anything really important, anything "legendary", comparable to d'Annunzio's speech at Quarto, to his flight over Vienna, or to the occupation of Fiume.

This passion of his, which urged him fatally towards the source of power like a moth flinging itself at the flame, was even more clearly shown after the end of the second World War. Who was on top? Who was ultimately going to come out on top? After the arrival of the Allies, Malaparte (at Capri, of course) became liaison officer to the U.S. Army, attached to the office of Military Information at Naples, and at the same time became friendly with Palmiro Togliatti. He was one of the first Italian writers to contribute to *Unità*, the Communist daily, signing himself with a pseudonym, Gianni Strozzi. Strozzi is the name of a ducal family in Florence (and the name of a well-known palace much admired by tourists); the mythical journalist was supposed to sound like someone open-minded and young ("Gianni"—Johnny—and not Giovanni), with a noble past behind him ("Strozzi"), who realized that the world was changing and that one had to be a Communist in Italy in 1944, just as one had to be a liberal in 1870, a war-enthusiast in 1914, and a Fascist in 1919, all so as not to be forgotten or left by the wayside. (Even d'Annunzio, elected a right-wing deputy, was at one point seized with suspicion that the Right counted rather less than he had imagined, and went over to the Left with the famous remark, "I'm going where life is. . . .") Later, Malaparte realized that the Communists were simply not going to make it in a democratic Europe rebuilt by the Americans and ruled by the great democratic parties of the masses. What mattered, he decided, were the people, the public, where everybody was.

*　　*　　*

ONLY IN NUMBERS was there real power. So he flung himself into everything that belonged to the masses—large circulation newspapers, the cinema, the theater—at all costs seeking success. He wrote two international best-sellers, *Kaputt* and *La Pelle*, synthetic works written in bad faith to shock and fascinate millions. He wrote and directed an interesting film, *Forbidden Christ*, and composed the music for it as well; it had a critical but not a box-office success, for its very qualities prevented it from reaching the mass audience which could not have understood it. He wrote and staged a revue called *Sexophone* in which, his face smeared with make-up and his lips reddened, he acted and sang. (He was howled down and lost 23 million lire out of his own pocket.)

His breathless and futile search for resounding popular success after the war was pathetic. It was born, I think, from his fear of being surpassed, of failing to be a man of his time; and it all made one feel dizzy and almost panic-stricken, as if one were watching balancing tricks or trapeze acts performed by an elderly, out-of-condition acrobat. However much he kept up-to-date and "ultra modern", a hint of his background remained. He wore thick, rebellious-looking sweaters, and lived an irregular existence without a home, camping out with friends. And yet he never seemed at all like a revolutionary organizer, a Marxist intellectual, or an angry young man, but only a romantic Bohemian in Paris, vintage 1910, a kind of "Dedo" Modigliani, dissolute but somehow elegant. The title of his revue, *Sexophone*, hints at all this, for it was a vulgar and pointless challenge to the taste of a public that hardly existed any longer (the lower-middle-class Italian of 1919 who was alarmed at the notion of saxophones and sex and Negro music). His weekly tirades in the revue *Tempo* contained the early ideas of Fascism and were apparently enjoyed mostly by men over fifty.

Over the years Malaparte seemed to forget that he was by nature a writer, a poet, a man of letters, and wasted his gifts in ranting and film making, in cheap skits and sketches and dubious journalism; he was too good to succeed with the masses, and too insincere to succeed with critical and thoughtful readers.

*          *          *

THE LAST TIME I saw Malaparte was the day before he left for China, on the journey from which he was to return condemned to death by lung cancer. We were at a reception for Ilya Ehrenburg, who was passing through Rome at the time.

The famous Soviet writer stood angrily in the middle of a silly little room, among flowery cretonnes, cream-colored curtains, and pink mirrors with figures of 18th-century ladies and courtiers cut in the glass: "period" surroundings that went back to 1935, the time when Italy was an "invincible" empire which "neither men nor events would cast down". Ehrenburg was surrounded by a group of Roman "friends of Soviet culture", young Communist intellectuals who carried little weight since they were ordered to admire in the same way whomever was sent to them. These youths were all pale, all bespectacled, and dressed in new suits like guests at a country wedding. They vaguely resembled one another, just like the relatives at a family ceremony, in fact; and their women, mistresses or wives, whichever they were, were all vaguely alike too, and all had the bedraggled and un-*soigné* air of women who had run away from home.

They all stood closely hedged around Ilya, to prevent him

seeing the empty spaces beyond and in the adjoining rooms, and those nearest to him asked him rather trivial questions. They all laughed heartily at his answers, though there was nothing funny about them, and turned to repeat them in Italian to those who were standing farther off, who laughed all over again. Either the importance of the occasion, or the fact that they saw no one around that they did not already know, made them nervous. There were those who wrote for the literary pages of the dailies, or for the cultural weeklies, or the learned monthlies; and a few more. There was I, but I didn't count. Every time they heard the bell ring as the door opened, they all turned as expectantly as a man waiting for a fish to bite his line, hoping the new arrival would be someone from the bourgeois world, some attractive opponent to seduce. But nothing happened. A few elderly non-Communists turned up, but they were familiar faces of people who sit among the distinguished visitors at Party congresses, who sign petitions for this and that, make enthusiastic trips to China, and to every congress beyond the Iron Curtain: unimportant folk who seemed quite uninteresting to me, and, for other reasons, even more uninteresting to the intellectuals of the extreme Left. The Marxists greeted them with a brief wave, unsmilingly.

Ehrenburg had shaggy, untidy gray hair, and eyelids half shut over eyes that peered about like those of an alligator lying awake in the mud. He wore a green shirt with a wide soft collar that left his neck free, and a brand-new, brilliant red tie with wiggles on it (undoubtedly bought in Italy). His suit was of an odd, rough, multi-colored material, a fake tweed woven with little flecks of red, green, peacock-blue, white, and yellow, the latest fashion in Moscow, very likely. And he wore sandals. The Great Revolutionaries almost all wore sandals, or shoes made of criss-cross strips of leather, or punctured with little holes, as if feet destined to show humanity's inevitable and scientific march forward are more delicate, more sensitive to heat than others. He stood patiently in the middle of the circle, letting himself be watched like an example of some rare disease shown to a group of medical students, chain-smoking long Russian cigarettes which he took from their cardboard package, dropping ash on his waistcoat, on his sandals, on the carpet. His fingers were stained dark yellow with nicotine.

Someone asked him: "What are you writing at the moment?" He answered in French: "What am I writing, what am I writing? . . . Can't a writer ever stop writing? It's like being sentenced without a hope of reprieve." Those nearest him laughed at once, the others laughed after them. Then someone asked: "Is it an ambitious work, something as important as your last novel?" (This was a rather daring political question. His last work had been *The Thaw*.) And he replied: "When you're writing, you always think you're doing something important. If not, you wouldn't write. Then, when you've read the reviews, you think again. . . ." He refused to say more, to talk of the theme of his work, to explain exactly what it was about.

Just then, at last, Malaparte came in. The young friends of Soviet culture smiled, relieved, and bade him welcome. They made way to let him through, and presented him to his foreign colleague. The two might have already met in Paris after the First World War, when the Russian was drinking absinthe in the cafés of the Left Bank with *avant-garde* intellectuals, in St. Petersburg during the Revolution, where Malaparte had been as a journalist, or in Berlin, the Berlin of George Grosz and tarts in boots, with riding whips, or simply at other meetings like this, in Russia or in Italy, on "cultural exchange" trips. Malaparte was tall and neat, wearing a rather tight brown tweed jacket and grey flannels, "English style", the uniform of his smart worldly youth. Only the sweater he wore instead of a shirt was meant to show his attachment to left-wing ideas, his open-mindedness. His hair was black, long, straight, and gleaming; his manner at once majestic and pleasant. Now that I think of it, they were indeed a pair. They were "rebels" from the early years of the century, their careers had sometimes been triumphant, sometimes difficult, according to whether their latest ideas had seemed useful or harmful to those in power. Malaparte, like the Russian, had always been pulled in opposite directions, between the rude and "barbarous" simple people of his country, and the mirage of a scientific, mechanized, on-rushing, and pitiless future.

Malaparte was to leave for China the following day. He had come to ask his Soviet colleague for details, for introductions to intellectuals in Peking, for advice and information. The Russian listened, watching him warily from under his eyelids. He refused to make any statements, perhaps because Malaparte talked indiscreetly in public, too casually, clearly, and enthusiastically, like every neophyte, of things that were new to him, whose dangers and undertones he could not guess; and therefore any conversation with him might be wrongly interpreted. All Ehrenburg said was: "When you come to Moscow, come and see me. We'll talk it over then and I'll give you all the letters you need . . ." And he listened in silence to Malaparte's reminiscences of Russia during the war. Very tactfully no one mentioned the fact that his reminiscences were those of a journalist who had followed the Nazi and Fascist armies. He spoke of the peasants he had met in the Ukraine. The young people round him nodded and laughed, to please their compatriot as much as any-thing, because at that time they had at all costs to foster the Party's popularity.

In the end the famous Soviet writer roused himself for the first time and smiled. It was when Malaparte told him what some old men in the Ukraine said to the Italian soldiers. They said: "Itali, Italianski, mir . . . mir. . . ." Now the word *mir*, as everyone knows, means *peace*. It is a word people can always agree on, one of the key words of Soviet politics. The Russian livened up, and hastened to translate it. "*Paix, paix*. . . . They meant that there was no war between them and the Italian soldiers, they were all peasants together." Too late Malaparte realized the trap into which he had made the other fall, but he was unable to stop, and went on bravely to the end: "No, no, thirty years before they'd had a load of candles from Italy, and still remembered them. They remembered the trade mark, and were trying to repeat the name somehow—the only Italian word they knew, *Miralanza*, [a well-known brand of soaps, detergents, and, in olden days, candles]. . . ." The famous Soviet writer again took on the patient air of some phenomenon displayed to the learned, and said hardly another word.

\*     \*     \*

MALAPARTE came back from China with two Italian doctors who had gone to fetch him, to die in Italy. A great many people, friends and enemies, met him at Ciampino. Malaparte was broken, destroyed by an interminable journey from Peking to Prague in a Soviet plane with no pressure control that had to keep stopping here and there in Siberia for various unexpected reasons. He looked like a ghost. As he came down the ladder, supported by friends, he looked about him and breathed: "Look, there's Moravia crying. . . ." Months later he could still repeat without a single mistake the names of those who had come to meet him.

Round his bed in the Roman nursing home a silent struggle broke out between the Christian Democrats and the Communists, each hoping to boast, after his death, that the great name had been one of their faithful followers. From his bed he craftily kept them doubting till the very end. Perhaps he was undecided himself: which power should one back on the brink of death? Which was better, earthly fame as a friend of triumphant Communism, or the supernatural viaticum of a good Christian? To play on the two opposing parties he saw them all, one after the other, and reassured them all—Tambroni, Minister of the Interior, Palmiro Togliatti, Amintore Fanfani, and Pietro Secchia.

The Christian Democrats had one advantage. He was nursed by two nuns who took turns, day and night, and never left him, and two Jesuits came to his bedside, Father Rotondo and Father Cappello. Father Rotondo was a man of culture, an intellectual who tried to convert the writer with subtle arguments. Father Capello was a holy, ascetic, mystical man, who tried to touch the poet's heart. Malaparte had no real religion. Son of a German father, he thought of himself as a Lutheran, perhaps simply because he had never been baptized. Anyone visiting him in the nursing home completely failed to understand, from his talk and from the objects he wanted near him, which party was in the ascendant. Below the window stood a table on which was a reproduction of Giovanni Pisano's *Madonna with a Belt* which is at Prato and so might be considered a reminder of his youth and not strictly a religious symbol; two Chinese porcelain lions, a reminder of Communist China but also of its imperial past: the arms of the city of Prato, a present from the Communist mayor, and a "Prayer of Saint Francis", a present from the Bishop of Assisi, beside a blessed crucifix; a small statue of St. Rita of Cascia sent by a peasant who had made the journey to buy it on foot, and a small statue of a popular Chinese writer. There were two photographs—a portrait of Pius XII and a snapshot of himself (Malaparte) talking to Togliatti.

And, as we all know, neither side really won. At the last Malaparte asked to be baptized and died a Catholic. But in his will he left the villa he had built himself at Capri to the Chinese Communist writers' union.

*       *       *

MALAPARTE's father was an eccentric, stubborn Saxon with whom he quarrelled all his life. His mother came from Lombardy, a northern Italian province. Not only was he not entirely Italian, he could not even boast any Tuscan blood, the blood of those he loved most, and understood and described better than many real Tuscans have done; nor did he even belong in Prato, his home town. In spite of this, few Tuscans were as Tuscan as he was, and few Italians as Italian; no one has shown, with more conscious satisfaction, the virtues and vices of Italians of every age better than Malaparte, who in fact seems more like a made-up "character" than a real man. Wasn't he a contemporary imitation of Pietro Aretino? Perhaps the explanation lies just there—in his mixed blood (he placed enormous importance on "blood"; one of his books is called *Blood*; and right to the end he refused a blood transfusion for fear of thinking another's thoughts and being animated by another's life).

Only a foreigner, perhaps, can manage to be so crudely

Italian. The "italianate Englishman" has been a "devil
incarnate" from the earliest days of the Renaissance, for the
synthetic reproduction of the qualities that seem most obviously
Italian in someone educated in another climate and another
religion has really devilish results. The fact was that Malaparte
was so conventionally Italian that he made all the rest of "us"
feel we were not Italian. Our country was not the "barbarous"
Italy he defended, an island in Europe, cut off from the life and
culture of the rest of the continent, and inhabited by men who
behaved as he did, but ("we" felt) a European nation, immersed
in a common Western culture, and needing to be saved from
"barbarians" like him. Which of us was right? Perhaps the
irritation he aroused in us was due to the fact that we secretly
feared he might be right; that he was the Italian, that is, and
that we were the foreigners.

# 5

# THE SICILIANS

THERE IS NO DOUBT in my mind that one of the few living Italian novelists of the first rank writing today, perhaps the best of all, is the Sicilian Leonardo Sciascia. This statement is not so bold as it sounds. The competition has lately become weak and scarce. Most well-known contemporary Italian novelists have stopped writing serious books for a variety of reasons: some are dead (like the Piedmontese Pavese and the two Sicilians, Vittorini and Tomasi di Lampedusa); some alive but resting on their oars (like Silone, Moravia, Soldati, and Carlo Levi); or some (like Pasolini) find the movies a more rewarding and less Procrustean field of activity.

Who is left? Minor provincial masters, promising young men who may or may not write anything durable in the future, and patient craftsmen who fabricate intricate pastiches, men whose efforts seem directed mainly to surprise or shock the ordinary reader. This is, of course, an old tradition in Italy, which goes back to the baroque saying of Cavalier Marino: *"È del poeta il fin la meraviglia."* Some of these books manage to astound some of the people all of the time (a few literally frighten them out of their wits) but do not seem to have what it takes to last.

Sciascia's books look as if they could. He appears to possess some of the gifts of a great writer. To begin with, he writes extremely well. (This is not indispensable, to be sure—Italo Svevo wrote wretched Italian, a spiky commercial jargon translated from the German with provincial idioms—but it is useful.) His use of language is economical, forceful, transparent, intense. He keeps a curb on his emotions. His books are original inventions, solidly constructed, conceived as one smooth unit from which it is almost impossible to cut a page, a paragraph, even a word. His reality is multiform and can be looked at from several sides. Though reportorial accuracy surely adds nothing to the excellence of works of fiction, the reader is stupidly pleased and reassured to discover that Sciascia's facts are as reliable as Hemingway's.[1] In addition to all this, Sciascia has one advantage many Italian writers envy him for. He is Sicilian.

\*     \*     \*

MORE FAMOUS Italian writers have come from Sicily than from any other Italian region of comparable size. (Among those best known abroad are Verga, Pirandello, Vittorini, and Tomasi di Lampedusa and, among the less known, Capuana, Di Roberto, Rosso di San Secondo, Brancati, Patti, to mention only a few.) In other words, Sciascia—like famous novelists from the American South—had the luck to be born in a defeated, impoverished, tragic, and misunderstood land where injustice and brutality prevail, where emotions run secretly beneath the surface like Carso rivers and sometimes explode violently like those of Homeric heroes. Indeed the scene in which Ulysses tirelessly slaughters his wife's suitors one after the other in front of his young son could have taken place anywhere in Sicily and not many centuries ago.

Sciascia has such deep roots in his native island that his books (like most Sicilian novels) seem to have written themselves out of family recollections, the reminiscences and gossip exchanged in the piazza, the *caffè*, or the *Circolo dei Nobili*, without any important inventive effort on his part. His incandescent hatred of evil, his love of liberty and reason shine through his tranquil, spare prose like the head of Minerva through thousand-lire banknotes when held against the light, and yet his love for his native country manages in the end to embrace everything, its evil vices as well as its virtues. In fact, he contemplates with the same affection and compassion the sunbaked landscape,

[1] Hemingway's description of Milan during World War I, for example is as meticulously exact as a scientific survey, down to the names of obscure streets, small hotels, bars, aperitifs, cigarettes, the habits and talk of the people.

the crumbling houses, the princes' *palazzi*, the garbage-littered streets, the starving and thieving children, the miserable victims of century-old oppression, the ignorant priests, the Mafia's cruel rule as well as its victims, as if he were proud, in a curious way, that such climatological misfortunes, historical catastrophes, heroic feats of resignation, and monstrous crimes could only happen among his people. This point of view, however, as well as the fact that he does not explicitly propose any sure-fire political panacea, prevents his books from becoming merely well-written tracts, as many similar ones are.

I must admit that my valuation of Leonardo Sciascia (whom I have never met) is not shared by professional critics. Only when pinned down in private eye-to-eye debate will an eminent Roman critic reluctantly admit that yes, in a way, when isolated from the contemporary scene as if he were already dead, Sciascia should be considered one of the three or four greatest, surely one of the most durable authors, perhaps even the *numero uno* of his generation. Publicly and officially, however, the same eminent critic will classify him only among the top twenty or thirty, in a group with other writers whose work is obviously transient but easier to catalogue, and whose Marxist or pseudo-Marxist ideologies and motivations are more fashionable. This is probably partly because Sciascia does not live in Rome, where trends and reputations are determined, belongs to no coterie, is rejected alike by the Marxists and the anti-Marxists, and does little to advance his career. He seldom leaves Sicily (as if, like Antaeus, he feared to lose his strength the moment he lost contact with his native earth). In fact, he does not behave like a Sicilian. Most Sicilians are always eager to flee from their island and are past masters in the arts of insinuating themselves into powerful coteries and of promoting their fames and careers.

That he keeps aloof from current fashions and admires discredited and obsolete models he readily admits in his preface to *Salt in the Wound*, a book known in Italian as *Le parrocchie di Regalpetra*. This work, recently published in the United States, was his first. He wrote it in 1954, when he was about 33 years old, an unknown elementary school teacher in his native

Recalmuto. It took him only a few days to finish the first draft of this chronicle of his little town during his lifetime; it was partly written in school while the boys drew pictures or solved problems of arithmetic. He did not know at the time for whom or why he was writing and what he would do with the manuscript once it was finished. Like most other autobiographical books, it was really written by the author for himself, in an effort to make sense of all the disorderly, puzzling, contradictory things he had observed through the years. It is a meandering and fascinating tale of events in Recalmuto (which he transparently concealed under the invented name of Regalpetra), couched in the unfashionable literary style of *La Ronda*'s writers.

*La Ronda* was a small but influential magazine published between 1919 and 1923, at about the time of Sciascia's birth, by young men back from World War I who were in revolt against the bombast and affectation, the decorative use of archaic words and twisted syntax, which plagued the Italian literary style of the times. They strove to write clear, simple, well-ordered, and polished prose. ("I liberated myself of all the Latinism that was imposed on my generation," Sciascia confesses.) The best writers in the period between the two wars had worked for *La Ronda* or had been influenced by it. But by 1954 they were mature or old men whom the younger generation derided.

Why *La Ronda*? Why such an unfashionable choice? Sciascia, being a provincial amateur buried in the heart of a distant island, far from the centers of fashion, might have thought *La Ronda* was the latest thing. On the other hand, he might have been born that way. It may be that his prose naturally belongs to the unadorned and muscular style of Italian writers before the Counter-Reformation and the Spanish rule, the style of Machiavelli and Guicciardini. Sciascia himself proclaimed his pre-Baroque preference for construction rather than ornamentation in these words: "It's more important for me to follow the evolution of the mystery novel than that of esthetic theories." These are, of course, fighting words in a country which cultivates esoteric literary cults.

Sciascia is just as difficult to catalogue from a political point of view. I believe he thinks of himself as a Marxist of sorts. His books are filled with immense Tolstoyan pity for the derelict, admiration for their courage, and the implicit hope that slowly, if other men like him go on writing honestly, denouncing things as they are, analyzing the historical and psychological causes of the Sicilian misfortunes, something will happen. "The poor in this town," he writes, obviously including himself among them, "have a profound faith in the written word: a slash of the pen, they say, like a slash of the sword, is enough to right a wrong or rout an injustice."

He is trying to deceive himself, of course. Sicilians do not read many newspapers. (Italians read fewer newspapers than any other European people, even fewer than the Turks, and Sicilians read fewer newspapers than other Italians.) When the poor talk about "words righting wrongs like a slash of the sword" they mean words written by officials, *notari*, lawyers, judges (Sicilians are particularly fond of protracted legal wrangles, mostly over land boundaries and wills), or by politicians in power, Mafia chiefs (who usually write little but who might redress a wrong or two in their own peculiar way), and surely not by novelists or poets.

Sciascia clearly is working hard to persuade himself that his own words may be useful, that his books may really help to change things. They may well be, in the end: they may change a few things. Who can tell? He has written several successful books in the last few years, two admirable contemporary novels (*Il giorno della civetta* and *A ciascuno il suo*), which have been distorted into shoddy popular movies, one ingenious historical novel, *Il consiglio d'Egitto*, and a series of essays.

\*　　\*　　\*

WHAT CURES does he suggest? When he tries to indicate a solution, Sciascia puts on not Marx's Prince Albert coat, nor Lenin's peaked cap, but the silk suit, powdered wig, and knee-breeches of a *philosophe*. "I believe in human reason," he says, "and in the liberty and justice it engenders, but here in Italy you're accused of waving a red flag as soon as you begin to speak the language of reason." In fact, many *benpensanti* are sure he is a Communist. (He might think so himself, for all I know.) On the other hand, it is pointless to define his exact political position. His politics are not important: his books are—*Salt in the Wound* above them all, the matrix of his subsequent works. All the principal themes he later developed are to be found in it. All his books are, in his own words, "one Sicilian book which probes the wounds of the past and present and develops as the history of the continuous defeat of reason and of those who have been personally overcome and annihilated in that defeat."

In fact *Salt in the Wound* is a powerful panorama of life in a Sicilian Middletown; it is not a philosophical or political diagnosis. It contains an incredible number of characters of all ages, political opinions, degrees of literacy, and occupations, all of them sketched with miniature-like precision. None of them is the impersonation of an abstract idea. None is a sociological specimen. The characters all seem like human beings. To all of them, individually, and to Regalpetra, collectively, all kinds of preposterous, terrifying, or funny things happen, things that obviously could happen only in Sicily.

The mayor of 1944, the man the American Army put in the chair, was murdered on November 15 of that year, on a rainy Sunday evening in the town's central square. A pistol was placed against his neck and fired. The mayor's friends were with him but no one saw anything; everybody fell back in terror from the crumbling body. He was a man who had many enemies. He spent his life dragging lawsuits from court to court, and had even quarreled with one of the leaders of the Mafia, who had been his business partner some time back . . .

A short analysis of local municipal politics:

In following the tortuous path of the municipal administration through the official records of the Council meetings, you seem to be entering a world in which an interplay of sophisms, of secret understandings and of deceit, of internecine warfare, cold and hot, is transmuted into pure arabesque. The only time a concrete relationship is established between the administrator and the citizen is when the mayor certifies births, identities, or deaths. . . . The bureaucracy, which in Sicily is a metaphysical institution (and is blasphemed as such), reaches an apex of consecration in the act of signature. When a mayor signs a certificate he's like a priest saying mass. For the rest of the day he is at peace with his conscience.

Sciascia is at his best when describing the wretched children in his own school whom he had to observe every day for several hours:

Thirty boys bored stiff. They split razor blades down the middle, work them a quarter of an inch into the wooden desks and pluck them like guitar strings. They exchange obscenities that by now I have to ignore—your sister, your mother. They swear, spit, make rabbits out of notebook paper—rabbits that move their long ears and end up as balls of paper if I suddenly call on them. And boats, and paper hats; or they color in the pictures in the textbooks, using the red and yellow so savagely that they tear the paper. They're bored, poor things. Stories, grammar, the cities of the world, the products of Sicily—but what they're thinking about is lunch. As soon as the bell rings they race out to grab their tin bowls; watery beans with a bit of margarine floating on top, a sliver of canned corned beef and a dab of jam that they wrap up in a sheet of notebook paper and go off licking, jam and ink together.

And:

The sons of the sulphur and salt miners are a little sharper than the sons of the peasants. The peasants take their boys to work in the fields during vacations and holidays; in May, when the beans are harvested, they stop sending them to school, unless they're sure to be promoted. This is why the peasants stop me in the street in early May, to ask how their sons are doing. I know why they ask, and I answer evasively as I can: "Perhaps he'll pass, he's not doing so badly." If I told the truth, the class would be deserted; not more than ten pupils would come to the final exams. Besides, I end up promoting more than I should, and defer those who should be in special schools to the October exams. These boys spend the three hours of school in melancholic fixation, their eyes staring straight, their mouths opening only to ask to go to the toilet. Those I send to repeat never show up for the October exams. The mothers don't want their sons to start the hard labor in the fields at twelve years of age, and they hide the truth from their husbands. I tell the mothers that it's no use; the boys don't study and will never pass. They answer that they hope things will change next year, or else their sons can go to night school where they'll be promoted for sure. And in fact one teacher at the night school gets three thousand lire for every pupil promoted, so you can imagine what goes on there.

He knows the humble Mafia of the little towns:

This is a Mafia Town. A Mafia of poses more than of facts, although the facts, if rare, are not lacking, and in the species of murder victims. There are a couple of Mafia chiefs, men with money and education; they go to the cafes arm-in-arm with ex-cons and then with the sergeant of the *carabinieri*. As soon as they see a sergeant they immediately play up to him, hang on him, guess his last desires. For them it's important that people who want to live in peace see them in the company of the more notorious members of the Mafia, and that the Mafia men see them on friendly terms with the cops. This game is their life.

\*          \*          \*

SICILY is, to say the least, baffling to Italians from other regions. To understand and govern the inhabitants, cater to their needs, and solve some of their fundamental problems have proven almost impossible tasks at all times. The attempt was made, with little success, by Greeks, Romans, Byzantines, Arabs, Normans, French, Spaniards, Neapolitans, Piedmontese, and the U.S. Army. Even Sicilians have seldom shown themselves capable of coping with the intricate mechanisms of their own life, certainly not the Mafia which does not always manage to run things as smoothly in its domain, which is Western Sicily, as its opponents think.

The reason why Sicily is ungovernable is that the inhabitants have long ago learned to distrust and neutralize all written laws (alien laws in particular) and to govern themselves in their own rough home-made fashion, as if official institutions did not exist. This arrangement is highly unsatisfactory (the inhabitants themselves endlessly lament their fate) because it cures no ills, in fact makes them worse, promotes injustice and tyranny, leaves crimes unpunished, does not make use of the Sicilians' best qualities, and has kept the country stagnant and backward in almost every way. It consists of a technique, or art, which is second nature to all Sicilians, both the decent, hard-working, honorable Sicilians, and the criminal minority, which includes the Mafia, that of building up one's personal power, and of acquiring enough power to intimidate or frighten one's competitors, rivals, or enemies, in order to defend one's honor and welfare at all times.

This is not necessarily always objectionable. Similar techniques have been pursued in many other countries and many fields of human activity by all sorts of respectable people who wanted to get ahead against stiff competition (at Versailles under Louis XIV, in Wall Street, Hollywood in its heyday, by big corporations everywhere, the Soviet Politburo, democratic political parties). It is, however, nowhere pursued as subtly, astutely, and ruthlessly as in Sicily.

Power has many sources. The first and nearest source is one's family. In Sicily the family includes relatives as far as the third, fourth, or fifth degree, collaterals, in-laws, relatives of the in-laws, godfathers and godmothers, best men at marriages, dependents, hangers-on, servants, and vassals. They all help or must be helped, as the case may be, in times of necessity. The power of the family is increased by the conquest of new vassals, by new alliances, association with other powerful families (some marriages are decided for strictly political reasons, as among royalty), association with powerful groups (the Church, large corporations, political parties), and, above all, by the capture of the gratitude and loyalty of influential friends.

One can cultivate both humble vassals and influential friends by doing them favors. One poor man needs a good (or a better) job, another a permit to carry fire-arms, the son of a third wants to pass his exams or be let off from military service, a fourth may be in need of a little loan; an official always wants a promotion, a professional man needs clients, a land-owner wants protection from cattle-thieves, a politician wants many votes on election day. They all welcome help. Influential men can, and often do, belong to the official establishment like policemen, judges, prefects, cabinet ministers, *deputati* (the State being considered by Sicilians as little more than the biggest Mafia of them all).

The island is therefore an intricate web of favors done in

exchange for other favors among men of all classes, from the humblest to the highest. It is, however, indispensable for anybody who wants to survive never to over-estimate his actual power, to gauge the power of all his possible opponents with the utmost precision, in order to occupy in society exactly the place he can actually defend with it, and to pursue only the aims he can presumably achieve. Disasters of all kinds can result from a miscalculation.

Power is used to intimidate and eventually to destroy rivals and enemies, mostly in ways which are not strictly criminal. Only in Western Sicily the *ultima ratio* for subduing the stubborn is death. A man who encroaches on another man's territory, brazenly seduces his wife or daughter, defies traditional prejudices, denounces another man's crimes to the authorities, and heeds no warnings must eventually be eliminated. (Why this should not be necessary in Eastern Sicily is a sociological mystery which has never been satisfactorily studied and explained.) As a result it is not surprising that the number of murders committed in the region is proportionally far higher than in other parts of Italy. It is surprising, however, that this number is not as high as one could imagine. This is because almost always the mere threat of death is sufficient to produce results. The threat does not even have to be spoken. It is in the air, in the consciousness of the people. Everybody involved is Sicilian, they all obey the same centuries-old rules of conduct, know their way about, are aware of the dangers of obstinacy. Nobody is a fool, everybody pushes the weak around and exploits them but prudently always gives way to the strong and ruthless.

All this is done with grace. Manners are almost always impeccable, even when matters of life and death are being decided, the language always euphemistic, and things never called by their own names. Foreigners seldom understand what any controversy is about; they do not know what is being left unsaid, because it is unnecessary to say it, or what is behind the dazzling smiles, the hearty embraces, the damp kisses on stubbly cheeks, the clasped hands, the compliments, the declarations of eternal friendship.

To be sure Sicily is no longer what it was a few years ago. It is still visibly changing; factories spring up here and there. Public works projects transform the landscape, cities have been cleaned up and enlarged. The people's standard of living has never been so high which, of course, is not saying much. But those who hoped to see the industrial revolution dispel the cloud of fear under which Sicilians lived for centuries (some optimists believed the industrial revolution to be the only cure for all the island's ills) are bitterly disappointed.

*          *          *

THE PATRIARCHAL Mafia of the villages, with its vaguely feudal code of honor, its old-fashioned manners, its dedication to patron saints and religious festivals, is on the way out, but a more vicious and dangerous, and less controllable Mafia has risen in the bustling cities. Its somewhat overdressed leaders are mostly men in their early forties, urbane, active, and tough. Some of them have university degrees. They handle immense sums of money, kickbacks from public works projects, manipulation of real estate restrictions, party funds, etc. These men enjoy a power the old Mafia never dreamed of, have international connections, shuttle by air to and from Rome, Milan, Beirut, or New York. They entertain bankers, political leaders, industrialists.

Only fools, idealists, and foreigners try to move without their guidance and protection in any business venture. Only fools, idealists, and foreigners, in fact, try to compete against enterprises enjoying Mafia tutelage and paying tribute to it, and this usually with disastrous results, for one thing only has been preserved from the old days: the new leaders still cultivate the power to order the death of anybody stupid enough to stand in their way. This, of course, they seldom do. In fact these men can often be compared to great statesmen of the past, whose unquestioned authority at international conferences was based on invisible and unmentionable armies and navies which they could employ at a moment's notice, but seldom had to. The cleverest contemporary Mafia men (as well as the cleverest statesmen of the past) never use the words: "Or else . . ."

This does not mean that men are not murdered almost daily by the Mafia in Western Sicily. The victims are undisciplined and ambitious Mafia men of low, medium, or high (but not the highest) rank who "took a step longer than their leg"; policemen in the line of duty; indiscreet or loquacious witnesses or informers; young and eager trade union organizers in country districts. The mortality of the latter is among the highest. They are particularly feared by the Mafia because they play without observing the rules and can easily cause more trouble than anybody else. They incite farm hands to strike at harvest time, incite them to rebellion, demand the local application of laws which are valid in other parts of the country, and give sleepless nights to Christian Democratic politicians, land and mine owners, and industrialists.

On the other hand, the Mafia does not bother with foreigners, journalists, and reformers. Foreign travelers are blind, do not know what is going on around them, and every year spend a lot of money in Sicily. They are respected and protected. The Mafia often orders some petty thief to return to them what was stolen from their cars or hotel rooms. To be sure, muckraking journalists try to write embarassing revelations about the Mafia from time to time, and often publish books of alleged Mafia secrets, but they are seldom to be feared. Their facts are almost always wildly inaccurate, but, even if accurate, could never be proved in a court of law, especially if the testimony of Sicilian witnesses is necessary. The most daring exposés always leave things as they are. Reformers are rare. They come and, as they tire of getting no results, and battling against invisible obstacles, they go. The best manage at times to change the surface of things in one or two villages but never the real substance underneath. They can safely be left alone to pursue their ineffective activities.

*        *        *

THE MAFIA was careful never to bother directly the reformer the whole world believes is its worst enemy, Danilo Dolci. It never thought him really dangerous, although it has occasionally taken reprisals against Sicilians who have helped him. To begin with, Dolci is almost a foreigner. He was born in 1924 at Sesana, near Trieste, in a province which had been part of Austria until 1918. His father (an Imperial and Royal, later Italian, station-master) had German and Istrian blood, his music-loving mother was half-German. Dolci therefore has no more than twenty-five per cent Italian blood, and border blood from the extreme North-east at that. He looks like a foreigner, tall (head and shoulders taller than any Sicilian crowd he leads in demon-strations), heavy, placid, blond and blue-eyed. (To be sure, there are many blond and blue-eyed Sicilians, most of them of Norman descent, but they usually look like nervous and thin Englishmen.) He could easily be taken for a prosperous Austrian shopkeeper, a Bavarian brewer, a Bolzano wine-grapes grower, the kind of people on whom *Lederhosen* look natural. Like most of these men Dolci speaks jovially and unguardedly, in an island where every word is loaded with hidden meanings and only the initiate has the key.

Dolci seems to think everybody is fundamentally nice; and that, if people only knew the real facts, they would draw his conclusions, share his hopes, and join him in his work. As a result, almost all the non-Sicilian people who come in contact with him, including the author of these pages, and also many Sicilians, find him irresistible, even when they realize he is doomed to go on chasing wild geese and never to produce results proportionate to his efforts and sacrifices.

When talking with him one is always tempted to believe the unbelievable, that, one day soon, enough people in Sicily will wake up and stop behaving like the Sicilians they are, and free their island from its tragic destiny, a destiny which is noto-riously due not so much to a limited number of exploiters, bullies, and murderers, as to the overwhelming multitudes of resigned, apathetic, and willing victims. One is seduced by Dolci's ebullient optimism, determination, his heroic acceptance of sacrifice, ridicule, and occasional punishment; by his sim-plicity and what is obviously a gentle form of madness. He is, in fact, as mad as many saints were in the past, a mad non-Catholic saint of today.

*          *          *

HE WAS BORN a Catholic and was a fervent and practicing one until a few years ago. After the war, he abandoned his studies in Milan—he was a student of music, and later of architecture— to follow the priest Don Zeno and work for him as a secretary. Don Zeno was a holy and controversial man who followed his inspiration rather than his superiors' instructions. He founded a village for abandoned children, was persecuted by the official Church, and was finally stopped from experimenting with dangerous ideas. Dolci, who was fascinated and inspired by the priest's conceptions, considers himself still a religious man but definitely not a Catholic.

After leaving Don Zeno, Dolci went to Sicily. He loved the island where he had lived as a young boy, when his father was stationmaster in a small town. Danilo chose one of the meanest and hungriest villages, Trappeto, to settle in at first, in order to meditate on a plan of action. There he married the cleaning woman of the house where he roomed, the widow of a fisherman with five children. (The couple have a few children of their own now.) Later he moved to Partinico, one of the Mafia strong-holds, where he gathered a group of followers and founded some-thing impressively named *Centro Studi e Iniziative per la Piena Occupazione*. It consists of a few employees and a mimeograph machine in a barn-like house, and is financed irregularly and insufficiently by contributions from all over the world, mostly from Protestant countries, although often by the Catholics in those countries, and by the royalties from Dolci's books.

Dolci's technique is simple and straightforward. He is a gentle and fearless agitator. He singles out one overdue but necessary improvement for a particular district, a dam, a road, a hospital, a school, an irrigation canal; convinces a lot of local people of its need; talks to key men who might help him or men who stand in the way; manages to persuade many village priests, mayors, doctors, schoolteachers; holds meetings and debates; publishes articles and gives interviews to the press. Finally, when the situation is ripe, he decides on a final demonstration to force the authorities to action. He wants them either to persecute him publicly or to hasten the construction of the project.

\* \* \*

DOLCI'S BOOKS, the ultimate source of his power, make fascinating reading, like most books dealing with the incredible facts of life in Sicily. They are more scrapbooks than books, carefully edited albums filled with newspaper clippings, quotations from official documents, facsimiles of bureaucratic letters, speeches, minutes of meetings, answers to questionnaires, children's poems, tape recordings of confessions, reminiscences, tales from all kinds of people, and an occasional little essay by the author. There is probably no better way to cope with such rich material.

In *The Man Who Plays Alone*—the title comes from a prudent Sicilian proverb, "The man who plays alone never loses,"—as in all his preceding books, he allows the facts to speak for themselves and seldom attempts to diagnose, or suggest cures for, the impressive collection of symptoms.[2] The authenticity of people's speech comes out even in translation. This is, for instance, the way a small *mafioso* explains some of the things a man ought to know:

An advantage of the Catholic trade unions is the assistance they can get from the Christian Democrats in exchange for help in getting them votes at election time. A recommendation from a priest, an archbishop, a cardinal . . . nowadays these people have some say, they have authority . . . a job in a bank, in an office . . . These people can help if they wish. And if they help a person, then naturally he will follow them: after all, they have provided his children with daily bread. When someone's been given a job, if he cannot return the favor any other way, he'll naturally try and get votes for them. The debt must be paid back. . . . Everyone will rally around a man who's in the money: he'll be favored by everyone, the authorities and the people alike. If one has money one becomes a gentleman. If you're in with the Government party, you're well off; but if you're against them, things will go badly for you. . . . A man with money finds all doors open, everyone makes way for him.

[2] Danilo Dolci, *The Man Who Plays Alone* (Pantheon, N.Y.), ably translated and annotated by Antonia Cowan.

Girolamo Leto, provincial secretary of the Liberal Party in Palermo:

. . . The Mafia, like the clergy, sides with power. . . . Today the real trouble in industry is not the *mafiosi* but the politicians who put pressure on to get jobs for their *clientes*; this is what is known as the "white Mafia"; the "black Mafia" shoots, the other kills without shooting. Politicians use the Mafia as an instrument to get power.

Michelangelo Russo, provincial secretary of the Communist Party in Palermo:

. . . There is a vast sea of bureaucracy. It's estimated that there are thirty thousand civil servants in Palermo, out of a population of 550,000, what with the Regional government, the State, the Provincial administration, the Municipal offices, and Regional economic organizations. From the numerical point of view, this category is most powerful. Since everybody knows that a job is not to be had through open competitive exams or on merit but only through string pulling, people turn to politicians in power in order to get the necessary recommendation. Once a man gets a job . . . it is unlikely he'll join any left-wing opposition party. Obviously he is influenced by how he got the job in the first place. . . . Our chief difficulty is that we have not succeeded in creating a mass party. At the moment our Party is weak, both as regards political initiative and in its lack of representation in the different strata of society. Another obstacle is the fact that our members are not sufficiently well educated to read widely or to assimilate and discuss printed matter, or to read our own publications.

A well-informed, readable, if somewhat prolix, travelogue-diary-reportage of Danilo Dolci's country was written by an American of Sicilian descent: *A Passion for Sicilians*, by Jerre Mangione, who is a novelist, former journalist, essayist, professor of English at the University of Pennsylvania and head of the University's creative writing program. Mangione and his wife lived near the Dolcis at Partinico and became their intimate friends; Mangione joined Dolci's staff for a while as secretary, adviser, and confidant. He went with Dolci to hunger strikes, sitdowns, demonstrations; sat with him at staff conferences; and apparently, like Boswell, never stopped scribbling in his notebooks.

In the end he had enough material to fill his useful and interesting book.[3] It contains more information about Dolci the man than other books I know, including Dolci's own. You can read all about this man's youth, maturity, private and public life, the genesis of his ideas, his adventures and hopes, his difficulties with authorities; you get a description of other people's (including opponents') views of him, and so forth. The book is readable, and, as far as I could tell, accurate and reliable. In spite of his Italian blood, however, Mangione is a victim of the view of Italy which is common among many of the lighter-weight English-language writers, both the professional *Italianisants* and the casual travelers, mostly women: the sentimental, compassionate, dewy-eyed view of the beautiful but unfortunate country, where the innocent and noble *contadini* are the victims of the machinations of cruel and avaricious villains. Why this view should please Mangione, for whom Sicily is the idealized home of his forebears, I understand. But he should also have learned from family tradition that Sicilian society is extremely complex, that one should be very careful when describing it, and that the people cannot be cleanly separated into sheep and goats.

It is curious to observe that Mangione has a distorted and partisan view of Italian history and misspells many Italian words. He writes: "[Garibaldi's] proved to be a false liberation of Sicily [in 1860]. Shortly afterwards the landowning barons, using gangs of *mafiosi* as troops, resumed their feudal powers, and continued to keep the majority of Sicilians in a subservient state." This is a series of over-simplifications. Garibaldi's liberation of Sicily from Bourbon rule, when seen in the light of nineteenth-century ideology, was a true liberation. The landowning barons found the competition of the new capitalist bourgeoisie increasingly irresistible in the decades after 1860. The Mafia was used by the new capitalists more freely than the barons had ever done. Its power really grew with the help of the new bourgeoisie, the men who bought Church land put up for

[3] Jerre Mangione, *A Passion for Sicilians: The World Around Danilo Dolci* (Morrow, New York).

sale. Garibaldi did not end feudal powers which were abolished forty-odd years before, when fiefs were transformed by law into private estates. The factors which kept Sicilians in a subservient state are innumerable and cannot be limited to one, the barons' conception of their place in society.

Mangione's linguistic errors are equally inexplicable. He repeats several times "*Siamo in accordo*" ("We agree") as if it were a familiar colloquial phrase. The correct form, of course, is "*Siamo d'accordo*". He writes "*guante*" instead of "*guanti*" (gloves); "*scusa*" between people who do not know each other, instead of the formal "*scusi*"; "*pianificazzione*" instead of "*pianificazione*"; and calls the well-known "*carabinieri*" "*caribinieri*", forgetting the parallel English word "carabineer". These mistakes are not unusual and could only be noticed by Italian readers, who do not read foreign books about their country anyway. There are perhaps only a handful of English-language writers who bother to find the correct spelling of Italian words, as if Italian were still an unwritten language, like some obscure African or Amazonian dialect, which everybody is allowed to write his own way, by ear. One is led to suspect (when one stumbles on one misspelled word after another) that facts are treated as glibly, which may be unjust in the case of Jerre Mangione.

\*　　\*　　\*

IN THE BEGINNING Dolci staged hunger strikes for himself and some of his followers. Later he preferred sitdowns which blocked public roads, cross-country marches of peasants, and unusually large public meetings. He even led delegations to Rome, to stand in front of Montecitorio, the seat of Parliament, placidly holding signs, or to explain the problem to ministers and *deputati*. Naturally the authorities handle him gingerly, with great tact, trying to avoid incidents.

Nothing immediate seems to come from his efforts. Only very rarely are the ministers convinced, the obstacles removed, the red tape loosened, and the project turned into a reality. But other useful, secondary results are produced nevertheless, whose consequences are not easy to estimate. Some people are taught the value of impatience, the need to defend their rights without waiting for the benevolent intervention of distant and absent-minded authorities; some learn that injustice can be resisted if defenseless people get together, exchange ideas, organize, and decide on a plan of action. One obscure and forgotten problem is talked about in public until it becomes urgent; newspapers begin to ask questions; well-wishers are aroused. Sometimes the leisurely itinerary of the dossiers, estimates, and engineering plans from one office to another becomes perceptively accelerated under the pressure of public opinion. Eventually (not always) the dam, school, hospital, road, or canal may be built.

It is difficult to determine how effective Dolci's methods are. Obviously, from a strictly traditional point of view, he should get no results whatever since he controls no real power, not the kind of power that intimidates Sicilians. He does not belong to a family, party, or awe-inspiring group; he has never ordered the death of anyone; he could not even defend himself and his followers in a real showdown. Furthermore, weak as he is, he has taken on, at one time or another, most of the dominant organizations in the island, the Church, the Mafia, the Government, the Christian Democratic Party, the Bank of Sicily, the police, and the prominent men. He even gives the Communist Party (which tries to exploit his activities) headaches.

In spite of all this, he has not been neutralized, deported, or destroyed. In reality, he is more powerful than people think, but the roots of his power lie outside the island. He is internationally famous. Foreign journalists, television cameramen, photographers, reporters from many parts of the world flock to his picturesque demonstrations. His books sell well in North Italy, Great Britain, the Scandinavian countries, and the United States. All this is the equivalent to a confederation of Mafia *cosche*. The fear of bad publicity stops the hand of the police. He is so well-known that he cannot be intimidated, roughly handled, or killed. (Moreover, the Mafia does not bother about him because, as I pointed out, it does not believe he is an immediate threat.) In fact he is not primarily what he belives he is, neither a political agitator nor a social reformer inflaming people with his arguments, but an unconscious and extremely able manipulator of publicity.

# *6*

# THE ARISTOCRATS

MANY ITALIANS used to live under the illusion that their country was more or less the one described by pocket encyclopedias, atlases, and geography textbooks. Wasn't there a Kingdom with its borders marked out on the map, wasn't there a King whose profile appeared on stamps and coins? Weren't there uniform laws, an army, a navy, a flag, just as in Europe's other great nations? In the days before the First World War, only the older Italians with good memories read the official descriptions with a certain skepticism. They still remembered how Italy had been hastily put together, under exceptional circumstances, by a courageous minority; how defects and shortcomings had been hidden or disguised for long; how old traditions and virtues had been discarded hurriedly for more modern and foreign ones—and, therefore, this minority feared that the construction was too flimsy to withstand a really hard test. But the younger Italians (who are today's old men) had learned their history in school and not by listening to family gossip, a history prettified and polished up like a popular illustration; and they regarded every expression of doubt as a betrayal. It was this generation's patriotic and optimistic zeal, in polemic with the older men and with reality, that gave Italy twenty years of dictatorship and a "strong" foreign policy. They governed Italy with absurd bravado, as though it were the Great Power of their imagination and the official rhetoric, and not what it was in reality.

When the picture-book Italy of the sentimental novels and the government-controlled press collapsed, there immediately appeared divisions which had been neglected, obscure forces and

tendencies which had been forgotten or concealed. With amaze-
ment, it was finally realized that Southern Italy is another
country which leads a life totally dissimilar to that of the North
(in consequence of which the same tax is mechanically exacted
in Milan and ingeniously collected in Naples by a thousand
complicated subtleties); that those provinces which had been
well governed in the past, such as the Veneto under the Republic of Venice and the Austrians, were also today the most obedient and loyal to the constituted powers, while those which had
been badly governed, such as the Legations and Sicily, were
perennially anarchistic and rebellious; that the Catholics and
the Church had remained silently hostile to the liberal state and
had formed an enclave almost without contacts with the official
world; that several regions longed for autonomy as for a liberation; and that the mass of the industrial workers were in secret
mutiny. In short, it was realized that the legal and moral
construction of the *Risorgimento* revealed, through large rents
and gashes, an older and more lasting reality, just as after an
earthquake or a bombardment a Baroque church will sometimes
show, under its stripped-off plaster coating, a Romanesque
framework.

                    *          *          *

THAT Italy does exist it would be foolish to deny. It is no doubt
a peninsula in the Mediterranean where certain well-known
historical events have taken place. It could also be defined as
the heritage of complicated and heaped-up masses of ancient
walls, *palazzi*, churches, basilicas, ministry buildings, abbeys,
convents, theaters, castles, hovels, porticoes, *piazzas*, noble seats,
universities, museums, fortresses, villas, and gardens (there is
one garden in Verona which since 1100 has belonged to the
family of the Counts Giusti, who for this reason are called the
Giusti del Giardino, "of the Garden") that compose our cities—
each city profoundly different from the next, yet all of them
Italian, that is, created by the same genius. One cannot easily
escape an architectural imperative which so forcefully imposes
memories, ways of life, a standard of taste, a special technique

for living together, that even foreigners begin to feel different after having lived in one of our cities for a short time.

In Rome, for example, beneath the walls of the Quirinale Palace, there is a small, open-air people's market, which sells fish, poultry, fruits, and vegetables, that would be unimaginable alongside Buckingham Palace or the Elysée. Under the columns of Palazzo Massimo, residence of one of the oldest families in Europe, by century-long custom homeless vagabonds still find a place to sleep. In the courtyard of the ancient *palazzo* of the Borghese princes stands a small fountain that provides excellent water (so famous it has given its name to the street, Via Fontanella di Borghese). Today the *palazzo* is rented out to offices, a famous club, private families, and a large antique shop, yet at meal-times, just as in past centuries, the poor people of the quarter—the old, the children, the fat housewives in their felt slippers—all go with a bottle or pitcher in hand to get their drinking-water, a thing that would be unthinkable in almost any city outside of Italy. Can the poor draw their water in the Duke of Argyll's residence in London?

Those rich moderns who buy some crumbling, decadent little *palazzo* in the heart of old Rome and renovate it with new bathrooms, an elevator, and *boiseries* of unpolished wood, must accustom themselves to the wine-shop across the way with its rickety chairs spread on the sidewalk, the shoemaker at the corner, the carpenter who works in the open air outside his shop, the wandering singers who come by in the evening, picking discordantly on a guitar. In almost all of Italy's cities the palaces of the great historic families are erected in the middle of the old popular quarters: they stand in a confused tangle of dirty alleyways that swarm with people, cats, dogs, chickens, donkeys, amid festoons of drying laundry. Not all the noble palaces at Venice are on the Grand Canal, while even those that face it with such dignity have a back entrance on land hidden among the narrow alleyways inhabited by the poor. Such an architectural plan imposed (and, in some way, still imposes) a living together of rich and poor, powerful and humble, which was one of the characteristics of Italian life, and as a result of which the holidays and

days of mourning were shared in common, not because the poor
and humble were *clientes*, that is, inferiors requiring protection
and help, but *famuli*, that is, members of the same great family
which embraces every social stratum.

Thus, Italy is without doubt its buildings and its walls. It is
also the people who live there, the Italians. But who are these
Italians? What have they uniquely in common? The answer is
very difficult. Is it religion? But their religion is the same as that
of other profoundly dissimilar European peoples. Is it the language they speak? Until a few years ago the language was above
all a written one, the language of a cultured minority. Down to
the Second World War, the great mass of the Italian population
felt (and perhaps still feels) more at its ease speaking its own
regional dialect, which is not a corruption of Italian but a direct,
ancient, and noble derivation from "decadent" Latin. In a
certain sense the current use of Italian as a spoken language is
the product of national independence and of the anxiety to hide
the most striking differences between the various provinces; it is
almost as artificial as the use of Gaelic in Ireland.

\*          \*          \*

ITALY is its people, the people of culture (that is, the conscious
inheritance) and the people who have never bothered their
heads over such matters, who do not know the reasons why they
behave "like Italians", why they eat, work, make love, do
business, raise a family, repeat proverbs, know how to survive
dangers, and know how to die when it is considered obscurely
necessary. In this sense, Italy is therefore not a touristic, geographic, philatelic, diplomatic entity, but rather a realm of the
spirit, so that one can say that many Italian citizens do not
really belong to it, while there are rare foreigners so ripened by
experience and study that they have become, sometimes even
without living in Italy for long, intimately Italian. True, one
cannot read the record of the national genius with the same
clarity in all of Italy's inhabitants. A section of the new industrial bourgeoisie, for example, consciously lived according to
patterns of behavior borrowed from abroad in the first half of

the century, from French novels, English governesses, Swiss private schools, American films. Their relations with the ordinary people (and with the social classes above them) are uneasy, guarded, embarrassed, and impersonal. Their wives find it easier to make their charitable contributions by mail, sending a check to some society, whereas the old-style Italian women, whether noble or bourgeois, still go to the needy families quite openly and without embarrassment to bring their bit of assistance and to gossip with them in dialect. Many of these new bourgeois live isolated in their school-book language, in the geological strata of their income bracket, inhabiting districts built just for them, cut off from the rest like the old European quarters in Chinese cities. Indeed, when they can do it, they also confine the poor people in concrete ghettos built at the city's periphery.

They often have the embarrassing desire not to appear Italian, to repudiate an awkward and inconvenient heritage, and so they glory in destroying the old cities in order to construct, in the vacuum they have created, residential quarters that seem as South American as possible, confirming with their blank concrete walls the modern and international generic qualities of the men who have built them. Observe, for example, the two almost identical buildings on Piazza Venezia in Rome. One building, the ancient embassy of the Venetian Republic, is uncertain, asymmetrical, superb, and full of dignity. The other, which is a modern copy of it built by an insurance company, repels us by its anxious need to be praised, trying to surpass its rival by neatness and a banal and arithmetical symmetry. The one great book that has come out of the new bourgeoisie, written by the son of an engineer and businessman who built small villas for the rich in the Rome of Victor Emanuel III, Alberto Moravia's *The Age of Indifference*, is a pitiless condemnation of this class.

In one of his letters, D. H. Lawrence wrote: "I hate city Italians. They wear ugly neckties." At a certain point all English travelers discover that "Italy is a *contadino* civilization". And there is some truth in it. Italy lives on (if at all) in its ordinary people, the peasants, the sailors, the fishermen, the artisans. In part it also lives on in the old aristocratic families. There is almost nothing that will help us to rediscover this Italy, since—outside of a few curious foreigners or some dialect poets— nobody has really studied it and attempted to define its characteristics. Many people are anxious to embellish the Italians or to improve them, but without first finding out what they were. Everything has been covered by the slime of receding floods of clichés, of sentiments straight out of the cheapest fiction, of hasty journalistic judgments and a morality that smacks of Sunday sermons. As a result, the Italians today are almost completely ignorant of those ancient rules—or ashamed of them without even knowing them clearly—which they have in their blood and which still sometimes succeed in making their life, if not the most just, prosperous, and efficient, unquestionably the most human, pleasant, courteous, and satisfying one in the world, so exactly fitted to man's measure that many foreigners feel immediately at home in it.

Almost all Italians—sometimes, unwittingly, also the new bourgeoisie—know how to do the same things, at a distance of centuries, that their ancestors did. If left to himself, an ordinary mason in an Italian village can still build a house of noble proportions. During the last war, when the country was a battlefield for two enemy armies, the peasants knew where to hide their goods, where to send their women and livestock so that they'd be safe, knew how to placate the soldiery with wine, gossip, and small favors, how to extricate themselves diplomatically from difficult situations, just as peasants had done many centuries before. During those years, Marquis Ambrogio Doria of the historic Genovese family which goes back to the year 1000, while living in his Montaldeo villa, discovered, rummaging through his archives, Cardinal Mazarino's letter to an ancestor and namesake, Ambrogio Doria, in which the Cardinal reassured him about the behavior of the French troops in Italy and included a proclamation to be posted up, addressed "*Aux Troupes de Sa Majesté le Roy,*" which would safeguard his house from looting. The Marquis's administrator immediately had the proclamation framed and nailed to the main portal, just as at that time on many other portals were affixed the letters of American generals, German colonels, or escaped prisoners grateful for the hospitality they had received. In the anarchy of those years and the immediate post-war period, there re-appeared in the passes of the Apennines the same bandits who had held up stage-coaches the century before, with the same technique, the same courtesy towards the women, and the same melodramatic arrogance and swagger. (The railroad services were interrupted, and the traffic ran, as in the past, on the old Roman highways.) In Rome one also saw how the Roman ruins had been created at the beginning of the medieval age. During the months of the German occupation and when the Allied Military Government first started, the people went out at night and stole, to build themselves shanties, doors, windows, roof-tilings from abandoned barracks on the periphery, from un-guarded houses or villas whose owners had run away, carried off Travertine slabs from the tops of walls, tore off bricks, columns, pilasters, ornaments, and, in a short time, made picturesque and very new ruins, identical with those ancient ones that filled the hearts of poets with so much emotion and which the tourists come to admire.

\*     \*     \*

THE ITALIAN ARISTOCRACY, which until a few generations ago was the ruling class, has a burdensome and useless heritage. As an empty bottle keeps the aroma of the wine it contained, so the aristocracy holds on to the memory of its past importance and dignity, of its duties, its responsibilities, and its art of ruling. It also remembers the ancient rules of life and preserves, in family libraries, the books and archives of the past, which are the culture and past of all. The intimate history of Italy is partly buried in the letters, notarial deeds, diaries, account books, testaments, and manuscripts which the noble families conserve in dusty libraries and which few people go to study, and partly in the oral traditions which are handed down from generation to generation. These noble families still own many of the historic palaces marked in the guide-books with three asterisks. (An old Venetian count slept in a room covered with frescoes painted, I believe, by Tiepolo, and woke up late in the morning, washed and dressed himself, encircled by admiring English, German, and American sightseers.) In a certain sense, theirs is the Italy which the foreigners really come to see, the only one for which it seems worthwhile to make the journey, the Italy described by English and German writers, the land *"wo die Zitronen blühn"*.

And yet, this Italy has only a decorative importance. In the present world the Italian aristocracy counts for almost nothing.[1] The memory of its past greatness and dignity has no doubt rendered the Italian nobility unfit for the daily struggle: its authority of comportment has become comic self-importance, its gentlemanly reserve has become isolation, and its cult of the ancient, useless virtues has been transformed into an embarrassing impediment. The nobles have not been able to survive either as gentlemen or by entering the world of affairs, except in marginal and sporadic instances, and then, sometimes, only by letting themselves be merged with the others. Their failure (in some way inexplicable, since many of them are nothing but the descendants of bankers, tax-farmers, contractors, and merchants) has pushed them into secondary positions, extras without any lines who often are hostile to the world that surrounds them and in which they have purely routine duties.

The fact that the taste and dignity of Italy's old life could not be poured into its modern one, that it was not possible, for example, to preserve completely that living-together of the different classes which went to make up the pleasure of so much of our existence, to retain the taste for beautiful, well-made objects, for elegant and disinterested deeds, all this is particularly deplorable because the old Italy, with all its defects, was a precious construction of man and, bereft of these things, life has since become more impoverished here than elsewhere.

---

[1] To a Milanese count who was reproaching him in 1924 for choosing his collaborators only from the middle-class *parvenus*, Benito Mussolini scornfully answered: "It's your fault. You are well mannered. At a party it's the boors who get to the buffet first."

Modern Italy had to be made, one might say, without the help of those who were perhaps more "Italian" than the others, as though it had been conquered by vigorous but ignorant foreigners and governed like a colony. The past has been forgotten or rejected, or, sometimes, unknowingly accepted after its return from abroad. Baldassar Castiglione's *The Courtier*, for example, did not serve as the model for the Italian gentleman, but the English model, which derives from this very book, was imitated instead by Anglophiles. In the same way, the memory of the "Gioiosa," the school created by Vittorino da Feltre for the Gonzagas, has almost vanished, while many Italians admired and envied Eton, which was a copy of it.

In Italy, it is true, almost nothing gets thrown away. Everything manages to scrape along somehow: medieval institutions, pagan rites, Spanish customs, archaic music, nineteenth-century liberalism, Fascism, old romantic socialism, Bakunian anarchism, legitimist principles in the Chateaubriand style, and so on. The country can be compared to a storeroom cluttered with putrescent and dusty antiques, which no one uses, and with new-fangled, graceless pieces of furniture that are gross imitations brought from abroad or even fake antiques, which of course are used every day. So Italy succeeds in being old, tired, decadent, useless, and, at the same time, crudely new and traditionless.

* * *

IN ITALY, these days, there are noblemen everywhere. There are still rich nobles, the owners of *palazzi* which have borne their names for centuries (some families actually living on streets named after them, such as the Guicciardini of Palazzo Guicciardini, on Via Guicciardini, or the Pucci of Palazzo Pucci, on Via Pucci, both in Florence, or the Borromei of Palazzo Borromei, on Piazza Borromei in Milan). There are nobles who are penniless and humble small landowners, not much different from peasants, and others who are clerks living in tiny city apartments that smell of cabbages and garlic. There are some who live off public charity, and, in the prison at Arezzo, there is a

Countess who was discovered to be the leader of a band of thieves. There are nobles at all levels of society and for all pocket-books, those famous in the international cafés and hotels about whom Igor Cassini wrote, the society figures who received invitations from Elsa Maxwell, and those about whom no one has ever heard a word. There isn't a small mountain hotel or seaside *pensione* which does not boast of a "Countess" among its guests. Obscure "Countesses" run private schools for foreign young ladies, and "boutiques" or antique shops in Florence, Rome, and Venice.

Today, many nobles in Italy are as phony as stage jewelry. After the fall of the Monarchy and the abolition of titles, there were ambitious Italians who profited from the situation by attributing to themselves absolutely imaginary family lineages. Other Italians succeeded, during the last weeks before his departure, in wresting from Umberto II patents of nobility of dubious value, since they had not been countersigned by the responsible ministers: these are known collectively as the "Counts of Ciampino", the Roman airport from which the King left Italy. Still others dug out of archives and family oral traditions noble rank to which they had a tenuous right and straight away added them to their calling cards. (Usually one learns about this from the servants over the telephone, since nobody has the courage to proclaim it openly. One asks: "Is the *signora* there?" The voice replies: "The Countess has gone out," with the tone of someone who wishes to correct an error.)

It is roughly calculated that the Italian Republic can boast of ten times as many nobles as there were under the Monarchy. Especially flourishing in Italy is the branch of the Emperors of Byzantium. In Rome alone there were, at one time, two such Emperors. One was (and still is) "His Imperial Highness Lavarello Lascaris Comneno, Heir Porphyrogenite of the Nomania-Paleologue, Prince of Turgoville, Duke of Savoy Villars, Marquis Oberto of Lavarello, etc., etc." The other was the comedian Toto, a Neapolitan who simultaneously resembled Pulcinella and the Duke of Wellington. On the stage he performed with the buffoonery of the *Commedia dell'Arte*; in the salons the ladies, honoring him with deep curtsies, addressed him as "Your Highness." Up to a few years ago his name was Antonio De Curtis. Then he became legally (the titles have been validated by a court) "His Imperial Highness Antonio Porphyrogenite of the Constantinian Descent of Phocis, Achaia, Flavio, Duke Comneno de Curtis, Imperial Prince of Byzantium, Prince of Cilicia, of Macedonia, Darbiana, Thessaly, Moldavia, Ponto, Illyria, Peloponnesus, Duke of Cyprus and Epirus, etc., etc." Relations were rather strained between Rome's two Byzantine Emperors. Each one watched the other with a certain distrust. They held court and distributed not only decorations of their Imperial Houses, but also noble Byzantine titles. There are people who flaunt countships, marquisates, and dukedoms acquired in this manner.

Obviously all these very recent noblemen are among the most rabid adversaries of the King's return, which is all the more embarassing since they should be counted, by personal preference and social position, among the most eager supporters of a monarchial régime. Some time ago, during dinner at Cascais, Umberto and some friends were discussing the situation and one of them proposed, if there was a restoration, to examine the nobility case by case. Laughing, the King instead proposed that all the titles should be confirmed without hesitation—"to reward," he said, "such demonstrations of faith in the institutions of the Monarchy." A weekly magazine, *Il Borghese*, used to publish in almost every issue a column called "The False Gotha", in which these new nobles and the titles they gave themselves were diligently listed.

\*     \*     \*

THERE ARE, to be sure, real nobles in key industrial and financial positions and other important posts. Count Carlo Faina of Perugia was president of Montecatini, the chemical monopoly. Count Giancarlo Camerana was, until his death, the vice-president of Fiat. Count Edoardo-Visconti of Modrone is president of Carlo Erba, the pharmaceutical company. The representative of the cotton textile industrialists to the Confederation of Industry was Count Policarpo Corsi of Bosnasco, whose grandfather was ADC to Victor Emanuel II. Marchese Emilio Pucci, a member of Parliament, is at the head of a famous dress and *colifichets* business. Prince Nicola Pignatelli d'Aragona Cortez, descendant of both the Spanish Royal Family of Aragon and of the conqueror of Mexico, Hernan Cortez—a Spanish grandee, is the Italian representative of the American Gulf Oil Company. Count Luchino Visconti—descendant of the Lords of Milan—is one of the best Italian directors and a member of the Communist Party.[2]

However, the occupation that the great majority of real nobles have written on their passports is "agriculturist". They own land, a few fields around the garden of an old villa or vast estates (many of which the agrarian reform cut down in size). In Southern Italy, until a few years ago, many nobles were the owners of those same tracts of land on which, right down to the French Revolution and the government of Murat, they had sole feudal rights. In Lazio, the princely families at one time possessed, and in part still possess, immense neglected estates given over to pasture land and traversed by the ruins of ancient aqueducts, which were acquired centuries ago when some member of the family happened to become Pope. In Tuscany, a few families were the proprietors of thousands of small farms, planted with olive orchards and vineyards. In Lombardy, even the water of the canals and irrigation ditches that flowed across other people's land was frequently the property of the nobles. There are nobles who are actively engaged in agriculture (many of them are actually university educated agronomists and farming experts, such as the Marquis Alfredo Solaro of Borgo, of a nearly thousand-year-old Piedmont family). There are others who rarely go to see their distant estates and confine themselves, while living in Rome or Naples, to pocketing the incomes from them. These are mostly Southern Italian nobles who were drawn during the last centuries to the Neapolitan capital of the Bourbon kings, in the same way that the French

[2] Many young nobles have in the past joined the Communist Party, as a gesture of aristocratic revolt against the vulgar and sordid bourgeois world.

nobles were compelled to live at Versailles. There are some who manage a few acres and live frugally; others, like Marquis Antonio Origo, who invest millions of lire in reclamation projects and new farmhouses for their tenants.[3]

Even today the Italian noble is happier in the country. The contact with the land and its people suits his character and traditions. He loves to shoot, he loves the patient slowness with which one faces the caprices of nature, he loves the withdrawn and isolated life together with a few friends and relatives, the conversations with the peasants whom he understands and who understand him. He knows and cultivates the art of "government". The word has nothing to do with politics. In the language of Central Italy "*governo*" means the guiding and care of all who are inferior, weak, undefended, and irresponsible— women, children, the old, dependants, and animals. All that cannot be taught, but is got by inheritance. The story is told how Prince Altieri of Rome, who had married a middle-class woman, was alarmed by the anarchic management of his large house. One day he gathered all the old servants in the kitchen and said: "You must be patient. It will take a little time, maybe four years. In four years you and I shall make a Princess of her."

As country folk they affect—or at least, affected until a few years ago—a crude ignorance or exaggerated scorn for the sort of knowledge which is useful in the technical and business world of today. The affectation sits easily on many Roman princes who, save for certain illustrious and well-known exceptions, are rough and uncultivated by ancient tradition. Also, in those regions dominated in the past by the Spaniards, the nobleman was ignorant almost out of duty to his caste. The barons in Calabria used to sign their names by a cross, to which the scribe would add the words "*quia nobilis*". Charles Felix of Savoy, King of Sardinia, defined the aristocratic point of

[3] It is interesting to note that the peasants with enlightened and liberal landowners, who teach them modern techniques and respect their rights, who build them schools and hospitals, are usually Communists, while the peasants with stingy and old-fashioned landowners are, on the other hand, predominantly devoted to the Church and vote for the Demo-Christian government.

view at the beginning of the last century, when *l'ancien régime* was fighting the liberals: "*Les mauvais sont tous des lettrés et les bons toujours des ignorants.*" Besides their attitude towards culture in general, the nobles showed and sometimes still show a strange indifference to art, when one thinks of the traditional protection which they gave in the past to painters, writers, poets, and scientists. When he visited art shows, Victor Emanuel III, a very cultured man with an infallible memory, liked to stop in front of a landscape of some town and ask the embarrassed painter: "What town is it? How many people live there? Are they hard-working and honest?"

\*    \*    \*

NOBODY in Italy is a purer and more typical representative of his own city, province, region, of the ancient ways of thinking, living, eating in a particular locality than the nobleman. In the noble families one speaks—or spoke until the last war—almost only dialect, the same dialect used by the people, though pronounced with greater elegance and having a more precise and richer vocabulary. Victor Emanuel III, though he was born in Naples and lived nearly always in Rome, spoke the Piedmont dialect of his forefathers. When Marshal Badoglio, Prime Minister during the dramatic month of July 1943 (Mussolini had fallen and was arrested, the Fascist Party was dissolved, the Germans were masters of a large part of the country, and the Allies distrusted the new government), proposed to the King to include in the ministry some old anti-Fascist politicians, he objected in Piedmont dialect: "*Ma i sun di revenant* (But they are ghosts)." And Badoglio simply replied, in the same dialect: "*Anche mi e chiel, Maest, à suma di revenant* (Also you and I, Majesty, are ghosts)." Although he was born when his family had not lived in Turin for two generations, Umberto II also speaks the dialect quite precisely—just as the children of English families transplanted abroad still speak their language after a century. Recently, when a count called a bottle of white glass "*buta*" Umberto correctly pointed out to him that the word he meant was "*carafa*" since "*buta*" is used only for green glass. After the war

in Turin the noblemen's club, The Whist, took in a bourgeois
club, The Philharmonic, whose quarters had been destroyed in
the bombardments. The servants of The Whist were most upset
by the union. They waited on the old members with deep-bow-
ing panache, while the others were treated off-handedly, un-
ceremoniously, gracelessly, like the customers of some ordinary
*trattoria*. The major-domo complained to Count Giancarlo
Camerana about the world's shabby decline: "Just look how
we've finished up. . . . Only we two, Count, speak the dialect."

Out of this contact with nature, out of the patriarchal "government" of large agricultural establishments and great houses
full of relatives and servants, the commanding of men and
animals, the slow passage of generations living within the same
walls, the nobles learned the ancient virtues, those which were
necessary and admired in yesterday's world but which, in these
feverish modern times, seem almost ridiculous and useless. The
Italian nobleman for centuries has been "the man on horse-
back". As the horseman dominates his horse (and things) not
with lively intelligence, rapid reflexes, and sudden decisions, but
often with the sheer weight of his buttocks and the position of
his body, with that lack of fear which also is a bit made up of
stupidity and slowness in recognizing danger, guiding the
animal with exact and invisible movements performed unconsciously and gracefully, avoiding sharp pulls at the reins, so, in
the same fashion, many noblemen today still reach their goals
by solid authority, courage, prudence, tenacity, perseverance,
precisely those dull qualities which one can find only in the
countryside.

Even today, their prime characteristic, in contrast to the
bourgeoisie's frantic anxiety and aggressiveness, is a strange
tranquillity and ease of life, almost as though they were unaware of the tremendous complications of existence. The best
nobles still train their children in self-control, firmness, courtesy,
still teach them how to use to advantage their close familiarity
with men, women, and the ordinary people. Many of them are
still masters of the art of conducting an intrigue, of defeating an
impatient adversary, of courting a woman (a technique which

calls for a subtle knowledge of the blind forces of nature). Lord
Chesterfield admired them and pointed them out to his son as
models of behavior, urging him to keep, as they did, "*volto
sciolto e pensiero stretto*" (in Italian in the original), that is, "an
open countenance and a closed mind." Words that have disappeared from speech must still be used today in describing
certain old gentlemen: they cultivate *tratto*, that is, elegance in
conducting one's affairs and in relations with others, and *il
portamento*, that is, the body's dignity, by which one moves, sits,
walks, or leans against a piece of furniture or wall with the
harmonious naturalness that recalls certain figures in Carpaccio,
Giorgione, and Mantegna, a naturalness which can now be
found only among old peasants and shepherds. Their ideal is still
that proposed by Baldassar Castiglione, whom no one reads: to
behave with decorum, to win the favor of one's superiors and
the friendship of one's equals, to defend one's honor and make
oneself respected without being hated, to inspire admiration but
not envy, to maintain a certain splendor, to know the arts of
living, to converse with wit and facility, to be in one's proper
place in war, in a salon, in a lady's boudoir, and in a council
chamber, to live in the world and at the same time to have a
private and withdrawn life. The ideal, like all ideals, is realized
only by a few. All, however, recognize it as a model.[4]

Since, however, their income these days is rarely sufficient to
support them, the great majority of nobles must work. I have
already told about those who occupy the few eminent positions
in the world of industry and finance. Many others have gone
into occupations where their traditional qualities can still be
useful. For example, they produce good wines. Wine, like a
noble family, is the product of generations, patience, and taste.
(The most famous Italian wine, Chianti, came out of the experi-

---

[4] These traditional characteristics are certainly not those of contemporary
Italians, yet they survive in the Italians, shown in either a good or bad light,
who appear in novels written by foreigners, precisely because, as I have said,
the historic Italy is the one which seems more Italian than the others, the one
that has taught the world and arouses the curiosity of travellers. Maybe it is
for this reason that the Italian, in light Anglo-Saxon literature, is almost
always a Count.

ments made by Baron Bettino Ricasoli at his Brolio Castle during the last century. Today some of the oldest families in Tuscany—the Antinori, the Spalletti, the Frescobaldi, the Sanminiatelli, the Pasolini, etc.—also produce Chianti.) Other nobles have entered diplomacy, where the art of pleasant conversation, of elegant intrigues, "the open countenance and the closed mind," still seem to be necessary virtues. As they did in past centuries, young nobles are impelled to go off on uncomfortable and adventurous expeditions, explorations in the Amazon, big-game hunts, and colonization experiments in Latin America. There are others, however, who exploit their good taste, working as interior decorators, antique dealers, organizers of holidays, and there was a great patron of the arts, Count Chigi Saracini of Siena, who yearly paid for concert seasons in his palazzo which attracted an audience from all over Europe. Many noblemen have opened shops of *colifichets* and sell extravagantly up-to-date merchandise. Many nobles are still attracted to military careers where they can "serve" and exercise the art of command, cut off from the modern world's confusion in a hierarchical order which agrees with their tastes.

But all this—the wines, the hazardous expeditions, the careers in diplomacy, the *colifichets*, the life under arms—doesn't amount to very much. The bourgeoisie are more numerous, better equipped, and trained even in those fields where gentlemen should naturally stand out, and the ancient traditional qualities are often more of a hindrance than a help. As a result, the nobles harbor the confused conviction that they are the victims of modern society, useless survivors fighting against a thousand enemies who wish to destroy and humiliate them.

\* \* \*

ANY PANORAMIC, general consideration of the Italian aristocracy is almost certainly inexact and can have only an anecdotal value. In reality, there is no "Italian aristocracy". Down to 1860, there was not one sovereign, one court, one style of gentlemanly life, but rather many courts, some very rigid in the Spanish and Austrian manner, others family-like, disordered, and pleasure-loving; bread-and-water courts and magnificent courts; and there were sovereigns to suit all tastes—tyrannies, glorious oligarchic republics, provinces under foreign domination, and, of course, the Papal States. And all this in continuous change, with borders that were redrawn at every treaty; and, at the passing of each dynasty, régime, and domination, with a flurry of negotiations, accompanied by inevitable confusions and discrepancies, it was necessary to acknowledge the previous nobles and to create new ones faithful to the latest master. This tumultuous, flood-like formation over ten centuries gave both the greater and lesser noble families sets of very different characteristics and traditions, which vary according to the title's antiquity and origin (whether from town or country, military or mercantile), the court in which the family was formed, and the province in which it had its roots.

It should first of all be remembered that the temper of the Middle Ages, the feudal and knightly spirit which shaped the soul of the nordic nobility, never succeeded completely in imbuing Italy, which always secretly remained partial to its own ideals and rebellious to any ideology alien to its true nature. Just as our Gothic churches are only Romanesque churches dressed up in German decorations, so, under the trappings of the knightly tradition, one can always catch sight of an Italian and Roman reality. It is known that fewer Italians left to go to Palestine to conquer the Holy Sepulcher than any other Europeans. It is also known that the Crusades mainly served as the occasion for Venetian merchants to open new markets in the Orient, and for the maritime cities to fit out fleets for the foreign knights who were leaving to fight the infidels. The knightly medieval spirit had the same luck in Italy as the ghosts, of whom there exists notoriously few examples. There are only two or three haunted castles in the entire country, which, moreover, were inhabited most of the time by Germanic conquerors.

Thus, an "Italian aristocracy" does not exist. The Piedmont nobility is the only one which is nordic, feudal, martial, formed around a single sovereign and subjected to a strict court. Several Piedmont families which originate before the year 1000, others established in the succeeding centuries—nearly all of austere customs, having been impoverished by the many wars of the House of Savoy—still maintain a rigidly decorous life in their boring, ancient provincial villas and raise their children with a firm sense of duty. It is chiefly Piedmont nobles who are still listed in the directories of the Italian Republic among the army navy officers and diplomats, all at the service of a sovereign who is no longer there. The Genovese aristocracy is composed of families of navigators and merchants, which are still today engaged in business affairs. The Genovese patricians did not have titles in their Republic, yet, when they travelled abroad or were sent as ambassadors, they gave themselves the title of "Marquis" for convenience's sake. They were also officially Marquises during the Italian monarchy.

The Venetian *patrizi* are doubtless to be counted among Europe's oldest nobility, some of them direct descendants of those small provincial chiefs, perhaps curials of the Roman Empire, who led the people to found a city on the lagoons to defend themselves against the barbarians. They set up a ruling oligarchy, the Grand Council, and, for more than a thousand years, until 1815, its members possessed no other title but that of *Nobil'Uomo*. After the Congress of Vienna, which made Venice an Austrian domain, the Hapsburgs proposed to give the patents of Count to those who wished them, the title of *patrizi* not seeming sufficiently splendid for their court. Many accepted, yet others refused, offended at being offered so common a title; it was only later that Victor Emanuel II made them all Counts. The Venetian lords are courteous, refined, amiable, and weary, burdened by their ownership of palaces, built on water, that are always threatening to collapse and must be continuously propped up and repaired at great expense.

The Milan nobility reflects that city's tortured and complex history. It includes very ancient nobles, ancient nobles, less ancient, recent, and very recent—titles from the Longobards, the Roman Emperors, the Spaniards, the Austrians, Napoleon, and the House of Savoy. Some Milanese nobles still own rich-landed estates, have large incomes, love music (the boxes at the Scala stay in the family for generations) and the good life, and are still somewhat distrustful of the industrialists and businessmen. At Florence the most ancient stratum is formed by the feudal nobility, descendants of Germanic warriors who came down into Italy before 1000—the Gherardesca and the Ricasoli; then there is the stratum of the country nobility which came to the city after having made their fortunes, and a group of bourgeois origin made up of bankers and merchants. In 1550, Cosimo de' Medici and the end of commerce on the Mediterranean forced all of them to put their money in the land, so that today they are solely landowners, notorious for their parsimony. In one of the great wine-making Florentine houses, they ask the guests at table to turn over their glasses if they don't want wine.

*          *          *

THERE are four very ancient families in Rome—the Caetani, the Massimo, the Colonna, and the Orsini. The other Roman nobles are nephews of the Popes who, having originated in other Italian cities, came to live in Rome to follow the fortunes of their families. The Rospigliosi, a Pistoia family known since the fourteenth century, were made Princes by Clement I. The Borghese, a Siena family in existence since the thirteenth century, were made Princes of Sulmona in 1610 by Philip III of Spain, in order to ingratiate himself with Paolo Borghese V. The Boncompagni come from Bologna, while the Odescalchi are bankers from Como. The Roman nobility was famous for its wealth, its sumptuous palaces, and its crude manners.

The nobility of Naples also divides into geological layers. Before the year 1000, there are the Caracciolo and Brancaccio families. The Aquino (that of St. Thomas Aquinas) and Sangro families are Longobards; the Capece, d'Afflitto and Dentice families (the last made famous at one time, to the readers of American newspapers, by the wife of Carlo, Countess Dorothy Dentice di Frasso, *née* Taylor, of Watertown, New York) are all Normans; the Balzo and Cito families are Angevins. The more superficial layers are of Aragonese, Spanish, Austrian, and

Bourbon origins. The Neapolitans believe they have inherited from the domination of the Spanish Viceroy the love for regal magnificence, which has ruined many families, and a particular touchiness about their honor and prestige. The Sicilian noble families are also numerous and inclined to sumptuous display. During the Napoleonic Wars, when the court of Naples was in exile at Palermo with their incomes greatly reduced, King Ferdinand prohibited the great Sicilian lords at the penalty of a fine from exhibiting themselves at the hour of the evening drive with more than four horses. The Prince of Terranova would then go out with six or eight horses, the fine's amount attached to the blinkers of each horse to facilitate the work of the gendarmes.

Even obscure families are very ancient in Italy. Among others, the nobles of several small provincial towns unquestionably descend from senatorial families of the Roman epoch, though often having no other title than *patrizi*, like the "*bourgeois*" of Geneva. There are tens of family names that surely go back further than the year 1000. The great majority, however, have relatively recent origins. At every change of régime, the new nobles reasserted old privileges (Maria Theresa at Milan only asked that the family prove that it had lived for three generations "*more nobilum*" in order to validate the title) and created new ones. To pay the costs of his wars, in 1772 Victor Amedeo II of the House of Savoy sold titles for three million, seven hundred thousand lire. The nobility's Book of Gold was reopened to the richest people at Venice after the war of Candia against the Turks and the war of Chioggia against the Genovese. In almost all the cities, with each generation, certain families disappeared and other new ones in some fashion obtained titles and, after a while, merged with the older and more illustrious nobles.

Only quite recently, almost on the eve of the French Revolution and the abolition of the feudal system, the question of the aristocracy's status was settled in nearly all the Italian states. In Piedmont, in 1687 they began to draw up catalogues of authorized coats-of-arms, and in 1738 they codified the norms for accepting a family's nobility. In Milan, rules were established in 1652 for admission to the nobility, and, in 1769, for the first time, it was forbidden that anyone bear a title which had not been recognized by the Court of Heraldry. The list of Tuscan nobles dates from 1750; that of Rome's noble families from 1746. The problem was faced by the new Kingdom of Italy in 1870 by the passage of a law which set up a Council of Heraldry. The first official list of Italian nobles was compiled laboriously between 1895 and 1900, and a final almost complete list was published in 1922.

*          *          *

ALL THIS has created a century-long confusion, which the nobles themselves can't make head or tail of. For instance, there never was a precise protocol in Italy for seating nobles around a dinner table. The scale of titles is useless. There are Longobard Counts who were sovereigns of their small medieval states and obscure Neapolitan Princes who were recently titled and have very modest origins; there are simple patricians who can boast of a very ancient lineage. Vicar-Counts who represented an Emperor, Princes of the Holy Roman Empire, Merchant-Counts of the Renaissance and the late Kingdom. Sometimes an attempt is made to place the guests according to the antiquity of their titles—an absolutely impossible feat. In Venice precedence was given to the "foreigners", that is, the nobles from other cities in Italy. Usually, the guests are seated in the order of their age, as though they were simple bourgeois or all had the same rank.

Nor did the rules of precedence established by the House of Savoy simplify the problem. Title did not constitute rank at the Quirinale Palace. The monarchy had issued out of a bourgeois revolution.[5] The order of precedence was that so-called of "General Marquis Luigi Federico Menabrea", aide-de-camp of Victor Emanuel II, who set up a system by which the last of the

---

[5] Following a plebiscite, Victor Emanuel II was proclaimed King and bore his title both "by the grace of God" and "the will of the nation", as was written in all the documents. At Parma the monument to him is inscribed "To the Elected King".

Knights of the Crown of Italy passed ahead of the first of the Roman Princes.[6] Privately, it was another matter. In the King's military and civil household, attending the Queen and Princes of the blood, were traditionally gathered members of the illustrious patrician families. Moreover, since in the Kingdom's first years the nobility was still in large part the ruling class, the public position of many aristocrats seated them at table in more or less the place to which, in other courts and at other times, their titles would have given them the right.

The truth was that the House of Savoy looked with distrust on that assorted *antipasto* of nobles of all shapes and descriptions which they had inherited with the Unification. At bottom, the only true nobles for them were still their own, the nobles from the Piedmont, whose families had served and followed them for centuries, just as the only castles, landed estates, villas, and country seats were their own, those of the House of Savoy, and not the ones belonging to other princely families which the unification had turned over to the Royal house. The Savoys had easily granted titles to Italians and foreigners, not always for special merits and on particular occasions, as was done, for example, in England, but here and there, a few at a time, without rigid criteria, to anyone who asked for it with sufficient persistence and was supported by political recommendations. This lack of serious discrimination irked the old aristocracy and confirmed it in its suspicion that the King was doing everything to diminish its prestige. That the Kingdom of Italy at the start of the century was dominated by the bourgeoisie was a fact before which the King had to bow, since it certainly was not dependent on his wishes. Nevertheless, there is no question that the King also took a bitter pleasure in adapting himself to the new conditions, even when personally disagreeable. Perhaps he bore the same distrust towards his throne and the anarchic and mixed-up country he had been called to reign over, as Letizia Buonaparte had felt for her son's Empire. When Theodore

[6] There wasn't an army major or a railroad station-master in Italy who wasn't a Knight of the Crown. Victor Emanuel used to say that a cigar and the Cross of Knight could not be refused to anyone.

Roosevelt came to Rome on a private visit, the King told him bitterly: "I am educating my son to become the first President of the Italian Republic." In fact, that is just what he became, for a few days, at least, in 1946.

*          *          *

LIFE in an Italy which was not yet industrial, whose wealth lay in the people, the land, the ancient traditions, the palaces, the ingenuity, and the works of art—this life was still, as has been said, dominated by the nobility. The coming to power of the democratic and nationalistic Left on March 18th, 1876, marked the end of the ancient hegemony. Until 1876 the political and ruling class, which had helped the revolutions and fought in the wars of Independence, was largely composed of nobles. If the aristocracy was not liberal, many liberals were aristocrats. Ettore Carafa, the Duke of Andria and General of the Partenope Republic, was compelled to lay siege to his own fee, Andria, in order to abolish his own feudal rights in 1799, and he finally had to destroy the place because its inhabitants did not want to renounce feudalism and loyalty to him. (The King later condemned him to death.) From 1849 to 1876 almost all the prime ministers were noblemen. The general who entered Rome on September 20th, 1870, at the head of Italian troops was Count Raffaele Cadorna. Ambassadors, prefects, important magistrates, and ministers came from the aristocracy, and also, at that time, some of the great financiers, businessmen, and the first industrialists. Inevitably their influence was felt in many fields— in economy, the elegant form of dispatches, the probity of public life, the soberness and good sense of political policy, the taste shown in the monuments and the style of the uniforms, and the general disinterestedness and decorum which they imparted to the new Kingdom.

It should be noted that the positions held by all these noblemen were not owed to their titles but rather to the fact that in a provincial country, which had remained outside of European history for centuries, they could be numbered among those who had had the chance to study, had traveled abroad, spoke foreign languages, possessed highly-placed friends everywhere, and were often the only people who traditionally pursued careers in public life. Moreover, since they owned land, they controlled the sole important capital of the period. Then, from 1876 on, only one of the prime ministers was a nobleman, Antonio Starabba, the Marquis of Rudini; all the others were of bourgeois origin. Gradually, also, the high positions in the state, the majority of seats in the Senate, the key posts in the world of business affairs, almost everything, with the exception perhaps of the great landed estates, passed from the nobles' hands into those of others. During these same years, the character of Italian life, both public and private, slowly changed—one saw it in the taste expressed in the buildings, the conventional forms, the relations between superiors and inferiors, the courtesies, the graces, the sense of the state, even in the typography of official documents. Of course, this was not only due to the decadence of the Italian nobility, but could be traced above all to that natural evolution all over Europe of which the Italian nobility's decadence was only one of many aspects. A partial historian wrote:

It was after 1876 that the real Italy came out into the open, so much inferior to romantic dreams. The government declined appreciably in honesty, dignity, good-breeding, competence and style. Mere cleverness prevailed over real knowledge, and politics undermined administration.

There was, however, one factor which was different in Italy— though the aristocracy, as in other European countries, proved itself incapable and reluctant to assume its new duties, which it scorned, only a small part of the bourgeoisie was properly trained, had firm faith in itself, and solid traditions.

Then, at the end, the epoch of Gabriele d'Annunzio arrived.

*          *          *

DURING the last decades of the century, that varicolored hotchpotch of illustrious and ancient, less illustrious, unknown, totally new, genuine and almost genuine families which, for good or ill, went to make up the aristocracy's Book of Gold, began searching confusedly for a new unifying principle. The Kingdom was new, life seemed to be changed, new industries and fortunes were being built, railroads were reaching out almost everywhere—it was necessary to be modern. The old traditions—save for the traditions from the Piedmont, which alarmed the other Italians —seemed to have been left behind and appeared dangerous to the principle of Unification. Everybody was looking for models to imitate. There was no time to be lost. The cavalry sent for a lance from the German Uhlans at Berlin to copy and hired a famous Austrian horseman as their instructor. The statesmen debated the national problems in the halls of Montecitorio dressed in *redingotte*, just as was being done at the Palais Bourbon. (The Parliamentary Rules of Order had been taken directly from the Belgians.) The cotton-mill owners of Milan played at being Englishmen, some of them even going fox-hunting in pink coats. The bankers were studying their German counterparts.

In those years, servants waiting on table in the old houses suddenly became mute, just as in England; until then, they had always been permitted to participate respectfully in the conversation. Many nobles tried to prepare their sons for their responsibilities by sending them to the universities to study. Other nobles began serving their new King with punctilious faithfulness. Still others, following the pattern of some English Lords, plunged into voyages of exploration and hazardous big-game hunts. Some nobles threw open their old *palazzi*, redecorating them in accordance with the period's taste, gave large receptions, frequented high international society, married the daughters of foreign nobles, and traveled all over Europe visiting their friends. There were also humble country Counts, belonging to the newest group of the nobility, who enlisted in the old Piedmont regiments and felt obliged to behave like the descendants of the Crusaders, scorning all dangers, putting on haughty airs, sometimes challenging peaceful-minded bourgeois to duels or throwing away part of their inheritance in wild gambling. In other words, the Italian nobles for the first time set about acting the part of "nobles"; they ceased to be patriarchal, with a place in the people's ancient way of life, in order to live a fictitious literary and choreographic existence.

What had happened was strange and complicated. In part, it was the product of the times throughout Europe; in part, the aristocracy adapted itself hastily to its new functions, just as the bourgeoisie was doing, and searched in its past or in the past of others for anything which could be useful. Out of this search the feudal traditions came, traditions which were quite new for many nobles and which are today thought to be part of a century-old heritage. Moreover, the nobles, issuing under pressure from their provincial habits and the torpor of centuries, were forced by a number of factors to imitate foreign modes. There were, for example, the English Nannies—women of ordinary families but pervaded by a religious veneration for titles, genealogies, and royal houses—who were inevitably imported to educate the young Italian nobles as if they were sons of members of the House of Lords, teaching them virtues which here would only be an impediment, and moral vices, such as haughtiness, reserve, and snobbery, which have rarely been seen before in Italy. Then there were the American or English women who had married a Count, a Duke, or a Prince and expected their mates to behave like their similars elsewhere. Between them, English Nannies and foreign mothers raised in the last decades whole generations of Italian nobles, converting them into deracinés from Italian life, with sometimes admirable yet completely alien qualities, people who were discontented with themselves, their existence, their country, their condition.

At this point, between 1880 and 1890, Gabriele d'Annunzio came into vogue, a poet of great talent, as snobbish as an English nurse. The son of a modest family from Pescara, short of stature and prematurely bald, saturated in classical studies and Italian history—from which he took only the ornate and showy— d'Annunzio had begun his career as the society reporter on a newspaper owned by Prince Sciarra, a patron of the arts. On the basis of his society notes he then wrote a novel in which the Italian aristocracy, the new Court, and Rome were depicted for the first time as a fabulous world, populated by overwhelming personages, marvellous women, very refined gentlemen who, in a heavy atmosphere of licentiousness and death, spent their time, far above all gross daily concerns, in erudite and subtle conversations, perilous, impassioned love affairs. D'Annunzio despised the bourgeois conventions and virtues. Instead he sang the praises of the nobility and of those who, like himself, had been ennobled by nature; he glorified the love of risk, pomp, and the picturesque. In his successive works, there was reflected the disquietude of a new, impoverished, and bored Italy, the young generations's anxious thirst for power, the cult of heroism, war, and blood. Skipping over entire centuries of sobriety and seriousness, d'Annunzio settled on the Italy of the late Renaissance—a defeated Italy—and the Byzantine Empire, or rummaged through other epochs crowded with decadent splendors and turbid disorder in search of the fantastic, cruel, and over-refined. Out of this work there came an Italy which pleased everyone to some degree—save, of course, serious, level-headed people—but which was particularly attractive to a large group of the new nobility. A style was born, a theatrical pastiche, false and literary, which served to fill a vacuum and nourished the furious, irrational faith that Italy was vowed to a great destiny just at the moment when the country seemed quite insignificant in comparison with the great foreign powers and even with the hopes of the last generation. And, lastly, it revealed a function for Italy's gentlemen and nobles, which was that of pointing the way to the future by their magnificent deeds, their admirable examples (piloting the first airplanes), a future which would be just as glorious and vaguely picturesque as the past.

D'Annunzio had very little success abroad, where his over-wrought and feverish style was almost completely incomprehensible, yet in Italy he enjoyed the sort of fame which only "the divine Aretino" had had. Every word, image, gesture, and love affair of d'Annunzio's resounded in the lost, uncertain, and discontented souls of countless people. The young noblemen became his fervent followers and adopted his ideals, even going so far as to model themselves after his characters, to speak, write, live, and dress like him. Women of great noble families fell

desperately in love with him and risked scandal and dishonor to
have affairs with him. Hordes of other women adored him from
a distance, dressing like the heroines in his novels and throwing
themselves into decadent love affairs in provincial towns. They
forced their lovers to behave like d'Annunzio's heroes, speaking
in a lyrical language composed of archaic, incomprehensible
words, and decorated their houses with rubbishy bric-à-brac,
just as d'Annunzio did and continued to do until his death.
Greyhounds and horses became fashionable. The Duke d'Aosta,
the King's cousin, husband of Princess Elena of France, even
wrote his letters in a handwriting almost identical with that of
the poet, on large sheets of handmade paper adorned by
Renaissance engravings and sybilline mottoes.

*       *       *

BUT not everyone was modern and d'Annunzian. The older
men (and the most ancient and substantial families) continued
secretly to live in their patriarchal way, on terms of close
familiarity with their servants and dependants, tranquilly certain of still being themselves, unconcerned about the rest of the
world and its absurd conduct. Even today, when the bourgeoisie
and the aristocracy which is most *à la page* are dressed by fashionable tailors and are models of elegance, the old, traditional
aristocrats still have their clothes made by some ordinary tailor
at a minimum cost. Prince Barberini used to go to drink wine
and play cards almost every day at a certain hour in an *osteria*
near Piazza Navona in Rome, a hang-out for street cleaners and
coachmen. At Palermo, in the *palazzo* of the Duke Fulco della
Verdura, visitors are still announced by the ringing of the tower
bell. The Duke, a New York and Paris jeweller, is one of the
most prominent men in international society. Yet in his house,
still inhabited by his mother, the Duchess, the porter won't stop
anyone from entering—as, indeed, was the custom in all the
*palazzi* at Palermo. Anyone who wishes can walk in and go
through the master's apartments. However, the bell is always
sounded—one stroke for a woman, two for a man, three for the
Duke, and a stroke-and-a-half for a priest, who is considered

something halfway between a man and a woman. (At every stroke there is a great emergence of heads from the upper floor windows and the courtyard to see who has arrived.) Some years ago, the Duke's father came across a beggar in the ante-chamber doing an excellent business collecting alms.[7]

The descendants of the d'Annunzians, of foreign mothers, the products of the English Nannies, are today chiefly social figures, making up a "high society" which never existed before in Italy. (The "rulers" of Roman society, the late Princess Jane of San Faustino and Princess Isabel Colonna close behind her, were bourgeois of foreign birth.) These "social figures" possess the names which readers of the newspapers are familiar with—even today old-fashioned noblemen and gentlemen would regard it as a dishonor to read their names in the newspapers, even in connection with some serious and legitimate event; in Rome they receive American millionaires and movie stars, send gossip columnists bits of indiscreet information, brag about their invitations to English castles or villas on the French Riviera. All this—the cultivation of frivolous friends in various parts of the world, the passion for certain sports taken up for solely fashionable motives, the pursuit of showy invitations, the balls and great dinners in the old palaces, the breathless running back and forth over Europe just to be present for an evening, a day, or a week-end at a particular place—is generally done by Italian nobles without apparent effort, without vulgarity, with grace and a sure knowledge of the persons involved, as becomes people of good breeding. Yet, despite all their care and gentlemanly tact, the activity in itself, the regarding of one's function as purely decorative and one's real purpose in life as that of obtaining a social success, is essentially vulgar.

In contrast: Duke Guido Visconti of Modrone was a soldier, a career officer in the cavalry, who had acquitted himself well in Libya at the head of his Saharan troops. He was not a Fascist. During the last war, he got himself transferred to a parachute division which was employed at Marmarica, in a desert of

---

[7] In the eighteenth and nineteenth centuries, beggars on the stairs and in doorways were the nightmare of English travelers in Italy.

blazing stone, without water, with meager supplies of ammuni-
tion and old artillery pieces which shot eight kilometers to the
English guns' fifteen. In the front line for months, the Duke used
to say half seriously: "Who are these English? Social *parvenus*.
Who are these Windsors, Saxe-Coburg-Gothas, Hanovers? All
newcomers." Guido Visconti of Modrone died heroically. Two
brothers of the princely family of Ruspoli, Marescotti and
Costantino, also died in the fighting at Marmarica. None of
them was Fascist. On the contrary, they had regarded the new
régime with distrust and hostility and had dreaded a war fought
at the side of the Germans, which they knew would surely end
in defeat. At the war's outbreak they had asked to be sent to the
front—as one of them wrote to his wife, "to do my duty as a
soldier." Count Paolo Caccia Dominioni of Sillavengo, painter,
architect, veteran of the First World War (he claimed to be "the
only Knight of Malta who fought with the *arditi*", the com-
mandos of that day), officer in the Engineers and anti-Fascist,
organized the first group of "saboteurs" in the Italian Army,
with whom he succeeded at a certain stage in retaking Tobruk
by demolishing its defenses with dynamite. The deed was
inexplicable to his friends who knew his dislike of the régime
and the war. Before he left for combat duty, one of his friends
asked him: "You know that the war is going to be lost. Why are
you leaving?" Count Caccia replied: "There's no doubt, the
war is lost. But let's try to lose it as well as we can, with dignity
and honor."

*          *          *

TO DIE heroically in a hated war, obeying leaders one despises,
are extreme examples. But there are many more reflections of
the aristocratic tradition in everyday Italian life.

To tell the truth, in their early years the children of Italian
noble families are almost unaware of the names they carry.
Since there aren't private schools in Italy just for aristocrats, the
young noble, enrolled solely under his surname in a state-run
school, gets lost among his bourgeois classmates. He learns to
defend himself, relies on his own resources, picks up useful

curse-words, observes the simple existence of ordinary families, goes through his first amorous adventures. Afterwards, throughout his life, he keeps friends from all classes. The children of the nobility enjoy mixing with other groups, since the others have greater freedom, nobody watches their every move, and they are much more easy-going and spontaneous. Nothing frightens the young noble more than bringing his family's importance to his companions' notice. He is even reluctant to invite them to his home and is terrified at being picked up at school by a liveried servant or an English governess. But, later on, the moment inevitably comes when each person must resign himself to being what he is.

Many nobles put off that day as long as possible; they continue to mix with and be lost among their bourgeois friends, in rebellion against their family, archaic customs, and the annoying weight of tradition. Yet almost nobody is able to escape his fate for long. Gradually, they resign themselves: first it is a matter of habit, then pride at being what they are. Many tell how "the day" suddenly swooped down on them—at the death of their old parents, when the palace or villa, the small house or fields landed squarely on their shoulders. No matter how broad-minded, irreverent, and up-to-date they are, no matter how convinced that the nobility's claims are a ridiculous impediment in modern life, the sheer weight of the walls, the old halls, the ancestral portraits, the paintings, the archives, the boxwood hedges, the burden of dependents who surround the family, the accounts to be kept—all this compels them to attend to their affairs and, little by little, they become resigned prisoners, docile links between past and future. They must fight tooth and nail to preserve what they own, to hand it down to their own children, educating them properly so as to fit them for their particular duties. As they grow older they discover with bitterness that they have come more and more to resemble their fathers, grandfathers, and uncles, that they unconsciously repeat maxims which used to seem ridiculous, that they also praise the obscure provincial magistrates and undistinguished soldiers whose portraits happen to be hanging on their walls. All this, take note, not with the pride and boldness of the past, when it was a question of sure advantages, but rather out of resignation, discipline, the abandonment of the idea of any sort of serious career. (Who, in Italy, would be operated on by a Marquis who was a surgeon, or would listen to the work of a Duke who was a composer?)

There is today, in this discipline, in this sacrifice of themselves for the sake of their name, something more than the old *noblesse oblige*. Many aristocrats, describing their war adventures, say: "If I didn't have the name I bear, I would not have done it." It is an ancient rule which, however, also often holds true for men of honor without ancestors. In today's nobleman there exists a sort of sharp antagonism, one might almost say an impotent defiance of the world which is hostile to him and does not value his qualities. It seems today to drive many nobles to exasperated sacrifices, in which there is evidently a certain desire to somehow disappear. Those disappear who give up all pretensions and become a part of the bourgeoisie, who "go bourgeois" (the only daughter of a Roman nobleman who married an actor, the young nobles who change their names, their cities, or country in order to start a new career, etc.). Those also disappear who withdraw to cultivate their traditions, sacrificing themselves for the continuity of their family, living in a vanished period of history, artificially maintained within the walls of their *palazzi*, as one reproduces an exotic climate to preserve rare and delicate animals. And, finally, those disappear who, in wartime, have not merely done their duty but wished to die and destroy their family, almost as if to show by their behavior what ancient blood means and to revenge themselves, by a brave deed, for all their peacetime humiliations. In this wish to disappear is implicit the admission that their virtues (and vices), which they do not know how to relinquish, are useless today. But are they really useless to a world which is becoming harder and more inhuman just because it lacks those very virtues (and vices)?

Out of the everyday struggle in bourgeois society there emerge powerful men, the founders of great industrial dynasties and fortunes. They establish, as they have always established in past centuries, the great new families who make alliances among themselves and control entire provinces or branches of human activity. They construct, as they always have, mansions in the city and villas in the country. Sometimes they also manage to obtain a title from some sovereign or the Pope. Gradually, as has always happened, they attempt in some way to learn the simple secrets which the nobles once knew—the art of living, of ruling, responsibility towards inferiors, but, above all, that one simple art which always evades them: how to make their families endure, how to educate their children in such a manner that they do not dissipate their inheritance in the space of a few decades, how to establish a tradition of continuity which goes beyond mere self-interest and the individual's caprices, the day-by-day pleasures, and which imposes sacrifices on each person.

How does one survive intact through the vicissitudes of history? How does one live through the centuries? This is the secret which the bourgeoisie will perhaps never discover. Yet, without this secret, apparently one cannot give dignity to public life, cannot encourage the arts, cannot placate man's crude passions. In past centuries the newcomers used to imitate the older models and follow their example. In this century when the ruling class in Italy may eventually come to feel the need at last for learning the ancient civilized arts, the aristocratic families—convinced of their traditions' futility, cut off from the world that created them—shall have utterly forgotten all they knew and no longer have anything to teach.

# 7

# GRAMSCI, A FOUNDING FATHER

SHORT TIME AGO, in the Italian Chamber of Deputies, after announcing my party's vote in favor of a Communist proposal for the abolition of movie censorship, I concluded, "It is superfluous to point out that Liberals have been against all kinds of censorship in all countries for centuries, while Communists are against it only when and where they are not in power." I sat down as the extreme Left booed me. All this had happened before. Whenever the occasion warrants it, either the Communists or the Liberals make similar proposals, the Liberals more often than the Communists; a noble debate follows. The Liberals draw the neat distinction between permanent and occasional love of liberty; the Communists boo; then an overwhelming majority (Catholics, neo-Fascists, Monarchists, Republicans, and Socialists) buries us under an avalanche of nays.

As I was leaving on that particular day, the young, erudite, and inexperienced Marxist-Leninist who had just spoken on behalf of his Party ran after me and said, "This you must admit, that the Italian Communists have always been in favor of liberty!" He was visibly hurt that doubts should be cast on the sincerity and intellectual consistency of his motives. I did not argue. I knew he had no doubts that liberty (real liberty, and not the *trompe l'oeil* variety which bewitched our grandfathers and is still held sacred by the bourgeois) could be secured in no other way than by serving one of the most tyrannical, bureaucratic, and dogma-ridden organizations ever invented by man. I reassured him. Yes, I said, the Italian Communists have always declared liberty was their ultimate goal. He looked relieved and thanked me.

This apparently contradictory belief, that pyromaniacs make the best firemen, that one can further the cause of the angels by joining the devils, is undisputed among Italian intellectual Communists. The rank and file do not worry about such metaphysical matters; they wholeheartedly belong to what they rightly think is a pitiless, centralized, and well-knit organization, which will destroy all class enemies, conquer the world, and run it autocratically, according to inflexible scientific rules, in the interest of the proletariat. They would like nothing better than a good bloody revolution tomorrow morning but they know they have to be patient. In the meantime they enjoy occasional street brawls and disorderly strikes, which are good for frightening the government, intimidating the American embassy, and extracting concessions from the capitalists. Few ordinary card-holding members ever felt qualms of conscience. They dearly loved Stalin; considered forced-labor camps a sad necessity; cheered the Soviet tanks in Budapest; and now are tempted to applaud Mao, the leader of a comprehensible form of paleo-Communism.

The intellectual élite, on the other hand, who have run the Party since 1924 with absolute power and no back talk, were continually tortured by secret doubts while Stalin was alive. Even loyal Palmiro Togliatti had to struggle with his conscience. He told Ignazio Silone in 1930: "The forms of the proletarian revolution are not arbitrary. If they do not correspond to our preferences, so much the worse for us. And what is the alternative? What happens to the comrades who abandon the party?"
. . . Many intellectuals were shocked by Khrushchev's Twentieth Congress speech, tore up their cards after the Hungarian revolution, are frightened by the ultimate consequences of the Chinese schism, and openly deplore the primitive excesses of the Red Guards.

Can it be said that there are two parties in juxtaposition, the party of the intellectual leaders and that of the rank and file?

To be sure, the difference between the two is almost invisible to the outsider. The intellectual leaders appear to him on the surface to be as enthusiastic, orthodox, and disciplined as any ordinary member; they end up by following Soviet decisions, particularly in foreign affairs. (After the outbreak of troubles, they all sided with Nasser against Israel, "a tool of the imperialists", as soon as *Pravda* took its stand.) Yet, if one looks a little more attentively, one discovers that there is often something vaguely heretical about them. To be sure, their writings quote Marx and Lenin, but just as often are based on Italian historical writers, Italian philosophers from Vico to Croce, none of whom was particularly noted for his revolutionary spirit. Communist examples and teachings from the Soviet Union and other Communist countries are painstakingly adapted to local prejudices and social conditions, until at times nothing recognizable is left. Above all, they cherish the Italian Liberal tradition from the Parthenopean Republic of 1799 to the Carbonari society and the Garibaldi expeditions. They show an odd respect for all the barricades of the eighteenth and nineteenth centuries, which established those very liberties which their followers consider ridiculous impediments to progress, mere decoys for sentimental fellow travelers.

Once, years ago, when Gian Carlo Paietta, an energetic young chief, stormed the prefecture of Milan at the head of a tumultuous crowd, and called Togliatti in Rome from the Prefect's own phone, the leader did not hide his displeasure: "Get out of there immediately," he said. "What do you think you're doing? Lenin said that either one carries out a revolution to the end or one does not start one." When Togliatti was wounded by an assassin in 1948, his last instructions to his lieutenants before being wheeled to the operating table were: "*Siate calmi. Non perdete la testa* . . . Be calm. Don't lose your heads." To be sure, the cadres all know they might one day have to lead a real revolution and have to kill and deport thousands of opponents, including women and children. But they confess privately their hope that their opponents, being intelligent Italians, will know in time when the game is up, will see the folly of putting up a pointless show of resistance, and will resign themselves to the inevitability of historical forces. One might say the leaders of the Italian Communist Party dislike revolutions just as much as studious staff officers dislike the untidiness of war.

This curious situation, in which a party of millions of fanatic, uncultivated, and easily influenced people has always been efficiently controlled by a relatively small number of mild scholars, most of whom abhor violent words, wear glasses, and speak with soft voices, has proved to be a very successful one. Had the party been led mainly by sectarian terrorists as certain other Communist parties are, it would have been weak and vulnerable. Indeed, this proved to be so between 1921 and about 1923, when the Party was led by its founder, Amadeo Bordigo, an engineer from Formia, who was an uncompromising, intransigent, stubborn revolutionary. Bordiga commanded an enthusiastic mass following, but divided the Left opposition, managed to frighten the bourgeoisie out of their wits, and helped the Fascists gain power by rallying all the timid to their side. As a result, the Party was practically destroyed and driven underground. On the other hand, an organization composed of a few thousand bookish students of history and philosophy, vaguely in love with liberty and anxious to free man from century-old injustices, would have been equally doomed to failure. The last movement of this kind was the *Partito d'Azione*, organized clandestinely during the time of Mussolini. All leaders and no soldiers, and probably including the finest and noblest minds in the country, it once and for all showed the practical ineffectiveness of the formula. Its members filled the jails, died heroically in the Resistance, left a priceless heritage of doctrine and examples, but never managed to win one seat in Parliament when democracy was re-established.

*     *     *

TO BE SURE, not all Communists are happy with the present situation. One impatient young member, an excellent novelist, recently compared the Party to an old galleon, loaded with money, men, and guns, and becalmed in the middle of the ocean. Dissatisfied critics accuse the leaders of being fat bureau-crats in love with the status quo, old men whose aim is not the revolution but the enjoyment of power in a free society, and point out that they did nothing when they could easily have staged a *coup d'état* immediately after the end of the war. The Party was still armed, the Americans had discharged their soldiers and abandoned their weapons to rust on foreign beaches, the Italian bourgeoisie was dispirited, and the State in almost complete decay. Nothing, however, happened.

Stalin himself thought the Italian leadership too bookish to be effective. "Look at Togliatti," he told Vladimir Dedijer. "He is a good theoretician, he writes good political articles, but will never be able to rally the people and lead them to victory." Togliatti was known as "the Professor" in the Comintern secretariat in the 1930s. It has also been pointed out that the middle classes which the Party sacrificed so much to assuage have not been pacified. They still distrust and fear it. The Party's overtures to democratic parties, its loud declarations in favor of liberty, parliamentary institutions, and peace are looked upon by most of its opponents as signs of duplicity and transparent Machiavellian tricks.

All this Byzantine sophistry and high culture are undoubtedly causing many simple card-carrying Communists to abandon the cells. Nevertheless the number of voters grows at every election, both in absolute figures and in percentages. At present one Italian out of four votes for the Party candidates. Nothing has stopped this growth, neither the Center-Left coalition nor the rising standard of living of the working classes. The Party is now a major factor not only in Italian internal politics (every party's position is now more or less determined by its relation to the Communists), but also in European affairs and Western defense plans. It even forced the Church to consider coming to terms with it. It has not placated the fears of the middle class, to be sure, but this time it has surely prevented the rise of a violent and armed extreme Right faction. The Party is so influential and learned that it is now affecting the thinking and the plans of all Western Communist parties to a greater extent than the mother party, the CP of the Soviet Union, now does. It is even influencing the younger and more liberal thinkers in the Soviet Union itself, who like the Italians' disapproval of political dictatorship over the arts. Some experts believe that if conditions do not change some day, probably within ten or twelve years, the Italian Communists will control enough votes to attract other parties to form a strong coalition government. This would be a final triumph of the intellectual elite. That day they will have fully succeeded in creating, out of a violent, immature, illiterate, and impatient mass following, a moderate, realistic, cultured and prudent movement—the only kind that could possible conquer power, and do so without provoking international complications and internal reactions, while receiving the blessings of the Church, and perhaps even the approval of the State Department.

\* \* \*

THE SUCCESSFUL FORMULA Togliatti patiently employed for almost thirty years, pretending to abandon it when the Comintern disapproved, and resuming it when the going was good, was not invented by him. It was devised long ago by one of his friends, a fellow-Sardinian, with whom he had studied at the University of Turin just before the First World War. His name was Antonio Gramsci. He is now considered not merely a hero of the Party but one of Italy's most brilliant and original thinkers. No modern Italian intellectual whether of the Right or the Left can be considered entirely free of his influence.

Gramsci, born at Ales in Sardinia, January 22, 1891, was one of the founders (not, as the Italian Communists like to believe, The Founder) of the Party in 1921, a delegate to the Cominterm in 1923, the leader of Italian Communists in 1923 at the age of 32, and was elected a member of Parliament in 1924. He was arrested two years later, in violation of the law guaranteeing immunity to members of Parliament, and sentenced to twenty years in jail. He died in a Roman clinic in 1937 of neglect and inadequate medical care. He left a vast number of newspaper articles, a few essays, several reports, and many letters, but his main contribution to political thinking is contained in the thirty-two notebooks which he filled during his detention, covering almost every aspect of Italian life, from literature to social life, from religion to economics, from the remote past to the Fascist present and the probable future.

Two important books on Antonio Gramsci have appeared recently, one in Italy, the other in the United States, and they should attract the wide attention which his personality and achievements deserve. Both carefully avoid the reverent exaggerations or suppressions of the official Party studies, which have obscured Gramsci's real work. *Vita di Antonio Gramsci* by Giuseppe Fiori is the work of a young Sardinian journalist, historian, and novelist, who has lovingly reconstructed his subject's native environment, questioned surviving relatives and contemporaries, collected anecdotes, and dug up forgotten documents and publications, to produce a lively portrait of both the public and private person. The result is both an authoritative and readable book, a rare combination in Italy where authoritative books tend to be verbose, untidy, and incomprehensible, and readable books are rarely authoritative. In fact the book has not only become almost a best-seller in Italy, but it will probably be considered the definitive work on Gramsci. The American work, *Antonio Gramsci and the Origins of Italian Communism* by Professor John M. Cammett, published by Stanford University, is a more specialized study. It gives as much attention to the public figure as to the political scene, the Italian working-class movements after the First World War. It clarifies a number of intricate problems which Italian writers often mistakenly take for granted and seldom bother to explain to themselves or to foreign readers. Cammett's useful study is solidly based on original and shrewd observations and on carefully established facts.

The two books complement each other almost perfectly. Both writers were lucky to have gathered their material at a time when many controversies were over, important private files had become available, some secret government archives had been opened, and the Party itself had timidly published for the first time a few embarrassing documents which it had kept buried for years. Both books are essential to an understanding of the Party's present policy. What position should the Party take toward the Center-Left coalition of Catholics and Socialists now in power? Many foreign observers believe the Party is neatly split into two discernable schools of thought. This opinion seems confirmed by debates in the official ideological magazines and the Central Committee.

The first school of thought is said to believe the Party should fight the government without mercy, in Parliament and the streets, as one more bourgeois travesty; that it should try to rescue the Socialists from the unnatural embrace of the Church, which is corrupting and destroying them; that it should attempt to form a new, anti-clerical, secular coalition.

The second school is said to classify the government as a typically feeble, progressive, democratic bourgeois movement which must be aided at all cost. The Party therefore should approach it without undue animosity, nudge it gently toward an increasingly independent foreign policy and an irreversible left-wing reform of society. The ultimate aim should be the formation of a large and stable alliance of Catholics, Socialists, and Communists, easily dominated by the Party elite. This last view, of course, is believed to be championed by the intellectuals, while the first is attributed to old Stalinists and the rank and file. In fact the rank and file are naturally attracted to protest and violent opposition: they feel comfortable being where they have always been. They find the present government particularly easy to hate. It could not have been set up without direct American help; it is certainly paralyzed, and one of the most inept governments since the end of the war. And easy to fight. It finds it embarrassing to resist the workers' requests and almost impossible to maintain order against workers' demonstrations.

What would Gramsci choose if he were alive? Of course, he himself did not always follow a pure Gramsci line. What he would do today is virtually what the Party is actually doing: encouraging the rank and file to express their dislike of the government as loudly and violently as they can. (It would embarrass the coalition to have no opposition from the extreme Left.) But, with the judicious use of parliamentary votes and the threat of social unrest, the Party tries to influence important foreign or internal policy decisions, meanwhile smoothing the way for its eventual entry into the government majority.

\* \* \*

GRAMSCI HAD MOST of the requisites of a great rebel leader. He was, to begin with, the descendant of expatriate rebels; his name is of Albanian origin; his great-grandfather had fled to Italy from Epirus in 1821 to escape Turkish oppression. He belonged to an impoverished middle-class family. (His grandfather had been a colonel of the *gendarmi*, an exalted rank in the Kingdom of Naples; his father had studied law at the University until the colonel's death and financial losses forced him to accept a miserable job in a Sardinian village.) Gramsci was extremely intelligent and eager to learn, but humiliatingly discovered that lazy and stupid boys from well-to-do families could go to school, but that almost all the bright poor were supposed to go to work. His native island was a distant and marginal section of Italy, where most of the inhabitants scraped along at a North African level of subsistence and only a few lived comfortably. Gramsci always spoke with a thick Sardinian accent, as thick as the Corsican accent of Napoleon or Stalin's Georgian.

He was furthermore a hunchback. Vladimir Degott, the Comintern emissary who met him in 1919, described him to Lenin as "a stupendous, interesting comrade, small, deformed, with a head so large it does not look like his own." The large head was handsome in his youth, with deep and thoughtful blue eyes behind *pince-nez* glasses, and a well-designed expressive mouth. Unfortunately, his voice was so thin he could never address large meetings. When he made his only speech in Parliament, in 1925, all deputies (most of them fascist by that time) crowded around him to hear what he was saying, and Mussolini, who could not leave the Prime Minister's seat, cupped a hand behind his ear. If Gramsci's dwarf size and tiny voice prevented him from becoming a rabble-rousing tribune, they made him a more dangerous man, the lone thinker who disdains evoking drifting emotions but distills durable explosive ideas.

He believed his deformity would always keep him from having normal relations with other people. When the Russian girl who was to become his wife fell in love with him in 1923, he confessed to her: "For many, many years I have been accustomed to think there is an absolute, almost fatal impossibility for me to be loved by anyone." He was sickly, tortured even in youth by insomnia, headaches, and nervous breakdowns, which often prevented him from concentrating and gave him occasional forms of amnesia. He was, however, indomitable. The amount of work he managed to do, both when he was young and free and when he was in jail, would have exhausted a stronger man.

Somehow, with the help of his family's heroic sacrifices, he went to school and, in 1911, won one of the scholarships reserved for Sardinian students at the University of Turin. (His name appeared ninth in the list of winners; number two was Togliatti.) Gramsci studied the humanities, specializing in philology, for which he had a particular inclination, but avidly followed a number of other and sometimes unrelated courses. He read omnivorously. At that time, Turin had a particularly distinguished faculty; on it was represented almost every contemporary view. It can be said that Gramsci's fundamental eclecticism dates from his years at Turin. He embraced socialism but always in later life refused to accept its rigid dogmatism. He particularly disliked positivism, then fashionable among the Left, and sectarianism. He always strongly believed that the Party should collaborate with all working-class movements, whatever their beliefs, and try to form occasional alliances with democratic bourgeois groups. He was fascinated by the great problem of Italy, the power of the Church, which had worried Machiavelli and every Italian patriot since his time. He wrote: "In Italy, in Rome, there is the Vatican, there is the Pope; the Liberal State had to find some sort of agreement with the spiritual power of the Church; the workers' State will also have to find a similar arrangement." He also wrote: "I don't go to

church. I am not a believer. But we must be aware of the fact
that those who believe are the majority. If we keep on having
cordial relations with atheists alone we shall always be a
minority."

He was impressed chiefly by the open-minded Liberals, like
Luigi Einaudi, a professor of economic theory, or Piero Gobetti,
a friend and colleague, who founded the review *Rivoluzione
Liberale*, and died at twenty-six from the effects of savage Fascist
beatings. And by the Liberal Benedetto Croce, who was not a
professor but dominated Italian intellectual life at the time.
Strict socialists despised him as a "class enemy", but as late as
1917 Gramsci bravely wrote: "Croce is the greatest thinker in
Europe today." Much fascinated him in the older man's
writings, most of all his firm denial that history would automatically do the work of man and would generate progress if
left to itself. Gramsci believed with Croce that the future was
shaped by the will and the ideas of man, and by "man" he
secretly meant the philosophers. He wrote that "every revolution has been preceded by hard critical thinking, the diffusion
of culture, and the spread of ideas among men who are at first
unwilling to listen, men concerned only with solving their
private economic and political problems." The best revolutionaries, according to him, were to be found in the reading
rooms of Public Libraries, where Marx, Lenin, and he himself
had spent so many hours. This belief in the essentially revolutionary character of culture is at the basis of his faith in the
historical role of Italian intellectuals, a faith which the Party
still holds. He also believed with Croce and Gobetti that liberty
was the shining goal of man's endeavor, or, as he put it, "the
creation of a society in which there could be the greatest
amount of freedom with the minimum of coercion."

At the same time he was a Marxist, one of the most profound
students and original interpreters of Marx's writings. As Cammett explains:

The ideas of Croce and Gentile were closely related to those of
Marxism in Italy. The connecting link was Antonio Labriola, a
Marxist who matured in the Hegelian school at Naples. Hence the

gap between idealism and Marxism was not a difficult one to bridge
. . . Gramsci's voluntaristic approach to fundamental Marxist
problems makes his work especially appealing to intellectuals, many
of whom had thought Marxism wholly deterministic. Moreover he
was able to express his Marxist thought in the language of other
philosophies, often exposing the weak points of those systems by
comparing them, in their own language, with corresponding Marxist concepts. There is a tendency to place Gramsci's work, described
as "left wing idealism", midway between Croce and Marx or between totalitarianism and historicism. Undoubtedly, Gramsci's
extreme historicism sometimes led him away from the opinions
generally accepted by Marxists. Thus he implied that economic laws
were not really laws in the "naturalistic sense" but "laws of tendency" in the historicistic sense. Gramsci also doubted the wisdom of
"mechanically" asserting the objective reality of the external world
—as though the world could be understood apart from human history.

Italy's entry into the war in May 1915 gave Gramsci his
first opportunity. What he thought was to be an irremediable
handicap turned into an asset. When all the young able-bodied
Socialist leaders from Turin were sent to the front, he was left
practically alone to carry on. He abandoned his studies and
plunged into dangerous political work. Turin was (and still is)
one of the three great industrial centers of Italy. The war had
enlarged its plants and filled them with workers from the countryside, raw material for the revolution, who had to be in-
doctrinated, organized, and led. Social tension was extreme;
disorders were an almost daily occurrence. They were actively
promoted by the Left Wing of the Socialist Party, which was
against the war, and was among the few to answer Lenin's
Zimmerwald appeal. Gramsci tirelessly wrote articles and mani-
festoes, addressed meetings, delivered lectures, took an active
part in the organization of strikes. He acquired precious experience. This was his first real contact with ordinary human beings,
the chosen people of his own particular faith, the industrial
proletariat. As he wrote his Russian wife in 1923: "How many
times I have asked myself whether it is possible to attach oneself
to a mass of people when one never loved anyone before . . ."

*        *        *

AFTER A workers' uprising in 1917, he was elected secretary of his Party's section. He considered himself on the extreme Left, in revolt as much against the Socialist leadership as against capitalism. The Italian chiefs were then elderly provincial figures of another era. Most of them wore romantic whiskers of all shapes, drooping black neckties, and wide-brimmed hats. Most of them were sincere and honorable men, but, in the eyes of the young, superficial, inept, and verbose. They were men who tried to hide their incapacity and irresolution under rhetorical appeals to sentiment or apocalyptic pronouncements of the most blood-curdling kind. Each served his own particular interpretation of socialism, from extreme moderation to extreme radicalism, and fought all others tooth and nail. As a result, when the war ended, while the bourgeoisie was disheartened and the forces of law and order were impotent, the Party lacked the cohesion, the clear ideas, the sense of responsibility, and the discipline necessary to exploit the unique opportunity history was offering it.

*        *        *

IN 1919, when his friends and collaborators came back from the war, Gramsci founded the *Ordine Nuovo*, a weekly mostly dedicated to ideological debate. It wanted to purge the Party of lukewarm and timid members in order to promote the revolution as soon as possible. Another faction led by Bordiga had been formed in Naples at about the same time with vaguely similar aims. It also published a weekly, *Il Soviet*. Yet the sophisticated *Ordine Nuovo* group had little in common with Bordiga's Bronze Age followers, except the desire to exploit the situation, the mistrust of Socialist Party leaders, the enthusiastic acceptance of Soviet guidance, and unlimited admiration for Lenin. Bordiga was fundamentally a sectarian who rejected encumbering alliances, not only with the Catholics and bourgeois democratic movements, but also with the whole Socialist Party. He was a sworn enemy of Parliament: he wanted his men to abstain from voting and to keep their names out of the candidates' lists. The Turin group, considering that most of Bordiga's enemies were, for different reasons, their enemies too, decided to play along with him for the time being. This is one of the earliest occasions on which Gramsci was induced to follow a non-Gramsci line.

The Third International was, at the time, anxiously watching the situation from afar. A victorious revolution in Italy, which the experts considered possible, would have given great help to the struggling Soviet régime. Moscow sent a stream of observers, emissaries, and secret agents, most of whom were uncertain and ill-informed, to prod the Italians, report on progress, and guide them to victory. Who was to be supported with money and advice? Lenin, who always thought reformists more dangerous than the secret police and the capitalists, naturally wanted the Italian Party purged of all moderates, and looked benignly on both extremist groups, Gramsci's and Bordiga's, though he felt more sympathetic to the *Ordine Nuovo* intellectuals. He enthusiastically endorsed a diagnosis of the situation, written mostly by Gramsci, which had been sent from Turin. It included the prophetic words:

The current phase of the class war in Italy could foreshadow either the conquest of power by the revolutionary proletariat or the rise of a tremendous reactionary movement organized by the owners' class and the governing élite.

On July 20, 1920, Lenin wrote: "We must simply say to the Italian comrades that the position of the Communist International corresponds more closely to the views of *Ordine Nuovo* than to those of the present leaders of the Socialist Party." He also attacked Bordiga, a member of the delegation to the second Comintern congress (to which Gramsci was not elected): "Comrade Bordiga forgets that the struggle to destroy Parliament must also be conducted in Parliament . . . Parliament is one of the arenas of the class war." But while the Turin group appealed to the philosopher and scholar in him, Lenin, the ruthless revolutionary organizer, could not forget that Bordiga carried with him almost 90 per cent of the extreme Left.

In January 1921 the Socialists gathered at Leghorn for their seventeenth congress. Gramsci was a delegate, but did not speak. The orders from the Comintern were to expel all reformists. Bordiga took a vigorous stand for the elimination from the Party of practically everybody; although he was supported by some agents of the Comintern, he lost. Historians now know that his and Lenin's radical proposal was a mistake. The Party was no longer on the offensive, the sole arbiter of a prerevolutionary situation, as it had been only two years before. It was now fighting for its life against armed and organized Fascist reaction; it needed all the allies it could keep, in particular the reformists who controlled some of the best strongholds, the thousands of municipal administrations. The day after his overwhelming defeat, on January 21, 1921, Bordiga led his men and the *Ordine Nuovo* delegates to another theater, the Teatro San Marco, and founded the Italian Communist Party known at the time as the *Partito Communista d'Italia*, a rump movement of all-out extremists. Officials were elected immediately. Bordiga was acclaimed the undisputed leader; his henchmen seized the majority of the posts on the Central Committee and occupied every position on the executive with the exception of one. Gramsci had difficulty in getting elected to the Central Committee and did not make the executive.

Years later he wrote reflectively: "The Leghorn schism, which detached the mass of the proletariat from the Comintern, was one of the greatest victories of the reactionary forces." Why had he not spoken against a line that went against his shrewd and more enlightened views? After Leghorn he took a subordinate place and loyally ran the *Ordine Nuovo*, transformed into a daily, as an orthodox party organ. The exchange of ideas ceased. Older comrades still reproach Gramsci for having expressed his lucid criticism of Comintern tactics and the ruinously sectarian Party only in private conversations with close friends. If he had behaved differently, they speculate, he could perhaps have deflected the course of history, for as a result of the Leghorn split and Bordiga's leadership, the Fascists' March on Rome was without serious opposition. Gramsci however, knew that he could carry only a small percentage of the rank and file even in Turin, most of them his own close friends, and not all of these all the time.

What he faced at Leghorn, and later when he was in control of the Party or in jail, is the agonizing dilemma intelligent Communists struggled with sooner or later. When the leaders of the Comintern are wrong, should one carry on a hopeless fight for one's ideas, lose, and leave the Party, or should one keep one's mouth shut, swim with the tide, and wait for a better moment? Twice again after Leghorn Gramsci had to face the same decision. The second time was in Vienna, in 1924. He was, by then, the Party chief, and his choice carried far greater weight and had wider repercussions.

Two years earlier, in May 1922, he had been sent to Moscow as the Italian representative to the Comintern, where he arrived desperately ill, with a nervous condition which almost completely prevented him from reading and writing. He had a high fever and tremors in his arms and legs. He was taken to a rest home at Sebranyi Bor to recuperate. One of the inmates was Eugenia Schucht, a Russian girl brought up in Rome, whose sister Julka often came to visit, and eventually became his wife. To Julka he wrote what are surely among the most endearing love letters in Italian and the most lucid political analyses. She bore him two sons, Giuliano and Delio, who are now Soviet citizens, one a violinist in a Moscow symphony orchestra and the other a marine colonel in Leningrad.

While Gramsci was recovering, the situation in Italy had become disastrous. The Fascists had seized power, Mussolini was Prime Minister, and the Communists were facing not only the onslaughts of the Black Shirts but also the efficient persecution of the police and the *carabinieri*. Most of the leaders were in jail, including Bordiga. The Party was without hope, reduced to a few scattered and isolated groups with few capable leaders, and little opportunity for organized action. Since Gramsci was the only one free to move, he was sent to Vienna in 1923, put up in an unheated laborer's furnished room, supplied with a half-witted secretary and not enough money, and nominated Party leader.

At this time the Soviet experts had finally come to the conclusion that the Leghorn split had been a grave mistake. The
instructions from Moscow, based on the third and fourth congress of the Comintern, aimed at an immediate reunification of
all workers' movements. Gramsci was ordered to convince the
comrades still at large once again to join forces with the
Socialists. At the end of 1923 and the beginning of 1924, he sat
in his little room wrapped in blankets, and wrote hundreds of
letters. There was nothing wrong with the new line except the
timing. Controversies on the defeat of the Left by the Fascists
had been raging for more than a year. Socialists and Communists had become unreconcilable enemies. In his jail cell, Bordiga, still theoretically in control of the Party, rejected the new
instructions outright, and proposed to break off relations with
the Comintern. He was enthusiastically seconded by a majority
of the Central Committee and by the rank and file.

*       *       *

WHAT WAS GRAMSCI TO DO? He knew, of course, that the
instructions from Moscow, although correct, were practically
insane at that moment. He also knew that Comintern support
was the only hope. He knew that Bordiga did not present a useful alternative, for he was only a mad romantic visionary. Gramsci did the best he could, maneuvering between two impossible
positions. "I had to keep to an eel-like course, to keep the Comintern happy and the Italian comrades more or less together," he
later admitted. Zinoviev complained at the time that "Gramsci
makes vague promises; and when he fulfills them, the result is
the contrary of what one expects."

The last time Gramsci had to face a similar dilemma was in
1930. This time he allowed himself to disagree openly with the
Comintern decisions. Probably because he had no direct responsibility, he could afford to take a brave stand, consistent
with his past beliefs and with his record as a student of Marx and
Italian history. In May 1924 he had returned to Italy. He had
been elected *in absentia* to the Chamber of Deputies and thought
he would be protected from arrest by parliamentary immuni-

ties. A month later Matteotti was murdered and the Fascist régime was shaken to its foundations. Law-abiding bourgeois and timid conservative abandoned it in droves for the time being. The Communist Party could cautiously start to reorganize, a few newspapers and magazines appeared again, workers began meeting indoors. Gramsci lived quietly. His wife and elder son joined him in Rome for a time, and he resumed his former Turin life; he spent his time reading, writing, talking to the workers and cultivating friends, not necessarily all of them Communists. He finally defeated Bordiga at the Party congress held in France, at Lyons, by drawing up a series of proposals, based on his own interpretation of the new Comintern line, in favor of collaboration with all anti-Fascist groups. He made one speech in Parliament (against a bill allegedly designed only to outlaw Freemasons and all similar secret sects). He wrote an essay on the *Problema del Mezzogiorno*. He also addressed a brave letter to the Communist Party of the Soviet Union in indirect defense of Zinoviev, Trotsky, and Kamenev. It never reached Stalin. Togliatti intercepted it, thought it impolitic and imprudent, and sent Gramsci an answer which is now said to be lost. Gramsci read it in the offices of the Soviet embassy in Rome and probably tore it up. This was his last important political act as a free man.

* * *

AFTER THE ATTEMPTED assassination of Mussolini on October 31, 1926, the Fascists passed the "exceptional laws" ordering the immediate dissolution of all opposition parties. They established a "special court" for the "defense of the State" and carried out mass arrests. Gramsci was among the first to face the tribunal. On the request of the prosecutor that "we must stop this brain from functioning for twenty years," he was sentenced to twenty years, four months and five days imprisonment. He was confined at the penal house of Turi, near Bari.

While Gramsci was in jail filling his notebooks, the Comintern official policy was once again abruptly reversed, to facilitate Stalin's struggle with the rightist opposition. All Communist parties were now expected to break relations with the Socialists. The Italian leaders were flabbergasted. Those few who had emigrated to France and were free had only recently managed to convince their most recalcitrant followers to make peace with the Socialists. How could a resumption of hostilities be justified? Some of the heroic founders of the Party, Ignazio Silone among them, either resigned or were expelled. Togliatti believed that because only Soviet support could keep the organization going, Comintern orders were to be obeyed at all cost and was busy branding all dissidents as traitors and expelling them. Still, he thought it prudent to inform the comrades in Italian jails of what had happened. Among the emissaries dispatched to Italy was Gramsci's brother Gennaro, who was one of the few people allowed to see him in Turi. This is how an authorized biography of Togliatti[1] related Antonio's reaction to his brother's revelations: "Although Gramsci could not know all the details of the struggle [between Stalin and the Right opposition led by Bukarin], from his penitentiary cell he gave his full approval to the most severe measures taken against the dissident comrades."

*    *    *

THE TRUTH was something else. Many years later Giuseppe Fiori found Gennaro working as a cashier in a suburban drugstore in Rome (he was run over by an automobile and died in 1965) and asked him what had really happened. This is what Fiori wrote:

Gennaro told his brother all he knew. Antonio was shocked. He agreed with the point of view of Leonetti, Tresso, and Ravazzoli [the dissident group]: he did not approve their expulsion and rejected the new Comintern line, which he believed Togliatti had accepted too quickly. . . . When Gennaro returned to Paris, "I went to see Togliatti," he said to me, "and told him: 'Nino [Gramsci's family nickname] is completely in agreement with you.'" This was an unexpected end to his story and I asked him the reason why. He could not understand why I was surprised. His answer to Togliatti

---

[1] *Conversando con Togliatti*, by Marcella and Maurizio Ferrara (Rome, 1953).

seemed to him the only logical conclusion to a logical reasoning. He
explained that he feared his brother would be accused of "opportunism" both in Paris and in Moscow as soon as his real position was
known. Therefore he had protected him. "If I had answered differently, not even Nino would have been saved from expulsion."

Fiori's publication of Gennaro's testimony provoked violent
reactions. Polemics ranged in the Party national weekly,
*Rinascita*, and its Sardinian counterpart, *Rinascita Sarda*. There
were denials, confirmations by Fiori, letters pro and con written
by veteran ideologues who had taken part in the 1929–1930
decisions, old Communists who had been in jail with Gramsci.
In the words of Giuseppe Berti, one of the original founders
and one of Nino's old friends, Stalin's orders "took away from
the workers' movement the essential weapon of a united front,
essential to bar the road to Fascism and Nazism, above all in
Germany, in the years in which such a weapon would have
been most effective." Subsequent disclosures in non-Communist
publications, some of which were only weakly denied by the
Party organs, revealed that Gramsci had not hidden his real
thoughts from the more orthodox Communists with him in
Turi. They were shocked and as a result he had been treated
as all convicts treat a traitor or spy; nobody came near him or
spoke to him for months. It is now believed that Togliatti was
fully aware of Gramsci's position, in spite of Gennaro's pathetic
lies, and had given orders that all contact by the Party with the
sick man should cease. Nobody went to see him in Turi nor, a
few years before his death, in the private clinics where he was
free to see friends. It is doubtful, however, whether Gramsci
would have received an emissary of the new Stalinist Central
Committee: he never expressed any desire to see any Communist
whatever, new, old, or dissident.

*          *          *

WHY WERE THESE FACTS revealed, or allowed to be revealed?
Why were the denials so weak? There is no doubt that a few
months ago, thirty years after Gramsci's death, the Party carefully considered the partial disclosure of the truth and thought

it useful. It allowed the revelations to leak gently, bit by bit, so as not to shock the sectarian old men, nor drive the illiterate rank and file into Maoist splinter groups; and ambiguously so that it could deny everything if need be. Why then were these disclosures thought necessary? Obviously, in the new international situation following Stalin's and Togliatti's deaths, it had become essential for the Party to demonstrate that the man officially known as the Founder (Amadeo Bordiga is still a nonperson), the creator of the bridge between Italian Hegelianism and Marxism, the inventor of liberal-Marxist theories, the only Party leader whose work is read and admired by non-Communist intellectuals, had not been mistaken in his view of what we now know was one of history's most critical moments. It was important not only because it helped to establish Gramsci firmly as the sole Patron Saint of the Party but also helped to strengthen his position as one of "the two original thinkers the Communist movement produced since 1917," as George Lichtheim writes in *Marxism* (the other, of course, is Lukács), and the inspirer of more and more intellectual rebels in foreign Parties.

The revelations also helped to prove that while Gramsci was right, Stalin was wrong, and that the most disastrous mistakes committed by the Italian Party were the result of Moscow's bad Marxist interpretation of contemporary events, and ill-informed meddling. To be sure, without Comintern hospitality and support, the exiled Italian leaders could not have lived and worked between 1922 and 1943. Yet nobody now tries to deny that the Leghorn split and the fight against the Socialists facilitated the Fascist *coup d'état*, as the isolation of the German Party later helped Hitler to take power. Both these defeats, provoked by unenlightened orders from the Comintern, not only were among the causes of the Second World War, but also irremediably discredited, weakened, and retarded all Communist Parties and damaged the proletarian movement everywhere. How could intelligent men trust an allegedly scientific approach to politics which could justify such grievous misjudgments of reality?

Finally, the disclosures were considered necessary to prove that there is an uninterrupted coherent ideological trend between the 1919 *Ordine Nuovo* group and the contemporary Party. This is mostly true. Even Togliatti, who had to impose the will of the Comintern and expel some of his best friends with ignominy, later spoke of "*force majeure*", of the "meandering course of the revolution", and did not hide his personal preference for Gramsci's dislike of sectarian policies and his sympathy for united fronts. When the documents become available, surely they will show how unhappy the Comintern leaders were with Togliatti's fluid interpretation of their directives. The Italian Party now stands openly for its "Founder's" views. It believes in "polycentrism," or the right to interpret Soviet views in the light of local exigencies; believes in class alliances, in collaboration with progressive bourgeois movements, including the Catholics, to transform society in a way which makes a Communist takeover easy when the time comes; the exploitation of all the opportunities offered by bourgeois democracy, including freedom of the press, freedom to organize, to strike, to demonstrate, free elections, and the revolutionary use of parliamentary institutions. It deplores sectarianism and terrorism. Cammett points out:

There is indeed a continuity from the *Ordine Nuovo* period to the political letters of 1923–1924, from the Lyons Congress of the Italian Party to the Popular Front. Opponents of this kind of Communism have denounced it as "opportunism" and "reformism," but others have interpreted it as a "realistic response" of the Communist movement to the economic, political, and cultural conditions existing in modern capitalist states.

This "response" is particularly difficult in Italy, which is neither a modern capitalist state nor a primitive backward country, but an intricate and misleading mixture of both. It is a country that has been governed for centuries by foreign rulers and petty princelings; a country whose identity has been assured mainly by its intellectuals and artists, and whose revolutions were never made by the people as a whole.

In December 1933 Gramsci was freed, and was allowed to

enter a private clinic in Formia for the urgent treatment of his many neglected ailments. Later he was transferred to a better clinic in Rome, the *Quisisana*, where, in August 1935, he was visited by a medical luminary, Professor Cesare Frugoni, who declared him in a desperate state. He had Pott's disease, tuberculosis of the lungs, dangerously high blood pressure, recurrent crises of angina, and gout. On April 27, 1937, he died, six days after his prison sentence had expired. His sister-in-law, Tatiana, who assisted him till the end, gathered all his papers and his notebooks, which contain the essence of his thinking. The central core of Gramsci's political philosophy is probably to be found in his reflections on Machiavelli. Like Lenin, George Lichtheim writes, Gramsci "had intuitively grasped the theory and practice of a revolution in a retarded country where the masses were suddenly hurled upon the political stage under the leadership of the Bolshevik vanguard." He believed the Party of his day had the role Machiavelli had assigned to his imaginary Prince, or, in his own words:

The modern prince, the myth-prince, cannot be a real person, a concrete individual; it can only be an organization; a complex element of society in which the cementing of a collective will, recognized and partially asserted in action, has already begun. This organization is already provided by historical development, and it is the political party: the first cell containing the germs of collective will which are striving to become universal and total.

This passage might well be recommended to the Italian intellectual Communists who admire Gramsci, believe in liberty, and think an Italian Communist régime would not be totalitarian, but would respect the fundamental liberties and the rights of the opposition. Lichtheim points out that Gramsci's criticism of totalitarianism was directed really at Mussolini's régime, "but could be applied word for word to Stalin (under whose rule Gramsci would have been unlikely to fill entire prison notebooks with philosophical reflections)." He adds:

We owe it to the accident of this gifted writer's incarceration under Fascism that there is such a thing as a Marxist critique of totalitarianism, "from the inside," as it were. The various opposition groups which split off from the Russian Communist party in the 1920's and 1930's produced a great many critical reflections on the operation of the régime, but—with the doubtful exception of Trotsky's last writings—nothing like a principled rejection of the central idea of totalitarianism, which is quite simply the idea of a social order created by force: perhaps the most "un-Marxian" notion ever excogitated by professed Marxists.

In his copy of Machiavelli's *Prince* Gramsci had marked this passage:

I say that every Prince must desire to be considered merciful and not cruel. He must, however, take care not to misuse this mercifulness. Cesare Borgia was considered cruel, but his cruelty brought order to Romagna, united it, and reduced it to peace and fealty. If this is considered well, it will be seen that he was really much more merciful than the Florentine people, who, to avoid the reputation of cruelty, allowed Pistoia to be destroyed.

A Prince would prefer to be "merciful and not cruel". Justice imposed from above by tyrants is to be abhorred. But then he has a job to do and it must be done.

# 8

# A GLIMPSE OF MUSSOLINI

I saw Benito Mussolini dozens, possibly hundreds, of times. He saw me only once, one afternoon in the castle at Tripoli. I was presented to him by the Minister of the Press and Propaganda with the words: ". . . and this is Luigi Barzini." The dictator looked hard at me, then pursed his lips, raised his chin, and for a few seconds said nothing. He seemed to be considering that fragment of information, and the pause was embarrassing. At that time there was always something gauche about being presented without shaking hands (which was something strictly forbidden by the Party); for a handshake is rather more than a mere greeting, it is a kind of symbolic gesture like the handshake country traders give at fairs to seal an agreement. One never knew what to do.

At last, after a rather long interval, the *Duce* spoke. Dragging out the syllables, he said: "*Ju-ni-or*." I was then little more than a boy, at least thirty years younger than the far more famous "Senior", my father, and felt like answering: "Obviously," but checked myself. Dictators have no sense of humor.

Somehow I felt I knew Mussolini extremely well. On military maneuvers, at ceremonies, on state journeys, where I had been sent as special correspondent for the *Corriere della Sera*, I had always pushed up close to him so that I could watch him at my ease and for a long time. He had a small cyst like a spring potato on his bald head; he had a dark oval mole under his chin (it must have bothered him when he was shaving); his teeth were the color of old ivory, and they were small and separated from one another, the kind of teeth that are supposed to be lucky. Once, in Sicily, I watched him in a military field Mass. With

folded arms, he stared angrily at the chaplain's back as if trying
to pierce holes in it with his eyes. At the elevation he neither
knelt nor bowed his head. I don't know why: maybe he wanted
to prove to himself that he was the same *esprit fort* he had been
in his youth; maybe he didn't know the custom, or refused to
make a public act of homage to anyone, even to God. That day
he was wearing boots of thin leather with very fine, pliable
soles, the kind of soles you sometimes see very old men wearing;
and, as he stood straight and stiff and motionless throughout the
whole Mass, perhaps without noticing he kept raising and
lowering the tips of his toes, rhythmically, in an almost invisible
gesture of impatience.

It was the same impatience that he always showed outside, an
irritated impatience: at generals who explained maneuvers to
him, at maps that unfolded too slowly, at the officer who didn't
come quickly enough when he was called, at the driver who
didn't bring the car around fast enough, or at someone's slowness in thinking over a reply before giving it. But perhaps this
irritated impatience served to hide his own uncertainty and uneasiness. One evening before the war, at Palazzo Venezia,
during a reception in honor of Halifax and Chamberlain, I
stood near him for some time, in order to observe him closely. He
was wearing tails, fastened in front with matching buttons, cuff-
link style. The unfamiliar clothes, the presence of distinguished
English guests, the smart company, the elegant and occasionally
beautiful young women, made him unconsciously behave in a
very unusual way. There was no doubt that he now saw himself
not as a Renaissance *condottiero* but as a man of the world, a lady-
killer, a charming and courteous host, and gallant as well. At
one point, as he went from room to room, he found himself
beside two pretty young foreign girls, possibly Lord Perth's
daughters. Gesturing (he spoke no English), he took them over
to a showcase, where fifteenth-century Italian jewels were on
show, and pointed them out to them, to make them look really
carefully, and, still using only hand motions and grimaces, held
forth on their beauty, value, and workmanship. His way of
gesturing (the same platform style that had such an effect on

crowds) when he was only a few inches from his listeners and at the same level was obviously excessive. He gesticulated with hands and arms, with his whole body, and twisted his face in so awkward, so clumsy a way that I was upset. His were not the smiling, fluent and natural gestures that southerners used in order to make foreigners understand them. They were pompous, theatrical, melodramatic; the kind, it then struck me, that the Doge of Venice might make in the second act of the opera *La Gioconda* in some provincial production; or the way the supporting players in *La Traviata* behave when they are trying to suggest aristocratic enjoyment at the dance at Flora's. The two English girls were also surprised and ill at ease, and looked at him incredulously. Then, moving a little away, they began laughing nervously, trying to stifle the giggles that rose up inside them.

The dictator's behavior had, to tell the truth, always filled me with disquiet, the kind of paralyzing embarrassment you feel with shy people or, in dreams, when you find yourself naked in a crowd. In the most characteristic moments of his speeches (which I sometimes heard in the line of duty), when he leant confidentially forward towards his audience, for instance, with an omniscient smile on his face, and some ironical remark on his lips, or when he raised his whole body to give greater solemnity to the words he was going to use, and emphasized them, one by one, with grimaces and gestures of his upraised arms (and the crowd went wild), I often turned my head away, as if forced to see a close relation or friend make a fool of himself without being able to help it. Sometimes I even closed my eyes.

Twice, though, I felt unembarrassed. At Gela, during a tour of Sicily, I saw him dance. He had stopped on the beach of some unsmart bathing place to have a swim, followed by a string of ministers and party officials, and after lunch he asked a girl there—perhaps a clerk or school-mistress—to dance with him. This time he was calm and smiling. History wasn't watching him. He was surrounded by his own people, colleagues and subordinates who feared him, and for whose opinion he cared nothing. The girl he had chosen was young, fat and sweaty, like the peasant girls of his native village, Predappio, at the beginning of the century. He wasn't, of course, a great dancer, and no doubt would have felt easier if the band had been playing the mazurkas and waltzes he had known as a young socialist, the music of rustic outdoor dances. But he made up for his inexperience by using his exaggerated gestures, swaying his body, inventing little turns on the spot, and stamping his feet to the tune's mechanical rhythm. Getting heated, he stopped almost at once (to applause and laughter), and invited the rest to copy him. Then all the others seized hold of unknown local girls and flung themselves into the dance as if the fate of the nation depended on it.

Another time, too, I was not the least bit embarrassed; on the contrary, I was impressed. We were in the Bolzano area for some big maneuvers. It was an awkward moment: war with Ethiopia was imminent, and peace, people said, was in danger. All the leading powers of the world had sent special military missions to take a close look at the preparations and the morale of the Italian troops. Russia had actually sent a national hero, Marshal Budyennyi. The United States had sent a Colonel called Grey Cotton Pillow, a name as soothing, soporific and peaceable as the current politics of his country. England, Germany and France had sent generals, colonels, and majors, specialists in the various branches of military science. Also there, I forget why, was the Maharajah of Kapurtala, in a tight double-breasted suit and a small black bowler, looking like an old-fashioned plainclothes police *commissario*.

One morning, at dawn, Mussolini set off to watch the result of the fake battles. He was in his red sports car, and behind him came the guests, an endless train of cars, all the ministers and under-secretaries in uniform, the whole of the Italian General Staff, all the world's officers in their splendid field uniforms and the Maharajah of Kapurtala. Here and there they stopped to question a commander about the way the maneuvers in his part were going. Mussolini, surrounded by soldiers, hands on hips, listened frowningly to the few words the scarlet-faced officer managed to stammer out, and then left, almost at once. After several hours of this wandering, on a straight road, he suddenly stopped the car. He got out, while the others stared at him to see what he was up to. He went over to a low wall, turned his back on everyone, and unbuttoned his trousers. There wasn't the slightest doubt what he was doing.

There was general uncertainty. Men trained to take instant, difficult decisions were bewildered, puzzled, uncertain, looking at one another with an embarrassed, questioning air. Many of them looked away at the distant view, the top of the Alps. At last, it was the English who rose to the occasion. A tall general got out of his car, went with his long strides over to Mussolini, and stood beside him against the wall, in the same position. The other members of his mission followed suit. Then the French plucked up courage and, after them, all the rest. Everyone ran to the wall. Only Budyennyi never stirred. He watched the scene, frowning, trying to decide if his rank entitled him to copy Mussolini or not. Perhaps he thought it would have been improper; perhaps only the Soviet Union has managed to retain last century's lower-middle-class prejudices.

## 9

# THE ITALIAN MISTRESS

EUROPEAN CHILDREN took for granted, years ago, that there were two kinds of women: women like one's mother, aunts, grandmothers, sisters, cousins, family friends; and the others. The others were habitually called "them"; "one of them," *une d'elles, una di quelle* were the common euphemisms. When one absent-minded grown-up started talking about "them" in front of children, the other grown-ups winked, coughed, and pointed with their chins to the little tots. The topic changed abruptly. Young ladies were asked to leave the room when "they" were mentioned.

There was, children knew, something mysterious about them which nobody, not even chauffeurs and waiters, who were generally reliable sources of illicit information, would reveal. One studies "them" whenever one could. One saw them at a distance (or imagined one saw them) in the city, during the winter, but one could really observe them at close quarters and at leisure only in summer hotels, the huge and stuffy *palazzi* in the Alps, by the foaming sea or a flat green lake, where guests changed every night but Sunday and the music played Schumann among the potted palms after dinner.

These particular women were more beautiful, wore better clothes and bigger jewels than mother and mother's friends, walked more elegantly, turned their chins up and closed their eyes when they laughed. When they were alone, they sometimes had a bored or melancholy expression, like actresses after the show. They were often fond of children (they never had any of their own) and sighed deeply when caressing a little curly head.

Father was the only one of the family who sometimes talked

to them. Waiting for his wife to appear in the morning at the
beach or, in the evening, dressed for dinner in the lobby he
would fill a few empty minutes exchanging polite pleasantries.
When mother appeared, he would stop the conversation cold,
without a concluding nod. Mother looked calmly through the
woman as if she were a ghost, as transparent as the air itself.

I must have been eight or nine when grandmother took me
and my little brother and sister to visit "one of them." Grandmother was a widow who lived alone, travelled frequently, and
despised stuffy prejudices. I was old enough at the time to know
what the woman was, but pretended I knew nothing. She was
the mistress of a famous Milan jeweler, a small and dapper man
with impeccable shirts, whom I had seen around town.

It was the Christmas season. The woman lived on a quiet side
street by the Park, in a tiny flat. It was very romantically
furnished with bric-a-brac, Oriental incense-burners, brocades
strewn everywhere, exotic plants and old church paraphernalia.
In this dimly-lit and perfumed ambiance she had set up a little
Christmas tree and an elaborate *presepio* just for us. There were
gay packages, ice cream, pastry and chocolates enough for a
whole school, all waiting for us.

She embraced all three of us hysterically, laughed loudly for
no reason at all, continually thanked my grandmother, and
tirelessly wound up the Victrola to fill the shy silence with music.
She was on the verge of tears when she watched us unwrap our
gifts. They were splendid gifts: military uniforms, trains, dolls,
construction sets. Nobody had ever given us such expensive
things before. She wept when we left.

\*          \*          \*

THESE WOMEN were a recognized institution in Italy, years ago,
as well as in most Catholic countries on the Continent. They
were recognized but carefully fenced in by rigorous etiquette.
When dining out with one of them, for instance, a man did not
salute ladies he knew entering the restaurant. This was embarassing, because she knew the man, knew the ladies, knew why

he did not get up and bow, and knew why the ladies went by his table with raised chins and eyes forward.

It was embarrassing and cruel. But she usually took the little incident as a matter of course. Perhaps she talked a little more animatedly than necessary for a moment or laughed too loudly at some banal remark. Often enough she lowered her eyes and went on eating as if she had noticed nothing. It was part of her life.

If the existence of these women was not officially recognized, they constituted nevertheless the predominant subject of ladies' gossip. Ladies were mesmerized by them and secretly envied their adventurous freedom. They knew their names and nick-names, curious habits, expensive tastes, caprices, loves, and recorded their fortunes and misfortunes. Some of "them" were indeed as famous (or as much talked about, anyway) as glamo-rous actresses or sopranos.

Take Marina, who lived in Florence, and was surely one of the three or four most beautiful women in Italy. She was the mistress of the very smart son of a great financier. The young man fell from a horse, while riding in the Cascine, and was in a clinic with broken bones set in plaster when his father went bankrupt. Marina sold her jewelry to pay doctors and hospital bills and only left the young man when he was back on his feet. Or take Elena . . .

There were, in Italy, years ago, hundreds of these stories, with endless romantic or dramatic developments, like real-life soap-operas, cliff-hangers or serial novelettes. The ladies were particularly worried by marginal cases. This point fascinated them all, for obvious reasons: at what precise moment did a lady (a certified, patented lady) cease to be a lady? When was society forced to stop receiving her? The dividing line was only deceptively clear-cut. The common rule was that a lady could have any number of lovers, one after the other or all at the same time, and keep her rank; but she would lose it automatically the moment she accepted the first precious gift.

What exactly was a precious gift? The obvious answer was anything which could be easily turned into cash: jewelry, a villa, thoroughbred horses, a painting by a famous master. But could a lady not accept any of these things if she won a bet? Could a rich lady not accept a jewel which might appear precious in the eyes of her maid but not in her own? Everybody agreed that she could, of course, accept a book. But suppose the book was a very rare incunabula and the lady ill-informed enough not to know its exact market value: what, then, was the verdict?

There was, at the turn of the century, in Venice, a *contessa* who was one of the sweetest and most beautiful women in Europe. She was nobly married, lived in a sumptuous *palazzo* on the Canal Grande, was courted by every gentleman who knew her, including some of the most celebrated men in Europe. Kaiser Wilhelm II anchored his white and gold yacht *Hohenzollern* in front of the Doge's Palace, in his way to Corfu, to pay her visits, and had her portrait reproduced on one of the German postage stamps. King Alfonso of Spain would sneak incognito into Venice to spend a few hours with her. D'Annunzio described her beauty in immortal lines. Other admirers were less well known but wealthier. All this made her the crowned queen of Venice, *la dogaressa.*

She had, however, a questionable habit. She accepted precious gifts, diamonds, emeralds, rubies, pearls, surely not for their value alone, but for the girlish pleasure and sense of power they gave her. This taste of hers was endlessly debated by ladies everywhere in Italy and the great capitals of Europe. Did it disqualify her? It could surely not be ignored. On her birthday, she would give a party in her *palazzo* and proudly exhibit the gifts she had just received on a big table, as brides do before their wedding day. Venice society murmured it was not only the height of bad taste and ostentation, but also an insolent challenge to conventions and to all the self-respecting people who upheld them. Nobody, however, did anything about it. Nobody stopped inviting her. She was too beautiful and well connected (if that is the exact term).

One young aristocratic naval officer, many years ago, decided he would teach her a lesson. He told his friends he would send her flowers for her birthday, bouquets of exotic and rare flowers, as expensive as a diamond tiara or a Fabergé egg, and nothing else. The message would be clear. He wanted her to know that he considered her "a lady," in spite of everything, one who could notoriously accept only flowers, that all other admirers of hers were cads and boors, and that she should guard her reputation more jealously.

When he appeared at the party, she rushed to meet him, passed her arm under his, and dragged him in front of the big table loaded with trinkets. "You must have been mad," she cried loudly enough for all to hear, "to send me such a wonderful gift. I love orchids. I had never seen these before. They are the most beautiful in the world . . ." His orchids were in the very center of the table, the most prominent of all the gifts, stuck in a priceless ancient vermeil vase, her own, possibly more expensive than all the other jewelry and *objets d'art*. Everybody thought he had sent the vase too.

*       *       *

THESE CHARMING WOMEN still exist, of course. They have been with us since the dawn of history (some pictures in prehistoric caves remind anthropologists of them) and will presumably be with us forever, down through the science-fiction centuries ahead of us. To be sure they adapt themselves to the new times, but often do so only superficially. Some have not changed at all. They still, today, delightfully preserve old-fashioned habits, as carefully as old *contesse* in the provinces.

I know one in Milan who lives alone with a lap-dog and a maid in a tiny flat, tastefully furnished with authentic Louis XV pieces. She plays the piano and covers acres of cloth with petit-point embroidery; receives her mature gentleman friend discreetly and her occasional younger friends even more so; frequents little known but exquisite restaurants with him; and takes one or two trips abroad with him, but only to the biggest cities, where the chances of meeting acquaintances are small.

Such women are becoming rare. The majority are now decidedly modern. They live exciting lives, ski, play golf in the best clubs, drive their own Lamborghini, have open love affairs, throw big parties, cultivate delicate friendships within the jet set, are received everywhere, and can be distinguished from the certified ladies leading the same kind of life only by a diminishing number of qualified experts. The confusion is partly created by the fact that some of these women are now actually married to their gentlemen friends. They even get an international divorce—one of those *ersatz* divorces ingenious Italian lawyers can provide for the rich—before leaving one protector and passing on to the next, often a laborious procedure. Furthermore, many do not even know (or confess to themselves) to what category of women they actually belong.

The reasons why they persisted on the Continent down the centuries and will go on to the end of days is that they are delightful, convenient, and irreplaceable. They represent the perfect and only solution in a number of complicated situations, some of which are perennial.

There are young men, to begin with, who, for one reason or another, cannot marry. A playboy waiting for an heiress to save his family's fortunes is a common example. Or a Knight of Malta. A Knight of Malta is an aristocrat, who must prove his sixty-four immediate ancestors were aristocrats, and who must marry a young lady with a similar pedigree in order not to disqualify his progeny for three generations. Waiting for the perfect match, he might fall in love and entertain a tender friendship with a charming and chic bourgeois woman who lives alone.

Moreover, if he is one of the Knights *"professi"*, technically a monk, he has taken vows of celibacy (but not chastity) which prevent him from ever considering a marriage. If he married he would not only lose his rank but would have to give up the possibility of administering one of the fabulous estates with castle and revenues the Order owns. (There were many fabulous ones before the war, in Czechoslovakia, Hungary and Poland. There are only a few left in the "free world".) A *faux ménage* with a chic, pleasant, and well-mannered woman is, of course, also the answer to his problem.

A very common case is that of the hard-working businessman who discovers he is on the verge of middle age and that his wife is fat, slovenly, and cannot abandon the provincial habits of their struggling youth, when she cooked his *minestrone* and ironed his shirts. Years before he changed his tailor, shirt-maker, boot-maker, joined a few good clubs, bought a jet plane and a yacht, and learned the easy and confident manners of the successful man. He finds it indispensable to acquire an expensive mistress, a glamorous beauty who can brighten up his life, keep him company on his trips, and act as a sort of *main gauche* hostess. Furthermore, her furs, jewels, clothes, and general expenses are a useful advertisement for his firm's financial stability.

The story is told of a Milanese manufacturer who had a stormy time with his wife when she discovered he ran about with a girl who could almost have been his grand-daughter. A violent scene almost broke out at La Scala, on a gala evening a year or so ago, when the wife saw her rival in a box, splendidly dressed in ermines and covered with diamonds. The husband pleaded: "Don't be stuffy, darling. Everybody in my position has a mistress. Even my partner. Do you want to see his girl? She is sitting two boxes beyond mine . . ." The wife pointed her mother-of-pearl binoculars at this other woman and looked at her for one long minute. Then she turned to her husband: "What a choice! Vulgar, dressed in bad taste, loaded with cheap jewelry, and not pretty at all . . ." And she added with pride: "*Ours* is so much better."

The contrary cases are less numerous but should be recorded. A rich man equally on the verge of middle age finds himself tired and lonely, bored by money and responsibilities. His wife is still drunk with the power of new wealth. She leads a dizzy life, wears day-after-tomorrow clothes, travels frantically all over the world, redecorates the house at the smallest shift of fashion, and throws memorable parties for people she is not sure she knows.

He misses the provincial quiet of his youth, the taste of home-made food , old shabby friends. He discovers a forgotten sweet-heart, secretary, or retired school-mate and manages to reconstruct in her flat the modest middle-class surroundings he longs for. He watches television in slippers and shirt-sleeves, eats the garlicky food his mother used to make, and plays peasant card games (*scopone*, *briscola*) with old cronies, or the concierge and the cook when nobody else is available.

Such *ménages à trois* are seldom broken up by a *crime passionel*. Few wives kill their rivals today. Most of these are peacefully and tactfully accepted by all concerned. A man's servant will give you the telephone number where he is to be found (his mistress's) as easily as they would give you the number of his club. A man I know in Rome takes two cruises in his yacht every summer, one with *la signorina* (as the sailors know her) and one with wife and children. The *signorina* always leaves a friendly note for the wife about the contents of the refrigerator and the supplies which are running short.

When the husband is seriously ill or on the verge of death, it is the correct practice for the most jealous wife to let the other woman discreetly know at what times she can visit him without meeting her. This is what Queen Margherita did as long ago as July 1900, when her husband, Umberto I, was mortally shot in Monza by an Italian anarchist from Paterson, New Jersey. A courtier was graciously dispatched by the Queen to the King's mistress, the Duchess Litta, to tell her she could visit him for the last time. The two women wept in shifts.

It would be hazardous to conclude that such arrangements are invariably more pleasant, peaceful, and restful than legal marriages. To be sure, the precarious position of the second woman is a help to keep her docile and complaisant. Nevertheless, the particular difficulties of a *faux ménage* often embitter the sweetest moments. An infuriated mistress can be more implacable and less easily pacified than a wife.

There are diabolical women who can turn the precariousness of their positions into a source of strength. They are the fascinating and capricious *signorine* who are surrounded by suitors, can change partners at the drop of an emerald tiara, keep all their men on tiptoes (including the protector *en titre*), make them all run foolish errands, and force them to ruin themselves to satisfy extravagant caprices. (Such women are invariably very cold and unsatisfactory in bed.)

There are more invisible and unmentioned undercurrents of tension in irregular households than in regular ones. The fundamental problem is that of the future. In the welfare state no provision is contemplated for aged mistresses; they still have to look out for themselves. Take any one at random. She used to be a winsome manequin (dancer, actress, stenographer, manicurist, usherette, dressmaker, cashier) only a few years ago. She cannot go back to her trade, now a slightly fatter and lazier woman accustomed to the comforts of life. What will she do if the source of her income abandons her?

She clings to him for all she is worth and by the use of all feminine guiles. She may provoke his pity (she has abandoned a career, a husband and child, a fiancé; she has sacrificed to her gentleman friend the best years of her life). She may blackmail him (she has a bad heart, she will commit suicide, she will give herself to a life of shame). She may terrorize him (she will kill him if he leaves her). Can she be thrown away like a squeezed lemon?

In the meantime, she plays her cards so that he will be obliged to marry her in case his wife dies. (If the mistress is very skillful, she will force him to get some sort of divorce.) She might give him a child. She must be careful to have it abroad, possibly in Switzerland, so that it can bear the father's name. The law in Italy makes it extremely difficult for a married man to recognize his natural offspring. If the child is male and her protector has only daughters or no child at all from his wife, the battle is won. The mistress is invincible.

She also prepares for the worst. There are some who save money to buy a *boutique*, exploiting the good taste they cultivated expensively for many years on the other side of the counter. Others prefer real estate. They buy little flats in old Rome, which they furnish and rent to foreigners. Many do what they have always done: they accumulate jewelry. The reason why so many of them prefer thick gold bracelets which they wear from wrist to elbow is that gold can be readily turned into cash. Or precious stones, which they buy as knowingly as Amsterdam brokers.

All this—the discreet questions about the wife's health, the constant reminders of her moral claims, the threats, the request for gifts to celebrate anniversaries or great occasions, the complaints—ends by making many such relations drearier than regular marriages. Then there are her relatives, who are usually poisonous. They need jobs, recommendations, subsidies, expensive operations or interminable cures for incurable diseases, and embarassing interventions to get them out of various spots of trouble.

To part with an old mistress can be one of the most difficult, delicate, and expensive operations in a man's life, often much more troublesome than a church annulment. It is such a formidable task, at times, that many timid men go without a mistress for the fear of not being able to get rid of her when the time should come.

Take the case of Mussolini. His mistress was called Claretta Petacci. She loved him desperately, and she made his life wretched. Her motto was "*Nec tecum, nec sine te vivere possum*" (or "I can live neither with you nor without you.") He had to send her husband (an air force officer) to Japan, as military attaché, to get him out of the way; obliged serious newspapers to publish what her father wrote, who was a doctor with literary ambitions; reluctantly enriched her brother Marcello, who took advantage of his position to make dubious deals with many Ministries; made her sister Myriam a movie star.

Claretta spent her days at Palazzo Venezia, in a little apartment over the dictator's office, waiting for him to visit her between appointments. (People thought his mental powers were seriously weakened by her ardor.) She followed him into his North Italian retreat, when the Allies conquered Southern Italy; and she finally died with him, shielding his body with her own from the machine gun fire of a Communist partisan. He vainly tried at various times to get rid of her. But what could even an all-powerful dictator do in the face of such violent passion, generosity, loyalty, and spirit of sacrifice?

THE REASON WHY, in spite of everything, such women have always been with us is that they have been irreplaceable in a country which has been for so long without a divorce law and where, furthermore, the majority of the people (despite the Parliamentary majority, of which I was one) abhor the very idea of divorce. The family is in Italy, as in pre-Mao China, the fundamental institution, stronger and longer lasting than weak laws and fragile governments. A good mistress very often keeps a leaky legal household afloat. In a way, the future of the country can also be said to be entrusted to the spirit of abnegation and good humor—mental balance, wit, intuition—to the humane understanding of mistresses. What would many of us do without them?

*Part Two*

# PLACES AND HAPPENINGS

# 10

# ON THE ISLE OF CAPRI

THERE are many Capris, of course; superimposed, like the impressions made by different inks in a color reproduction, they form the ultimate and complete picture, which perhaps only the local gods can see. There is, first, the obscure and forgotten everyday home of the Capresi, who are born, live, and die here, as if it were a place of no special distinction, and who buy, sell, or inherit rocky olive groves, houses, or little vineyards, which—for others—are picturesque and poetic details in a divine landscape. Secondly, there is the Capri of the Neapolitans, who cross the bay on the white ferry boats with their children and grandparents to celebrate a feast day; for them it is more or less what Coney Island is for New Yorkers. (Capri, for the rest of the Italians, is a hard-to-reach and somewhat different summer resort, made more interesting by the presence of so many odd foreigners.) Then there is the Capri of travel-folders and all-inclusive tours. Baffled and tired tourists, dressed in nylon, dawdle a few hours between two boats, buy straw hats with the word *"Capri"* embroidered on the brim, mail blue-tinted post cards, and eat pizza. They are herded everywhere in a hurry; see little, as if in a trance; and are not interested in what they see anyway, as they only came to be able to say "I was there too." The Capri of the longer-staying tourists usually disappoints them. Why should it be so famous, they ask themselves; it is nothing like Cannes or Monte Carlo, has no row of palatial hotels on the waterfront, no Casino, no exclusive beach, no Sporting Club with gala *soirées*? Most of them leave with the vague suspicion of having been swindled.

"If you ask me," I heard a disgruntled American business-man say recently, "I'd give it back to the Indians."

Finally, there is the most famous of them all, the Capri of madcap foreigners, odd types, exiles, refugees, and playboys of the Western World, morally displaced persons of all kinds, the Capri, in short, of literature and legend. It is the Capri (in order of no particular significance) of Axel Munthe, Maxim Gorki, Norman Douglas, Krupp von Bohlen, Count Fersen, V. I. Lenin, and Roger Peyrefitte. It is true it no longer flourishes as it did at the beginning of the century, and, to a lesser degree, between the two wars. Fewer people now feel the urge to escape from their own countries and those that do no longer seem as outlandish as they used to be. Still, the fame persists of an island sanctuary where time out from the hard games played in the rest of the world can be enjoyed. Many still think of this Capri, mostly fashioned by their desire and imagination, as a place where they can "find happiness," or, at least, the delight of enjoying an unusual kind of unhappiness, where life is miraculously free from laws, man is not his brother's keeper, all pleasures and pursuits which do not endanger life and property (and a few that do) are considered licit, or acceptable (or inevitable), because *nihil humanum* the Capresi *alienum putant*.

The one-day tourists and other foreign travelers usually dismiss their bizarre countrymen who settle in Capri, or live here long periods of the year, as misfits, failures, pansies, cranks, black sheep, etc. (Note that there are few Italians of their kind among them. The place does not suit them. They prefer Paris, as Modigliani did, or any other distant and alien land.) Such definitions are superficial. They merely describe the visible symptoms of a deeper malady. Who are (or were) these refugees? Why do they leave well-ordered lives at home, sometimes with the frenzy with which peasants flee from the scenes of war and massacre? What is there on the island that provides relief from anguish? "Odd" they undoubtedly are, but also unhappy and baffled. There are a goodly number of suicides among them every year. A few are rich and own (or rent) beautiful villas. Some are decorously well off. The majority are poor, with money

enough not to go undernourished. Some are persons of taste and
sensitivity. Others are as simple as peasants and like to live with
peasants. Have they a characteristic in common? Aren't they
all in love with themselves, persuaded of their personal superiority and on the superiority of their views, hurt by other
people's disapproval, contempt, or persecution? Gorki escaped
from the Okhrana; Norman Douglas the fate of Oscar Wilde;
and Axel Munthe the sober judgment of the world's medical
associations. Unable to demonstrate their divine right to fame,
incapable of exacting admiration by producing authentic
masterpieces, or enacting "great and noble deeds" (or effecting
the humiliation or violent destruction of their enemies), they
flee in search of (more or less) the same thing: a suitable shelter,
a small stage on which to impersonate their favorite characters,
an indulgent like-minded public who will listen and applaud in
order to be listened to and applauded in turn, the kind of public
one finds at the conventions of amateur magicians, a public of
accomplices.

Obviously many places in the world possess (or possessed)
some of the features necessary for this consoling *mise-en-scène*; few
possess many. But only Capri seems to have them all, and, in
addition, a number uniquely its own. At one time or another, in
fact, such people gathered in Peking (before the war); in Ascona
on the Swiss shore of Lake Maggiore; on the Left Bank; in
Geneva in the nineteenth century; in Baron Corvo's Venice and
in Florence; in Taormina, Taxco, and Taos. Inevitably, most
of them drifted, in the end, to Capri; and they still come. Why?

*       *       *

THE FIRST REQUIREMENT is beauty. Not, however, any kind
of beauty; only an unusual and haunting beauty (perceived
only by sensitive souls). Strangely enough, it must be the glaring
beauty which children, wide-eyed tourists, amateur photographers, and collectors of picture postcards recognize at first
glance, the beauty that inspires Technicolor painters and sentimental ladies who are always moved to say, "If I could only
reproduce this sunset, nobody would believe it's real. . . ." In

short, the place must be the obvious paradise of the dilettante aesthete. The second easily-satisfied requirement is relative isolation. The crowd wants to be alone. It must be difficult to reach but not too difficult, and possibly in contact with some great, lively, interesting city. Climate? Not too hot and not too cold, all the year round. This is important not only for the obvious comfort and the economies it affords; it also allows the shedding of Nordic clothes and habits, and the adoption of new, daring, primitive fashions. As those who tried it in Montparnasse in winter well know, it is discomfiting to be a sub-zero bohemian. The fourth requirement is: fame. A refuge must be well-established before one flees to it; one ought to be reasonably certain to find there a suitable number of sympathetic fellow refugees. Surely, it is imprudent to be a lone pioneer in such matters.

One of the decisive and more important requirements is history. This strikes out the great majority of places, for what hermitages in the Western world, Australia, Oceania, or, for that matter, Africa, can boast of an interesting and inspiring past? Even Gauguin's Tahiti paradise and R. L. Stevenson's Samoa—here surely was beauty, good climate, isolation, and paganism—could boast only of a meager and scarcely documented past. The sense of history, of living on a stage echoing events, is necessary; it allows one to feel part of a century-old pageant, and to select, in a long and picturesque series of centuries, the period most soothing to one's restlessness. Once entrenched, one surrounds oneself with the suitable bric-à-brac.

"History", however, has another and more important meaning. The spot selected should have a long record of civilized living, should be a place where (I take the phrase from a travel folder) "time stood still". In other words it must be backward and decadent, not backward and primitive. Travelers must be able to feel themselves immersed in the graceful manners and habits of older days, admire the naïve peasant fiestas, enjoy the band concerts, or the fireworks, the folk-dancing, or the processions in honor of the patron saint. They must discover for themselves the quaint local dishes, the pleasant little wines, the homespun cloth, the wisdom, the local handicrafts, the bizarre superstitions. Such unspoiled places usually also boast of an ancient architectural style of their own, not to be found elsewhere, to which contemporary builders continue to conform (with only slight exaggerations) for purely commercial reasons. This adds to the illusion of being far from the everyday world. Such places are also, of course, inevitably poor, as poor, in fact, as the ancient world was. The native poverty, if it does not reach melodramatic extremities, undoubtedly enhances all pleasures. Foreigners are magically projected, on arrival, into a social and financial prominence unattainable for them at home; they become the object of many forms of respect and homage, for the natives' old-fashioned courtesies have become, in the course of time, distinctly servile. Their wages and hopes are so small that the foreign resident can afford to surround himself, often for the first time in his life, with cooks, gardeners, batmen, and boatmen, all apparently eager to please their master. Skilled craftsmen, masons, cabinetmakers, tailors are ready to satisfy his whims at a low price. He can also enjoy the occasional pleasure of being liberal and generous, protecting unfortunate and derelict persons, an attractive orphan or a handsome widow.

But, perhaps, this above all: foreign residents should never speak and understand the language of the natives—at least no more than what is strictly indispensable to getting along. Everthing, for them, must be veiled in a fog of incomprehensible sounds. The moment when the mutterings of the cook, the intrigues of the wine merchant, the squabble between servants, the confidences of local friends become crystal clear, the moment when the life of the village is no longer a strange and alien spectacle and the people in it become approximately understandable—this is the moment to pack and go. The feeling of having fled to the security of "a different world" is lost. This, fortunately, almost never happens. Such foreigners never permit themselves to learn the local language well enough, as if they instinctively felt the dangers of excessive familiarity. They usually limit their acquaintances to cooks, waiters, *concierges*,

*épiciers, boulangers,* shopkeepers, a few multilingual snobs, and
pimps. Are there, for instance, any other characters peopling
most of the foreign memoirs of expatriate lives in Paris, after the
first war? Did any of them have an idea of what was going on in
France during the time, or what the French artists were up to,
or who they were? Nineteenth-century travelers in Italy
assiduously visited the same mediocre painters and sculptors,
ignoring all the real personalities of the period.

*     *     *

IF THESE, then, are the requirements for an ideal shelter from
harsh realities, it is obvious that Capri has them all. Beauty?
Where else can one find so dramatic an island, surging from the
sea like the double-humped back of a sea monster, as if designed by Gustave Doré himself and ready to be etched for
Dante's *Inferno* or Milton's *Paradise Lost*? Here are sheer sugar
loaf rocks emerging from deep blue waters, the celebrated
Faraglioni. Here are multicolored precipices, where contorted
trees miraculously cling to overhanging walls of stone; idyllic
vineyards and gardens, where barefooted and sunburned
adolescents of both sexes, like fauns and nymphs, live the simple
Arcadian life, happy to serve the *Signore* for but a few pennies.
Here are flowers everywhere, bougainvillea covering southern
walls with bishop-purple tapestries, wild roses among the
Roman ruins, oleanders, pomegranates, and jasmin, all the
evocative flowers for the Nordic traveler. Chalk-white
peculiarly-designed houses are half-hidden in the green foliage,
or assemble in the two main villages around the domes of the
cathedrals. To walk in the quaint little streets, where only a
donkey with his loads can pass, is endlessly pleasurable. All the
twisted roads eventually end up in the Piazza, which has
rightly been compared to a miniature Piazza San Marco: the
two cafés facing each other, the campanile, the ancient houses
hunched round, the Cathedral, and the opening to the sky and
the sea at one side. It is a puppet theater stage-setting. The
public sits at the café tables, which leave only a narrow corridor in the middle through which everybody sooner or later is

forced to pass. New characters appear dramatically from the wings or arrive from the *funicolare* station, with their new bizarre clothes, a dog on the leash or a monkey on the shoulder, and are immediately appraised by all the old residents and classified.

Nor, dear friend, dare you miss the island coastline. You go slowly, possibly on a boat rowed by two sailors. Motors go too fast, make too much noise, smell, and cannot give explanations. The boatmen will show you grottoes of all colors: besides the famous blue one, green, white, pink, and red. (The names are mere exaggerations of the real hues, which are delicate and shaded.) You will see secret coves and tiny beaches ("where lovers can bathe unseen"), rocky little islands, and you will look up precipices hundreds of feet high, like those from which Tiberius pushed his enemies. "He used to watch his victim thrown to the sea after prolonged and exquisite tortures," says Suetonius. "A party of sailors were stationed below, and when the bodies were hurtled down they whacked at them with oars and boat hooks, to make sure they were completely dead." Other views from the island's height are so famous as to be commonplace. The bay of Naples is unsurpassable (or try, if you must, the Bosphorus, Rio de Janeiro, or Hong Kong). It has a final, almost lethal, quality of its own, recognized from ancient times. It is a different landscape at all hours and seasons: mother-of-pearl pink and grey on sultry summery mornings, when the mainland vanishes in the distance; somber and dramatic under the cobalt sky of a summer noon; silver grey, like a Channel view, the livid and purple sea whipped by rain, on stormy days. Or, at night, when Naples across the bay is nothing more than long beads of stars in the black velvet. This celebrated and mutable panorama, this beauty that is everywhere the eye comes to rest has always baffled painters, who were loving, devoted, enthusiastic, vulgar.

The climate is ideal. It is not as hot in summer as Milan, Paris, or London, not half as cold in winter. The same wardrobe can do for all seasons (with the addition of a cardigan and a raincoat when required). The legends that surround the island's remote past are remarkably rich and vague. Did not Ulysses sail by? Was this not the home of the Sirens? While many other places in the world can overshadow it in exact historical background, none can boast of a simpler and more fascinating past, empty of accurate and recorded facts, but rich in innuendo. The people are Phoenicians, Greeks, Byzantines, with a violent mixture of Saracen blood (for Saracens landed periodically and left visible traces in succeeding generations.) The few historians who have occupied themselves with Capri have been inaccurate and unreliable, but were useful to build the kind of atmosphere necessary for spiritual refuge.

Suetonius, of course, is their leader, and you cannot easily get away from him. Some of his sentences are now graven on stone tablets at suitable spots. He described the first of the villa-builders on Capri, Augustus, who, like some few in later centuries, preferred something small and inconspicuous—

modest enough and less remarkable for its statuary and pictures than for its landscape gardening and the rare antiquities on display. . . . For example, at Capri he had collected the huge skeletons of extinct sea and land monsters popularly known as "giant bones" and the weapons of ancient heroes. . . .

Capri's real patron saint, who built himself three, four, or five (some say twelve) villas, good for every weather and season, and enlarged Augustus' simple residence, was Tiberius. He went to live there in his old age.

A few days after he came to Capri [says the historian, to illustrate the Emperor's fastidious but understandable dislike of being annoyed by peddlers], a fisherman suddenly intruded on his solitude by presenting him with an enormous mullet, which he had lugged up the trackless cliffs. Tiberius was so upset that he ordered his guard to rub the fisherman's face with the mullet. The scales skinned it raw and the poor fellow shouted in his agony: "Thank Heaven, I did not bring Caesar that huge crab I also caught." Tiberius sent for the crab and had it used in the same way.

The old Emperor, who was nicknamed "the goat" for his hairiness and lasciviousness, left dangerous precedents.

He made himself a private sporting-house where sexual extravagances were practiced for his secret pleasures. . . . He devised little

nooks of lechery in the woods and glades and had boys and girls
dressed up as Pans and nymphs posted in front of caverns, so that the
island was now openly and generally called "Caprineum", because
of his goatish antics. Some aspects of his criminal obscenity are almost
too vile to discuss, much less believe. Imagine training little boys
whom he called his "minnows," to chase him under water while he
went swimming and nibble him. . . .

Students of such details can pursue the rest in Suetonius. Of
course, the historian has been accused of having been no better
than "a journalist", a "political pamphleteer", a "paid defamer"
of the Emperor's character. Scholars have tried to prove that all
his revelations were gross inventions. The specialists' debate
neatly divides the residents of Capri.

The natives, naturally, want to believe that Tiberius was a
great statesman of impeccable character and Suetonius nothing
but a corrupt and malicious liar. Tiberius is, after all, the most
illustrious of all foreigners who built villas on the island, complete
with swimming-pool and sheltered terraces for sun-bathing,
thus starting a fashion which (after an unfortunate lapse of many
centuries), has given jobs and relative prosperity to the Capresi.
To him goes their reverent gratitude. One of the best hotels
proudly bears his name (the *Tiberio Morgano*). If there were a
Capri Chamber of Commerce it would undoubtedly celebrate
the far-seeing virtues of the Founder and build him a bronze
monument. In the people's thoughts he has become a kindly
and beneficent grandfather figure, of whom it would be improper to speak ill.

The foreign residents, on the other hand, swear to the sober
reliability of Suetonius, gentleman and scholar. They tenaciously
cling to the horrible tales, the memory of the refined and cruel
pastimes, and the goat-like lecheries of the hairy old Emperor, as
examples from a happier era now unfortunately unattainable
even by the richest and most reckless. There is, for them, something rather heart-warming in the knowledge that such things
were done not far from where they live, perhaps even on the
exact spot where majestic ruins now rise among the dwarf pine
trees. The place where "Villa Jovis" rose (the house Augustus

built, which Tiberius enlarged and inhabited until the last few days of his life), is the goal of a pleasant late afternoon walk, a reverent pilgrimage, when the sun is no longer hot, after one's siesta and before an aperitif in the Piazza. The view from there is the same the Emperor and his victims enjoyed, a most romantic spot; the sun goes down into a blood-red sea.

\*       \*       \*

ONCE CAPRI was mostly famous for the quails which landed on it in season, tired by their flight from Africa, which the natives easily captured and sold to the mainland. The local Bishop lived, somewhat precariously, on a percentage of the profits from the hunt. Only once the island became involved in world events when, during the Napoleonic wars, Hudson Lowe (later to be appointed Napoleon's jailer on another island) was its governor in the name of His Majesty Ferdinand IV of Bourbon Sicily, and his ally, the King of England. The place was easily stormed by Murat's Neapolitan army, who routed a few hundred Corsican defenders. It is one of the very rare instances of a Neapolitan victory. In the 1820s, second-rate German painters began rediscovering the island. One of them, in fact, is credited with having re-entered the "Blue Grotto" for the first time in centuries, thus inaugurating the contemporary tourist traffic. The local inhabitants knew all along about the cave; they called it Gradola, but never visited it; they thought it filled with evil spirits. The wonders of its colors had never struck them as interesting or commercially useful. But their lives were to be changed, after centuries of courteous, resigned, civilized, hungry, miserable, and dangerous living. They are adaptable, capable, willing, industrious, skilled craftsmen. They are apparently still content with little money. They are diplomatic modifiers of truth, tactful flatterers, with a sure knowledge of human nature, its frailties, limitations, and its opportunities. Above all they have learned not to be surprised by anything. The famous Marchesa Casati, for instance, after the First World War, used to walk to the Piazza from Anacapri (she lived in "San Michele", Axel Munthe's famous villa, built, probably, on the spot of one of the lesser *dépendances* of Tiberius), covered with leopard skins, obviously naked underneath, with a live leopard on the leash and a peasant following her, holding aloft a large glass jar in which a rare oriental fish slowly swam. The *Capresi* looked at the scene as if it were nothing extraordinary and pitied the poor woman, for she was a foreigner. "Foreigner" means to them anybody not from their part of the world. All "foreigners" are, for them, somehow, slightly demented, literally outlandish, and mere children, when it came to the real matters in life, money, the purchase of land, enlarging and enriching one's family, the choice of suitable saints for help in various exigencies. Foreigners must be humored, helped, kept out of jail, entertained, served in all their whims, and delicately exploited. Even under Fascism, when the new Italian Imperium looked forward to the defeat of despised and decadent foreign democracies, such people were welcomed and protected. Local policemen and carabinieri behaved more like the attendants at an expensive and private insane asylum than like the stern servants of a Spartan totalitarian State. (The island was then under the personal protection of the Dictator's daughter, Edda, the wife of Galeazzo Ciano, the Foreign Minister, who built a villa.)

To all these attractions, one last (and not the least) must be added; the island's "magic powers of rejuvenation." Sickly and tired people are said to become healthy and energetic. Healthy people are supposed to brim over with unspent animal vigor. Middle-aged people watch their skins daily become "smoother" and their eyes are reputed to shine again with mischievousness as their flabby bodies become rounder and fuller. Dyspeptics abandon their diets and harmlessly take to lobsters with spicy sauces, spaghetti with red peppers, pizza at all hours, all washed down with ice-cold white wine. Such is the electric quality of the air; no sleep is necessary; a siesta suffices. Small wonder that residents find the time and energy to give themselves to pursuits scarcely suitable to their ages. Grandfathers and grandmothers are again tortured by the pains of love, burning with ardent passions sometimes for each other, more often for some youthful

local shepherd or wood-nymph. The fact that these adolescent
natives speak a language the foreigners do not understand (the
local dialect cannot be understood even by North Italians) adds
to the mysterious fable-like interlude. Young visitors are more
naturally the victims of the aphrodisiac atmosphere. What for
their elders is a splendid sunset glow, for them is the relentless
blaze of a summer noon. They become untiring and indiscriminate.

All explanations I have been offered for this state of affairs
seem embarrassingly inadequate. Doctors speak of "the sea
breeze," or the long walks necessary on a mountainous island
with only two roads where most communications are assured
by mule paths; or the siestas, the idle hours and the spicy food,
the sharp sparkling waters, etc. Obviously there is something
else—something Tiberius discovered in his old age?—emana-
tions from the nearby Vesuvius, underground radiations, the
enchanted presence of pagan gods? Nobody knows.

\*    \*    \*

EVERYTHING changes, and Capri has changed. Take the
clothes, for instance. Years ago, when linen suits were *de rigueur*
in most resorts and, at night, stiff shirts and dinner jackets,
foreigners on the island invented the comfortable habit of
wearing at all hours and in all seasons the clothes of fictitious
fishermen and peasants, blue cotton trousers sometimes turned
up as if to push a boat into the water at any moment, wooden
clogs or espadrilles, and cheap cotton jerseys. The women
adopted violently-colored dresses made of inexpensive cloth, or
even trousers, the narrow trousers of boys. The natives, to be sure,
wanted none of this. They dressed in the authentic clothes of the
poor in Southern Italy, shabby but dignified. Half of them
always wore black, the South's eternal mourning. None of them
wore vivacious colors and picturesque inventions. The Capri
bourgeois invariably wore city clothes, a felt hat, a stiff collar, a
necktie, and a dark business suit. It was then easy to distinguish
the Capresi from the foreigners at first sight. But now the natives
have been infected. Since the war they have taken to "the Capri

fashion," which they now, season after season, invent, encourage, and dispose of profitably in chic boutiques. Your boatman is no longer dressed like a boatman, but like "the Capri idea" of what a primitive and simple boatman should wear.

Consider the style of houses. Clearly, the original architecture was influenced by the Saracens. (Or nomad Arabs had been influenced by the Byzantines, who also ruled over Capri and Naples until the beginning of the Middle Ages.) The chalk-white walls, the uncertain shapes of masonry (erected without the help of lead line and rule), the stucco carelessly smoothed by the palm of the hand (as in the Near East), and the terraces built in such a way as to gather rainwater and funnel it into cisterns, all gave Capri houses a distinct character. Then the foreigners came and stabilized the design into a set pattern. (Something like this happened in Southern California, when the Anglo-Saxons imitated the local Spanish and Mission style left over by the Mexicans, and developed it so that it could ultimately be copied by Mexican business-men for their suburban villas in Mexico City.) The Capresi until one or two years ago built houses in a caricature of their spontaneous and traditional style. Now, for the first time, they have revolted. They are erecting the kind of resplendent and barbaric structures which are familiar enough in Brazil, Bahrein, Tokyo, Ghana.

More things, however, have changed in Capri than clothes and styles of houses. It has become a place of great fame. More and more people come for a few hours or days. They follow "the paths of Norman Douglas and Axel Munthe"; they dutifully see all the things that must be seen, read the suitable quotations from Suetonius, *South Wind*, *Siren Land*, and *The Story of San Michele*. They diligently buy and wear the outrageous clothes. They sit in the Piazza. They feel their simpler appetites stirred by well-being. But they are not refugees from anything. They are not seeking a new kind of life, nor are they athirst for new sensations. (In fact, they prefer the things and kind of places to which they are accustomed.) They crowd Gracie Fields' *Canzone del Mare*, which is an orthodox and luxurious bathing place, with swimming-pool, shops, bar, and restaurant. The cook there is a

North Italian who worked in grand hotels abroad; waiters in white scribble orders on little pads with carbon paper; the food is tasteless. All of it could be in Cannes or Palm Beach. It does not resemble Capri, where one swam from rocks, ate in disorganized little trattorie, on the shore, under makeshift awnings, splendid food served by the owner. For some nine or ten months of the year, I suppose, the old Capri still exists. The old-fashioned Capresi and the expatriates are still there. The odd characters keep on coming, even if inconspicuously. But they no longer hold the center of the stage. Few of them are distinguished or notorious. If you know who they are, you will, I suspect, recognize them. Above all, the memory of their predecessors persists, in the legend of Capri and its landmarks and showplaces; the red house where Lenin lived as a guest of Gorki (who kept a revolutionary school for Russian political exiles); the incredible villa of Axel Munthe, "San Michele," now the property of the Swedish Government, where tourists can admire the d'Annunzian bric-à-brac, the phony antiquities, and the cheap copies of museum masterpieces; the ruins of the aesthete Fersen's villa in its dishevelled park, now the property of an absentee Mexican. The memory persists in the names of a handful of residents, descendants of painters, poets, or drunks, and the look of some children, strangely blonde and Nordic, sons or grandsons of foreigners who married local peasant girls. The tradition persists in the very presence of the summer tourists, for they come to the island without quite knowing why.

*     *     *

OF COURSE, Capri is "no longer the same". I was reassured this splendid summer that the landscape, the memory of Tiberius, and the climate have not changed much, "but our people have."

"What a tactful love of money we once had! A young Capresi would endear himself to some wealthy and crotchety foreigner hoping to be included in his will after many years of service. He decently waited for his death before taking away his silver, linen, furniture, paintings, statues, and the contents of cellar and larder, to be sold in Naples. It all has now become blatantly commercialized. We advertise. We organize prepaid (or post-paid) tours from anywhere. We have become a branch office of the air and shipping lines. We want our tourists and we are getting them. We obviously want the island to become one of the most popular resorts of the world. We want everything turned into a *Canzone del Mare*. We are betraying the gods of the place for the hope of gross wealth. . . ."

All this is true (especially during "the season"). But it is not all. The world has changed more than Capri. A paradise pre- supposes a hell; an oasis, a desert. If a place is to remain a refuge, there must be other places to flee from. If persons are to enjoy a new freedom and abandon all hopes of respectability for it, they must be in fear of harsh and inhuman laws, obedience to which is the necessary price for respectability; if they seek indulgence, they must be tired of severity. In the world of today stiff collars are no longer always *de rigueur*. Men can dress informally and lead apparently disreputable lives with no calculable danger or visible punishment, almost everywhere. Vices which could once only be satisfactorily enjoyed in Capri (in a secret atmosphere of complicity, and even here with a slight, unlikely, melo- dramatic fear of jail or expulsion) are now flaunted in many other places. Where in the Western World are the severe fathers or the stern judges or the iron-fisted organizations or the oppres- sive societies? Who any longer disapproves of poets, or bohe- mians who merely want to "live like poets"? Imitations of those Capri trousers for women, once a symbol of emancipation from so many prejudices, are now mass-produced for sale in depart- ment stores. Capri is no longer an island; it has quite rejoined the mainland.

# DEATH OF A BANDIT

————

IT WAS in the autumn of 1933 that I saw a bandit killed. His name was Fraticheddu. In Sardinian this means "little monk," and is a nickname given to children who have to wear monk's habits, to keep a vow made by their mothers to some saint who cured them of some deadly disease. I was going round Sardinia for the *Corriere della Sera*, and journalism was a tricky business in those days. Pretty well every vital and important subject had been banned by the régime at some time or other, for one reason or another, and editors were wary of anything new or out of the way, even subjects that had not been forbidden but had not yet been officially pronounced upon. The papers were filled with endless and beautifully written descriptions of sunsets over the sea and dawns among the sand dunes, endless gloomy scenes of storm or rain (though even descriptions of the weather were not entirely safe, since it was forbidden to mention—say—snow in Naples, if there was any, for fear of harming tourism).

I had left with precise orders: to describe Sardinia without ever touching on three things—poverty, malaria, and banditry, which the régime claimed to have put down long ago. So that when the captain of the *carabinieri* quietly told me to follow him if I wanted to be in at the death of Sardinia's most famous bandit, I felt annoyed, in a way, at the thought of leaving my lunch half-eaten for something I couldn't write about in the paper, anyway. I was lunching, as I did every day, in a small restaurant in Nuoro, near the post office, where I had become friendly with all the local bachelors, officers and clerks and civil servants and the vet; and it was here that the news was brought

by the panting *carabiniere*. His chief listened thoughtfully while
the man murmured away, then wiped his mouth without a word,
and, taking his cap and belt down from the wall, gestured to me
to follow him into the street.

We drove off at once. It was two o'clock on a bright afternoon at the end of September. The bandit, I learned, had sheltered with one of his men at a farm not far from town. The car
took us only part of the way, to a point where horses, already
saddled, were waiting for us. In Sardinia the *carabinieri* used to
wear huge hooded overcoats, with the hoods flung back, like
those of the shepherds; black, and lined with bright red, which
showed whenever the wind blew their long skirts. We mounted
and began cantering silently through the low, twisted olive trees.
The light was clear and transparent, as it is in the mountains,
and we were on a high, undulating plain that sloped down to a
point where the land opened up, like legs flung apart at the
groin, and swooped downwards among untidy clumps of rock
and wild olive bushes. We dismounted and left the horses with
two men who were already holding the mounts of those who
had turned up before us.

It was then that we heard the first shots: first a few, then
more, and finally, after a pause or two, almost continuous firing
like hail on a tin roof. Behind the rocks and wild olive trees and
in the folds of the ground, everywhere, the *carabinieri* were
hiding, gun to cheek. We crept up to the edge of the slope and
got them to tell us where Fraticheddu was. But there was nothing to be seen. Two dark rocks, half hidden by wild olive
branches, hid the entrance to a cave on the opposite side of the
dip. There was the bandit, with his man, observing us and firing
at us. He had opened fire first (they told me) as soon as he
realized he was surrounded, but he had realized it too late.
There was no escape. They could kill him from any side, the
moment he appeared. Men were even crawling on the heights
above him, on the flat rocks that formed the roof of the cave.

*          *          *

FRATICHEDDU had been taken by surprise, because he had

made an inexplicable blunder. He had arrived there a couple of hours earlier, tired after traveling all night, and had stayed in the cave, as he had done before, on the land of a peasant he knew. The peasant hated him for having stolen one of his cows, but was terrified of him. When he arrived the bandid asked for water, bread, wine, firewood and straw, as usual, and for something else as well, something surprisingly useless, frivolous, modern and "continental." It was this request that was to cost him his life. He had never tasted *Pastiglie del Re Sole,* cough drops that had been advertised a great deal in the papers just then, and wanted to: perhaps he really had a cough. He told the peasant to send his son straight off to Nuoro to buy him a tin. It is a rule that nobody leaves a house where a bandit is hiding, and, to be doubly sure, no one who enters it leaves again. This time, no one knew why, Fraticheddu felt safe, safe to the point that he allowed himself something quite reckless. The son, a boy of 13 or 14, who was now lying flat behind a rock with the rest of us, came back with the cough drops and the police.

We did not see Fraticheddu die. All we saw was a man standing up on the roof of the cave, almost on the front edge of it, against the sky, waving his gun. Gradually the firing stopped. Then there was silence. The man, one of the Sardinian plain-clothes *carabinieri* who carried double-barrelled hunting guns and were dressed for a day's sport, had managed to crawl to the edge of the rock on all fours and from a couple of yards' distance had fired straight into the heads and bodies of the bandit and his man.

\*　　\*　　\*

WHEN WE ARRIVED on the scene, he was already stripping the bodies. The two men had fallen face downwards on the ground, their guns dropped in front of them, surrounded by cartridge cases. They wore the brown velveteen clothes that peasants wear for shooting, and heavy boots of the kind worn by infantry soldiers and countrymen. From everywhere on the surrounding hills men and women in Sardinian dress came running up, old and young shouting curses from afar and recalling stolen cattle, murdered sons, ruined houses; wild-eyed and shaking their fists, and yelling in an incomprehensible dialect. They two had been hiding there, waiting for the firing to stop. The *carabinieri* officers and I and a number of soldiers were looking in at the mouth of the cave to see the bodies; and in all the uproar, all the cursing and shouting, the plainclothes policeman, the killer, was calmly and coldly turning the corpses over like wax mannequins to go through their pockets. He wore a faded mauve corduroy jacket that had been washed many times and had three round holes, as big as cherry stones, in the back. They told me he had a score to settle with Fraticheddu and had refused to let up until he killed him.

Years earlier, he and another man, with their superiors' agreement, had taken to the bush and passed themselves off as "deserters". It was an old trick. Fraticheddu had taken them into his gang and seemed to suspect nothing. After a few days he suggested shaving them and cutting their hair, which had grown extremely long. One of the men sat down on a rock, laughing, and Fraticheddu put a napkin round his neck. The first *carabiniere* (the one who was now going through the dead man's pockets) had gone to fetch water, and was coming up a slope with the filled buckets when, far away, he saw the same scene he had left a few minutes before, but with one detail of it changed. His companion was still sitting on the rock, with a napkin round his neck. Fraticheddu, with his bandits around him, was still standing behind the man, holding the razor and laughing. But the fake deserter no longer had a head. It had vanished, cut off by the razor.

In no time the first policeman had dropped the buckets and started to run. The others fired the shots that went through his corduroy jacket, and chased him, but somehow he managed to hide and reach the main road, where he flung himself down exhausted and bleeding on the asphalt and fainted in his own blood. A car picked him up and took him to a hospital; and so he was saved. And now he was giving a sergeant a list of the contents of the bandit's pocket: a hussif of leather, tanned country-fashion and made by himself, with needles and thread in it, a wallet made in the same way with a few banknotes in it, and a *liaro di cabala*, the kind from which peasants deduce the numbers they play in the lottery, bound in the same leather. I thought of the long hours of boredom spent by bandits alone in the woods and mountains, often in the rain, hours they got through by making wallets and hussifs, and binding books. The heelplate of his guns, too, had been patiently covered in pieces of old rubber tyres to prevent it hurting his shoulder when firing, and the soles of his shoes were done in the same house-wifely, careful way. There was also a prayer book, a religious image, a belt of cartridges, and a full tin of *Pastiglie del Re Sole*, with only a single one missing.

*     *     *

WHEN the *carabinieri* went up the slope again, through the twisted olive trees, carrying the two corpses on their shoulders, the peasants in their local dress surrounded the two groups, completely hiding the bodies, and still shouting curses and shaking their fists. The policemen in long overcoats were holding the horses in two groups by their reins, and at the smell of blood and death the animals started shivering, bucking, neighing and tossing their heads. The men had a hard time controlling them. Before mounting mine I stroked its neck and spoke to it to calm it down.

# 12

# A KING'S LAST NIGHT

NE EVENING—it was June 12, 1946, to be exact—
General Graziani, aide-de-camp to the King, rang me
up at home to say he would be coming to dinner "with
a friend." A few days earlier my wife had been knocked down
by a Polish truck. We laid a small table at the end of the bed,
and had to fold the ornate cloth into four. There were four
places: the "friend", Graziani, Bergamini (the old anti-Fascist
editor), and myself; and my wife, sitting up in bed in her ban-
dages. The day had been a tumultuous one, and very hot. The
council of Ministers was in permanent session. For them, the
Republic (which a popular referendum had approved a few
days before) had already been born: De Gasperi was head of
State, Umberto a usurper. For Umberto, too, the Republican
victory was unassailable; all the same, it had not yet been proclaimed with the juridical precision that would make it seem
peaceful and legal even to Monarchists in the years ahead. He
was waiting for a definitive decision from the Court of Appeal.
For days De Gasperi had been coming and going by car from
the Viminale to the Quirinale, growing ever paler, more weary
and worried. I had been standing at the main door of the Quirinale for several hours during the hot afternoon of that very day
with other journalists and a silent group of onlookers, waiting
for something to happen. The English correspondents were
proud of the end of the dynasty, the Americans knew little about
it, the Italians (even Republican Italians) kept quiet. When the
Prime Minister's car came out we all flung ourselves in front of
the radiator and on to the running-board, to stop him and get
him to talk. Someone opened one of the doors a little: "How

did it go, *Eccellenza*? Give us a statement." "Stop badgering me, stop it!" the quiet librarian shouted with unexpected rage. De Gasperi's patient, flaccid, almost doggy face for a moment took on a terrible expression, one so unexpected that it frightened us, the expression of a Japanese warrior's mask. "*Via, via, avanti, avanti!*" he cried angrily to the driver.

Some people in Rome, outside the Quirinale, were still waiting for a decision from the Court, for another referendum, for a miracle. It was very hard for them to get used to the idea. I knew that, if he was to do things in the traditional way, there was only one thing left for the King to do, and that was to retire to the most loyal part of the country, the part that had given him a majority vote, declare that the referendum had been rigged and was therefore illegal, and wait. This meant civil war. I knew, too, that Umberto would never unleash it. Admiral Stone, head of the Allied Control Commission, had told him (but the advice was superfluous): "If the monarchy has to be defended by force, with the forces at our disposal we cannot guarantee the eastern frontier." The admiral had come to make his prudent point some time before, when he as well as others believed a victory for the King was possible. He thought there would be a rising in the Po Valley against the result of the referendum, and begged the King not to move or to do anything, to let things go their own way, because the Allies had more important things to worry about than defending the rights of the House of Savoy. According to Anglo-American sources, Tito was bringing his divisions up to the border. A third World War might very easily break out, and the Allies had no wish to provoke it, straight away, and on Umberto's account. What was more important was the fact that he himself was reluctant to start a war in any event. And it was this human, modern, reasonable, civilized reluctance to shed his subjects' blood for the sake of his crown that showed the monarchy had lost the old brutal vigor, which, in earlier centuries, had driven so many kings into the saddle at the head of their men, banners flying, drums rolling, trumpets sounding. It was the reluctance of this tall, courteous, sickly man in mufti to find more human victims, when hungry molochs were swallowing them up elsewhere—it was his innate inability to do so—that brought him closer to us, that made us regret he would not be king. Umberto was no longer a king who cured scrofula by laying his hand on the sick man's head, or chopped off his subjects' heads either. He was a king who shrank from bloodshed. He was one of us.

\*       \*       \*

SOME TIME BEFORE we had talked together in his office at the Quirinale. In that large, shadowy room, which had been the other Umberto's office as well, the greenish light of the table-lamp lit his face only faintly.[1] He then asked me what I thought of the referendum which was about to take place. He spoke calmly. Those around him professed the most exaggerated optimism, because they were in the habit of doing so, and refused to forecast anything but triumphant success. But the King and Queen faced up to the difficulties. The Queen, he said, was uncertain of the result. The King foresaw a small majority one way or the other, but was unable to decide which way the balance would swing. What did I think?

I said that I did not think a monarchist victory was likely. Why?

I explained. A defeat always costs kings their throne. Pressure from the republican side was fierce. Parties organized by the resistance, some of which were linked to the Allied organizations, underground movements provoked by the necessity to fight the Germans, and dominant public opinion, were decisively against the monarchy. The Allies, in particular the

[1] That evening, he told me he had seen a very long secret report made by Fascist agents when he visited a coast battery near to the little house I was living in during the war. The report was headed "*Talk between Barzini and Umberto*" and it said that the Crown Prince had had the road blocked by loyal officers and had talked to me alone for several hours . . . after which a motor-boat had been seen to leave the shore and make for the open sea. In actual fact he had merely sent me a note of greeting through an officer at the battery; he never saw me; and I owned no motorboat. "And surrounded by these stupid lies and denunciations," said the King, "one was trying to live and work and do one's duty."

British, supported a republic. To defeat Italy and leave the monarchy standing would seem to many of them as if they had not finished the job. Fascist propaganda, in the North, had pre-disposed the masses to the idea of a republic. The propaganda of the Salò republic was much the same as one saw scribbled on the walls just then. The government was republican, had been republican since the liberation of Rome. In a conformist country, unused to politics, the weight of official opinion, of propaganda, the weight of certain organized pressure-groups, would shift the few million votes needed to give the Republicans victory. Then, too, there was the ambiguous attitude of the Church which could not allow itself to be accused, later on, of having backed the losing side, and had not forgotten the role the House of Savoy had played in 1870, when it took Rome from the Popes.

Above all, I told him, what seemed significant to me was the attitude of the monarchy itself. The men the House of Savoy had brought in to rule Italy were no soldiers but mostly middle class men in mufti, in frock-coats and top hats. Theirs was the dynasty of the *Risorgimento*, of soldiers, large landholders, and aristocrats to be sure, but also lay intellectuals, engineers, scientists, industrialists and financiers. And all this conservative world, the old Right and the old Left, was now weary and disheartened Ideas had been dissipated, had lost their sparkle. The young, only vaguely remembering their fathers' old fashioned ideas in founding industries, newspapers and commercial firms, were merely preoccupied with what they could get for themselves. These people, I said, today believed that if they sent the King overseas, they would save something they loved even better—a remnant of power. They wanted a republic like that of President Thiers. Others weakly supported the monarchy only because they hoped that if they saved it the King would save them. "Italy is no longer in the hands of those who brought you to Rome," I said. "It is in the hands of those who had nothing to do with the *Risorgimento* and didn't want to, of people who haven't voted because they haven't had enough money, of women who never voted, of Catholics who didn't want to vote.

It's a different Italy. What do you expect? What do you think?"

The King said:

"It all depends on the results, of course. I might even be the King of this new Italy. A dynasty doesn't necessarily belong to one social class. Kings have always managed to rule by taking the people's part against the nobles, the bosses, the big shots. But if the results aren't definite, one way or the other, then I'm afraid of what will happen to the country. A monarchy with 51 per cent? It's terrifying to think of trying. It means going on the way we are now, wrangling bitterly in a way that humiliates all of us, a way that weakens everything; it means uncertainty, divisions, particularism, collapse. A 51 per cent republic? Some people say it could be easier, because the monarchists would come round to it. Coming round means barely accepting it. Will a weak republic, in time of crisis, get that primordial, instinctive self-sacrifice from its people that a much-loved monarchy manages to evoke, because it's rooted in the past, in people's awareness of their history? The self-sacrifice my family got from all kinds of people in the decisive moments, like during World War I?"

"Your adversaries are ready to fight a monarchical victory that's shaky or weak," I said. "They're ready to cut through the knot, and that's one of the arguments in favor of a republic, one which people who are scared keep repeating. Your Majesty, would you fight for your rights?"

Umberto said no. He shook his head in a puzzled way, surprised at my question, looking as incredulous as if I had asked him if he was going to take up fire-worship or cannibalism, ancient rites from another age. "Italians have suffered enough," he said. "They've shed enough blood. They must have peace."

"Then you've lost," I said. "Not because bloodshed's necessary. And I'm not questioning your courage in fighting. Everyone knows how you confronted death and danger at the front at Cassino. We know the monarchy could gather soldiers around it, brave men who would flock to the banner. I'm not talking of courage but of the will to fight, the wish to fight. On the other side they want to fight. They say so in the newspapers and at their meetings, they spread it around, and everyone knows. They're armed. The country knows this, and it can guess and feel the difference between you."

We were talking quietly, as if it were all about some other country, not ours, some other flag, not the one we had always known, he and I, ever since we were born, and had thought would never change.

"You may be right," he said. "I'll go by the referendum. Italians will always choose the right way. I don't want to buy my crown with money or with blood."

He said these words quietly but very firmly. Perhaps he had repeated them before to others who had tried to advise him how to win.

\*     \*     \*

SO ON THAT DAY, June 12th, we all knew that there was nothing more to be done. I knew, too, that the King would not go to his Royalists and there await his destiny. I knew that Italy was now a Republic, a 53 per cent Republic, born in suspicion, among fiery accusations that the result had been rigged, entirely lacking the clarity and purity that would have silenced even its most unshakeable opponents. For the Monarchists, it was the worst that could have happened: after a victory for the King they must certainly have hoped for a huge, crushing, reliable Republican victory, one that would remove everyone's doubts and stop everyone arguing. Only thus could life start up again.

That night, while the Ministers were in stormy session at the Viminale and Nenni was urging the reluctant De Gasperi to take a strong line, the King came to my home, crammed into a small car and accompanied by General Graziani. Next day the papers said he had spent the night at a hunting lodge at Castel Porziano. No one dreamt that he had gone to an ordinary little house in Rome, as the guest of one of those excited journalists who had spent the afternoon besieging the Quirinale, clutching pencil and notebook.

Umberto was very tired and overwrought. For days he had been receiving crowds of weeping people, unknown people trooping in on pilgrimage from all over Italy, old generals, veteran soldiers, loyal supporters of the House of Savoy, working-class men and women, Ministers, and the constant emotion had worn him out. It was not easy to be the last of his line to reign, and to leave a throne not through any fault of his own (the advantages of the throne he probably failed to appreciate, being born to them, and might notice only later, when he missed them) but because he himself sincerely felt he could be useful to the country in that position in the years ahead, and help to avoid upheavals in it. It was not easy, either, to leave at the most intense, dramatic moment. If he could have tucked himself away in some village and still followed our life, from outside, he would have been happy. Because he too was an Italian. But kings make awkward guests.

He tried, however, not to show these feelings, and he tried to behave in a way that would make us feel calm and comforted. He talked lightly, like a man who had left his worries behind on his desk and refused to let them spoil his dinner. But his sad, tired, patient eyes betrayed him.

What a strange person Umberto is. Years earlier, when I met him for the first time, and I was younger, more informal, and more irreverent, he made a curious impression on me. We were having dinner at a house in Milan. I had never seen him before. I watched him attentively, with a journalist's photographic eye.[2] Umberto was then the elegant officer, the handsome boy people thought a bit empty-headed, with smooth, clean-shaven, bluish cheeks, the prince who continued to be only in the cartoonists' caricatures, right up to the last day. Handsome, rather empty-headed boy? I wondered. The superficial description was not quite right. There was something more, which I failed to grasp. There was a very slight stiffness in his bearing, a way of bowing his head, an unconscious authority with which he spoke to his gentlemen in waiting and accepted people's bows . . . I tried

---

[2] I collected details about well-known people I had seen at close-quarters. I knew that Mussolini had a black hair sprouting from every pore of his nose, that the Duke of Aosta's reddish beard grew right up to his eyes, that Victor Emmanuel's hat was a Lock of London's, and plenty of other useless things.

to understand, tried to find a comparison just for myself, because I never thought I would be able to write it. Like everyone else that evening he was in evening dress, but it was the kind that a soldier would wear-off-duty, one that looked as if he didn't care how it was made and had none of the details that show its owner really understands such things. It was a good smart anonymous suit, the kind you see ready made in shop windows. Stiff, anonymously and correctly dressed, clean-shaved, tall, authoritative . . . I found an irreverent comparison: 'he was like a butler, one of those tall patrician butlers that when you are a child make your legs shake and dry your voice up, the sort that look through you as if you didn't exist. A butler? I tried out the absurd comparison. There was something in it but it wasn't quite right. An aristocrat? Actually he was not like one of the dukes and archdukes and grand-dukes and princes you meet in clubs, men with great names whose skin is folded into a thousand tiny wrinkles, who are old before their time, with weary, ancient blood in their veins and elegant clothes, with disarming, childish smiles, tiresome, feminine whims, and sudden bursts of anger. He didn't look like the dukes I had seen. What, then, was he?

When we came to the end of the meal I realized and felt ashamed. It was quite simple. I had come from America, from a world of back-slapping and hands in pockets and feet on the table. I was a journalist; and journalists, old and young, clever and hopeless, are always informal and judge a man only by the way he writes and by what is said about him. Appearances are often deceptive, good journalists often looking neglected and bad journalists impeccably dressed and behaved. Fascism, all around me, was a coarse, rowdy, childish, rhetorical world. So I knew precious little about points of style.

But when I thought back, at dinner, to the men whose physical presence, unconscious authority of voice and gesture and reserved and dignified bearing impress themselves on others, I realized that in fact these started with the coachmen of an old family, then the butler, and on, up and up, to the colonel of an old and celebrated regiment, then to the ambassador, and finally

even higher, to the King. Umberto was a king. He was a king in
a dynasty that had ruled uninterruptedly for centuries. The
discovery filled me with confusion and shame.[3] Not only that,
but the feeling of awe I experienced in front of him could be
considered one of the fundamental instincts of nature, like the
religious or gregarious instinct; it was one of those instincts
through which society draws its strength to make men live
together and sacrifice themselves for one another, "for the common good". I was facing the man who might one day be my
king, the hereditary chief of the great tribe of Italians.

When I saw him again, after the liberation of Rome, the
elegant officer and handsome young man no longer existed;
only, as I said, in the harsh caricatures of the left-wing press. At
the Quirinale he was *un uomo*. His baldness, the pain you could
see in his dark eyes, his patience, the control he had over his
expression, the seriousness with which he listened to vital problems being discussed, the careful, well-informed questions he
asked, revealed an unexpected maturity, the kind that sometimes comes to a young man who suddenly finds himself, at his
father's death, with a firm and business matters and brothers
and sisters all on his own shoulders. His day was an endless
stream of people; the few free hours he had he spent with the
disabled children in the Quirinale garden, who grabbed at his
clothes when he appeared among them, to make him stop and
play. ("*Sorrida*, smile!" a photographer called to him one day
when he was in the middle of a group of children. "Do you think
it's easy to keep smiling all the time?" he said.) The anxieties
of his position, the suffering caused by his country's ruin, the
daily torment of all those conversations and suggestions (faithful
servants advising behavior that would have been right in another
century, what with the Allies wanting orders of chivalry and
decorations, and the Ministers, teetering between the monarchy,

[3] I belonged the the generation that, starting from the revolutionary and
iconoclastic paradoxes of the years after the first World War was—with
great difficulty and spiritual hardship—discovering the proverbs everyone
knew, and the most elementary, obvious things—that Umberto was a king
belonging to an ancient dynasty, that appearances are deceptive, that when
it rains it's best to have an umbrella.

a Republic and a Regency, the new social planners and the wise
old men) were visibly wearing him out, day after day. Yet his
smile was still frank and reassuring, his manners were still calm,
and those who saw him went away comforted; the thought of his
being at his workplace in the Quirinale gave somehow a sense of
security to many older people.

\*          \*          \*

THAT EVENING of June 12th we did not speak of serious problems. I did not ask for interesting details which would have
turned these pages into a rich historical document, nor did he
give them. But the subject was always the same; however hard
we tried, we could not avoid it. For instance, Umberto spoke of
Portugal. When he was a boy at Racconigi, he said, the gamekeepers went to Portugal once a year to get some specially prized
pheasants and partridges from the Portuguese royal family's
estate. "If you're good," they told him, "we'll send you to
Portugal to see your aunt." He had never been to Portugal and
the unkept promise of his childhood kept coming back to him.
"Maybe I've been too good," he said, "and I'm going to
Portugal . . ." Then he spoke of the Ministers' last visits, some
of those Ministers who a few hours later must vote on the agenda
for the night of June 13th, proclaiming the Republic without
waiting for the Court of Appeal. He imitated the way one or
two of them had behaved. One, a ferocious republican who had
brought him some decrees to sign, flung them down on the desk,
rushed over to a far corner, and started sobbing silently, turning
his back and making signs with his hands that meant no one
was to come near him or speak to him, that he was to be left
alone. All this the King told us with a smile on his tired, sad face,
mimicking these people's gestures a little, but without bitterness.

Only one moment moved us deeply. It was when, recalling
a Sicilian village that had been mentioned, Umberto half-
closed his eyes and named all the villages along the northern
coast of Sicily, one after another, without missing a single one.
And he described some of them, to make us see them again, the
tower, the gate, the citrus-fruit orchards, the fountain. We had a

feeling that he knew all his country, yard by yard like this, from a tireless round of visits. Oh, not like one of us, who turns up unnoticed, eats in a cheap restaurant, and sleeps in a commercial hotel. No. He always saw places decked out and garlanded and gay. To him Italians were always dressed in their best, their faces always newly washed and shining, and the bells always rang for him from every bell-tower. Yet he loved this non-existent country, dressed up and clean as Holland, and he remembered it with half-shut eyes, village by village. He loved it with the tenderness we all feel for this land of ruins and of resourceful, indestructible people, with the tenderness which defeat had increased because it had removed the dreary irritations of fascism, its empty boasts of triumph and its leaders in their dark uniforms. We three, who stayed behind, felt how much the parting meant to him. And we changed the subject.

*       *       *

LATER I WENT to my newspaper office. From a telephone belonging to *Il Tempo* I passed on to Graziani the information that had come through a moment earlier, that the Ministers had decided not to wait for a final decision from the Court and had appointed De Gasperi. (Someone in the editor's office said: "It's a tiny *coup d'état*.") Then I heard no more. The King left the next morning. In the newspaper photographs he was wearing the same suit as he had worn to dinner the previous evening. He had not gone to bed all night. I was told that when they gave him the various choices—to arrest the government, to retire to Naples, or to leave without handing over power—he chose the last.

Umberto was a civilized man. There was nothing else he could be or do. Even his most implacable opponents who had been in contact with him had admitted his detachment. He would not be accused of clinging to the throne. All he hoped was to serve the country, which he certainly would have done if the voting had gone his way, if the crown had not come down to him so heavily encumbered, if he had lived at a time when a king could still serve his country.

# 13

# MILAN, A NATIVE'S RETURN

AT THE BEGINNING of the century Milan was busy, dignified, practical, but still a beautiful city. There were a few ostentatiously modern streets, proudly built to reflect the new industrial prosperity, which reminded one of Wilhelmian Berlin or *avenidas* in Latin American capitals. Most of the city was ancient. Many buildings (including *La Scala*) were in the late eighteenth-century neo-classical style, favored by Maria Theresa, Napoleon and Eugene Beauharnais, and the Archduke Ranier. Wars and revolutions, the Austrians, the French, and then again the Austrians had followed one another without any noticeable change in the official taste in architecture. Here and there were still proud rococo buildings belonging to the aristocracy, famous ancient churches, hidden among the winding little streets that dated from the Renaissance or the Middle Ages, which had the names of guilds. The inner ring of the old city still had its moat, the navigable canal, above which appeared very old gardens that drooped romantic foliage over the green water.

Frantic modernity was represented by the bicycles that whizzed by ringing their bells, by yellow trams and red taxis (it was Mussolini who had them both painted the same almond green), and by high, shiny black cars with curved brass horns, in which expensive-looking ladies sat in their fur coats with bunches of Parma violets pinned to their breasts, or serious gentlemen in stiff collars, with beards and whiskers. There were still plenty of horse-drawn cabs, called broughams, and private carriages too, which were distinguished by the shape of the whip (the cord left the handle, making a calligraphic curve instead of a sharp angle) and by the coachmen's top hats (with a black leather cockade on one side). In the morning ladies went out shopping in their carriages, which stopped outside well-known shops. Up to the First World War there were still a great many carts, far more than powered vehicles, and on summer mornings the gay cracking of carters' whips, as loud as shots, came in through open windows.

The rich industrial world was then beginning to overshadow the old aristocracy. Part of the aristocracy had favored Austria during the wars of independence, was profoundly Catholic, and now perhaps felt more closely bound to the new royal house, the House of Savoy, than to the new Italy. The bemoustached old king, Umberto, who lived in the old vice-regal villa at Monza, had been entertained by the great families at private balls, first with a certain embarrassment, later more enthusiastically; here and there, in some shadowy courtyards, were memorial plaques bearing a wan reminder of one of his visits to some elegant party. The nobles were mostly taken up with land, their own estates. Like the working people, they nearly always spoke in dialect. Theirs was a sharp-sounding dialect, with soft rolling r's, as ceremonious and precise as that of the ordinary people was broad, cheerful, and coarse. Only the nobles and the peasants remembered certain ancient complicated rites connected with their rich farmland, the times and ways in which water flowed in the canals to irrigate the meadows or fill the rice-fields, the raising of fat milch-cows, the obscure rules that governed the ownership of water-courses, drains, irrigation canals (girls' dowries often included, among other things, these cold water canals, as well as a box at *La Scala*).

The most prominent of the nobles, many of whom had no old titles but had made their money out of silk and tax farming in the eighteenth century, or through supplying Napoleon's army, despised the industrialists, though they envied them their new riches and uncomplicated ways. All the same, they sometimes let their daughters marry these *homines novi*, who accepted them even with modest dowries; the girls brought to their new homes aristocratic habits and taught their children the good manners of the old élite. The oldest of the nobles showed their love for the old Austrian Empire and the old ways quite without embarass-ment, indeed almost without noticing, and went to take the waters, for instance, at Bad Gastein or Karlsbad or Marienbad rather than at Montecatini or Salsomaggiore. They went hunt-ing in Hungary, Croatia and Rumania; their shirts and ties and "Virginia" cigars (which Franz Joseph favored), their manners, their way of paying court to ladies, the coffee they drank, their very faces, still had something of a Viennese air about them. Their second language, however, was French, not German, as it was for all the aristocracy of Europe, and they nearly always spoke it well, helped by the Milanese soft "r."

\*     \*     \*

EFFECTIVE POWER lay in the hands of the oldest industrialists, nearly all of them dealing in cotton. These were serious, often gloomy gentlemen. They had money, owned the *Corriere della Sera*, exercised moral and political authority, and had acquired social prestige. Their experience and their machinery were English. They nearly always knew English, the way priests know Latin, the language of their religion; they often went to England, to Lancashire on business and to London for fun, the way foreign priests go to Rome. They dressed in an English style, buying all kinds of imported things at *Bellini's English Goods*, the shop in the Galleria which until quite recently had the gilden arms of the United Kingdom above the door; and had suits made by Prandoni with the materials and patterns he imported every year. Prandoni was a famous tailor who had learned his job in London and had worked there at the end of the century; in his rooms above the entrance to the Teatro Mazoni he had signed portraits of his noble English customers in pink coats, as if to assure all those who came to him that when they left they too would be a little bit English. Luigi Albertini, the editor of *Corriere della Sera*, went to Prandoni for his clothes, and so did the *amministratore* Eugenio Balzan, who asked all the journalists of the newspaper to favor the same tailor.

The interiors of the houses of the *cotonieri* were not furnished in *art nouveau* style, which was thought frivolous and lacking in tradition, but in the more decorous one known as "English style", light woods in straight lines, chintzes and cretonnes from Liberty's in Regent Street. They had faultless butlers who never spoke (the aristocracy's servants were cheerful, familiar, and chatty), and fox-hunting and horse-racing prints on the walls; they drank tea (with a drop of cold milk poured first into the cup); they used beautiful writing-paper with the address in the corner, Bond Street style; and they had bound collections of the *Illustrated London News* and *Punch* in their libraries. Until the 'thirties Beppino de Montel, who was not a cotton but a silk man, an equally prestigious thing to be, owned racing stables (and what could be more English than thoroughbred horses?), was president of the *Clubino*, the young men's club, and had enjoyed the expensive favors of *La Belle Otero*, used to send his shirts to London to be washed and ironed, like the dandies of the Second Empire. It was well known that only the English gave starched shirts the pliable stiffness and dull surface considered indispensable. Most of the cotton-men were *liberali*, the way Albertini was, which meant conservatives warily open to the century's new ideas.

Commerce, the banks, and the new industries were in the hands of little-known, tenacious men, who were beginning to make their way. A few names were already known: the Bocconi brothers, the engineer Pirelli, the Borlettis, the Falcks. Most of these people came from the surrounding countryside or from the lakes, where the very first industries harnessing the waterfalls began. Many of these activities were supported by the big new banks, the *Commerciale* in particular, which was financed by German capital and run by two German Jews, Toeplitz and Goldschmidt. Many of these small industrialists in fact spoke German, not the soft language of the Austrians, which a few of the aristocrats with Viennese relatives still knew, but the harsh technical German of Wilhelm II's Germany, or the guttural German of Switzerland; some of them had studied precision engineering, commerce, and finance in the Rhineland or the Palatinate; or else engineering in Zurich. German technicians and managers were employed in their new firms and in the commercial organizations.

Many of the shops selling hardware and household goods were German, as well as those selling musical instruments. So were some of the chemists. An important pork-butcher, the best known in town, came from Prague. Young men who had studied in Switzerland and Germany, where they had become stiff, aggressive, punctual, and meticulous, all of which made them hard-headed in business; as soon as they could handed their children over to German governesses, of which there were plenty up to 1914. Household gas, however, was in the hands of the French, under the elegant title of the *Union des Gaz Universelle*, and their meter-readers wore caps with flat visors like those of the Wagon-lits conductors or the Third Republic's infantrymen. The culture of intellectuals, writers, journalists, and playwrights was French, and they addressed each other as *"voi"*, like people in the Italian translations of French novels or plays. Two or three cotton brokers who supplied the industry with its raw material, and a couple of dentists, were American (dentistry and Southern cotton being the modest activities in which the United States was then dominant).

\*        \*        \*

AT THE BEGINNING OF THE CENTURY Milan still seemed what it was, an old European city, one of small industrialists, merchants, craftsmen and financiers. Old houses, old streets, old arches and ancient churches; villas surrounded by old gardens reflected in small lakes, and a hundred secret gardens in the middle of the city; the flourishing old hotels that had known Stendhal; *la Scala*; the restaurants gleaming with brass and upholstered in red velvet (one bore the name of an Egyptian pastry-cook who had followed Napoleon from Alexandria to Milan); the kindly honesty of well brought up people; the resourceful, pleasant spirit of the working classes; good food; gleaming well-groomed horses; light carriages, hospitable homes; it all meant that although Milan was a commercial city it was also elegant, rich, cultivated, and civilized. The smoky industries were on the outskirts; the Berlin-like or South American avenues were few. Businessmen hungry for success lived in new houses, in new separate districts, without being much noticed, and social unrest ran secretly, like an underground river, to come up noisily in times of crisis, when workers struck. Respectable people then lowered the *Corriere*, took off their pince-nez and, waving them in the air, said: "What are we coming to? Things are really going from bad to worse. . . . How will it all end?"

\* \* \*

THE OLD MEMBERS of the *Unione*, the oldest club in Milan, did not feel secure. Every now and then distant, muffled sounds of tumult came through their windows, the sound of a trumpet when a Police *Commissario* (in tricolor scarf and bowler hat) broke up a meeting, and the hail-like sound of horses' hooves on the pavement, when the cavalry had been ordered to clear the streets. Noble owners of estates, country houses and large town ones, cotton men and bankers, great merchants and industrialists dealing in electricity, chemicals, iron and steel and machinery all wondered just who was stirring up the people. It was a known fact, that if the working classes were left to themselves, they would be still entirely devoted to the Church and the royal family, still faithful to *Sant'Ambrogio*, the patron saint, still respectful towards the rich, whether old or new, still attached to the best traditions, still hard workers (just as the middle classes and the nobility were, in fact), and always ready to give way to a fine carriage or to someone in authority. The rich wondered why a mere handful of ruffians could make the poor so besotted, could make them forget prudence and the law, and get them out into the streets to defy the cavalry, just as they had defied the cannon of General Gava Beccaris during the riots of 1898.

Who these agitators were was perfectly plain, because they made no effort to hide themselves. They were unsuccessful writers, briefless lawyers, hungry journalists and deputies and small-time politicians who had blown in from heaven knows where, with a day's growth of beard, a floppy black tie, a broad-brimmed hat, and any number of hare-brained ideas in their heads. They called themselves republicans, radicals, democrats, positivists, progressives, socialists, masons, materialists, atheists. They printed little newspapers, published manuals of popular science on Darwinism or translations of revolutionary tracts; they organized co-operatives, mutual aid societies, and trade unions. Some of them lived with Russian nihilist emigrées without marrying them (as Filippo Turati, the head of the Socialist party, did with Anna Kuliscioff, or Mussolini was later to do with Angelica Balabanoff). There were also some discontented priests of the new lay, secular Italy, crazy priests who under Austrian rule would have been suspended *a divinis* by the archbishop, excommunicated without delay and denounced to the civil authorities, but that now, in the confusion of souls after the conquest of Rome, he did not even reproach.

Although they were united in the face of the inexplicable upheavals among the lower orders, the nobles, the cotton-men, and the new industrialists were still suspicious of one another. The nobles were annoyed to find that, gradually, the industrialists had become much richer than they were; the industrialists who had really settled in (the second or third generation industrialists, that is) refused to believe that the shamelessly aggressive middle-class which was scooping up money wherever it could was really going to last. They laughed, for instance, at the Bocconi brothers, who had opened a huge multi-storied shop in Via Santa Radegonda where they sold ready-made clothes, and said they dealt in "ribbons and shoe-laces"; they laughed at the Pirellis, who made "rubber heels". They all kept on with their separate lives, greeting each other coolly in the street, not asking the others to their houses, as if by closing the door, by grading the angle of their bows, or by dropping a name from their guest-list they could divert the course of history. They watched each other curiously, the new rich imitating the customs and manners of the older rich, the middle-class imitating the rich, each slowly trying to penetrate the class above it. Inevitably there were infiltrations. Among the few links were the state schools, which brought the young together: in Milan (as elsewhere in Italy) the private school *all'inglese*, where good families educated their sons to be aware of their own superiority, and through which men at every level found school friends later in life, was never a success. Then there was business, which everyone went in for, without worrying where buyers and sellers and backers came from; and there were marriages, which gradually mingled the old and the new rich, the nobles and the middle classes, so that the faults and virtues of them all were often combined in their descendants. (Had not Giuseppe Visconti di Modrone married the niece of Carlo Erba, founder of the great chemical works?)

*        *        *

SUDDENLY, came the tempest of the World War I. In the months when Italy was neutral many noblemen, many middle-class conservatives, fervent Catholics of the middle and lower middle-class, as well as many of the working classes (more or less the same as those who had taken no part in the "Five Days" revolt of 1848 against Radetsky) favored the Triple Alliance, or at least non-intervention. Some were frightened of any war; some had no trust in the solidity of the new Italy; some had remained faithful, if not to the Emperor himself (who was still the man who, as a youngster, had fought for the defense of Lombardy in 1859) at least to the idea of authoritative, hierarchical governments, because they defended the traditional values, *Dio, Patria, Famiglia, Religione*, and *Proprietà*, without which society would collapse and life have no meaning.

The cotton-men, who were liberal and anglophile, like the most modern section of the aristocracy, were on the side of intervention: they were for the King, the new Italy as a "Mediterranean power," for d'Annunzio, England, and the young Prince of Wales who had rushed to the front wearing khaki like his soldiers. Many of the newest industrialists were also for the War, because it was the only thing that would give Italy its place among the great industrial powers of Europe. The radicals, the lawyers with their floppy black ties, and many intellectuals, were for the *Sorella Latina*, the "sacred principles," and the democracy that was being defended in Flanders. With them were also many fanatical socialists, some of them for muddled reasons; some hoped to see the War turned into a really world-wide conflagration, followed by the universal proletarian revolution. But the most serious and responsible socialists were for neutrality and universal peace. They found themselves on the side of the old Austria-lovers and many Catholics with very different ideals from theirs, just as they had fought with them against the new Kingdom from 1860 onwards, and against the industrialists and liberal values. After May 1915 all argument was silenced. The Milanese fought generously and with good discipline, and the city sacrificed a great deal of money and a great many dead. Its industry made a decisive contribution to the war effort, and many Milanese grew rich at the same time.

\*     \*     \*

THEN CAME fascism, and no one knew what to think. Many wore the black shirt (out of conviction, or conformity, or a sense of discipline), and shouted the same slogans. Nobles, cotton-men, industrialists, radicals, trade unionists, Catholics, social-ists, peasants, the poor—fascism had many forms and seemed the answer to each person's particular worries. In the confusion of those twenty years, between one war and the next, between one speech of the Duce's and the next, between one great battle or another to increase grain production or push up the birth-rate, the old class divisions and old social processes of develop-ment continued, but without any one group bearing the name it should, reading its own newspaper, or being clearly aware of what it wanted or was trying to do. The fascist idea of economic self-sufficiency had encouraged industries which stretched out on the outskirts of the city, but it had also encouraged the passiveness of the people of Milan in the face of Rome's arro-gance. This meant that the city's leaders, who had once been proud of their provincial autonomy, adapted themselves (or pretended to adapt themselves) more and more to the bureau-cracy in Rome and got into the habit of taking the night train to the capital to see ministers and get the problems they had jealously insisted on solving in the past solved by those in authority.

The fact was that the old landowners who produced rice, silk, and milk, in spite of their age-old prestige and glorious names, now hardly counted at all. Their villas and palaces were crumbling, and were sold to commercial firms or turned into flats and let. The new classes no longer tried to imitate the tastes and manners of the nobles. Many industrialists (especially those who had come up most recently, and had no traditions behind them) were fascists, or else adapted themselves all too easily to the times and used fascist protection to do business, make money, and consolidate their power. Under the same uniforms, the differences between the classes became more bitter. This was perhaps the dominant characteristic of the time. The Milanese no longer understood one another. It was unsafe to speak clearly, except to dear friends; the only ideas that were allowed were those of the régime. The old Milan survived, Catholic, provincial, reactionary Milan—certain somehow that fascism would prevent its collapse. The Milan of the 1906 exhibition survived, progressive, industrial and commercial Milan, and the *Duce* seemed to want to protect and strengthen it. Trade unionist and proletarian Milan survived, linked to a section of the party and to some internal movements. But secretly, without any of the others knowing it, each of these groups was nourishing its own resistance to the tyranny, minority groups, each one inspired by its own particular ideals. At the end of the World War II, these all came together, united by their common hatred into a brotherly alliance. But after fascism collapsed, almost nothing held them together. Some wanted the authority of the Church restored; some wanted the constitutional monarchy back; some wanted a democratic lay republic; some the triumph of Marxism and the dictatorship of the proletariat.

What united everyone (as it had united the Milanese for centuries) was the passion for work. Milan is the only city in the world in which "Good work" (*Buon lavoro*) is a greeting repeated every day by everyone. In confused periods of history, when no one knows what is going to happen, the Milanese of every class fling themselves into work, which makes them forget reality, bitterness and fear. "Work", please note; not gain. New industries were set up, old ones enlarged, world sales organizations created and large financial pools formed. For the second time in the history of Italy it was the work of the Milanese that saved the country.[1]

Once again, though, Milan had to defend her way of life in her familiar way. Long before, when the Spaniards set up their first viceroy in the city, the Milanese learned the necessary art of pacifying their distant rulers and earning their good-will and neutrality, an art they refined under Austrian rule. The court in its capital beyond the mountains and the seas must suspect nothing of what the Milanese were doing and must not interfere. Milan sent tributes and ambassadors, put on enthusiastic demonstrations for the viceroys, gave them parties and gala performances and illuminated addresses, and corrupted its governors with flattery or with gold. All this was merely in order to be able to carry on with their own business in what really mattered—work, production, the shrewd administration of public and private funds, the building of factories, the consolidation of families. After the Second World War Milan treated Rome exactly as it had treated fascism, or as it had treated Vienna, Paris, and Madrid.

In the short run, this made for a quiet life, but it was not entirely satisfactory. Milan never learnt to exercise a political power that was in proportion to its economic importance. The Kingdom of Italy wanted money for armaments the country could not afford to use in pointless wars. With money from Lombardy the Republic, often inefficiently, now finances projects that are often futile and sometimes damagingly utopian. Milan is silent, accepts the situation, applauds, and secretly goes on building, producing, and initiating new projects,

[1] The first time was after 1870, when the capital accumulated bit by bit in the eighteenth and nineteenth centuries from corn, rice, silk, milk, taxes and trade financed almost wholly the modernization of Italy, the building of railways, the rebuilding of Rome and the development of the first industries.

asking no one for help or for thanks. Indeed, it hopes that no one in Rome will notice the way some new scheme has flourished, thus avoiding being loaded down with taxes and tangled up in laws of Byzantine complexity.

*        *        *

THIS IS THE CITY I was born in, as I have seen it during my lifetime. I have seen it turned from a rich agricultural town, proud of its local cheeses and of the music in its theater and of its splendid houses and churches, into an industrial metropolis comparable with Düsseldorf or St. Louis. In about fifty years it has covered the ground that England and France took nearly two centuries to cover. It has done wonders. It has also had historical indigestion. Men, families, and social classes have, from decade to decade, had to adapt themselves to new responsibilities and tasks and ways of life. The city has had to assimilate unprecedented waves of immigrants who are profoundly different from its own people. (This is ancient history. The city is made up of the descendants of immigrants, transplanted there over the past two centuries; but until 1914 it was a case of people coming in from the nearby countryside, from the valleys and lakes and the Veneto, a few at a time, people who could easily be transformed into Milanese as they were inspired by the same ideals as the Milanese.)

The sudden, monstrous growth, the increase in population and in wealth, the incredible increase of activity of every kind, have put the very character of the city in peril. The new districts, many of them built where the twisted old streets used to be, are anonymous and characterless, made, someone said, by corporations for corporations, not by men for men as before. The Milanese mistrust of politics means that even in the city positions of authority are given to men from outside, and the actual administration is in the hands of a bureaucracy that mostly comes from other parts of Italy; and that it has not managed to protect some of its own honest, fundamental needs and traditions from "Roman corruption". All the same, there are signs that Milan will survive (I mean the ancient spirit of

Milan); that it might turn outsiders into Milanese and gradually get even Rome to listen to what it says. What changes the spirit of those who live in Milan is work, which no one can avoid. The demands of work well done, at all levels, forces different men to adopt similar ways of life. Cunning, which Italians elsewhere are so fond of, intrigues, administrative muddles and cooking the books snarl things up and hold back production; dishonesty, excessive prudence and lack of confidence do not suit the rhythm of machines, the enormous quantity of exports, and the daily advance of technology. It is work that has made the Milanese what they are and that might eventually turn the immigrants into Milanese.

# 14

# THE QUEST FOR LAMPEDUSA

I LIKE Sicily just as it is. I feel comfortable there, and love everything about it: roast swordfish, the pointless sharpness and precision of argumentation, the pitiless sun, the orange-groves with their green-black leaves shining like painted tin, the motionless sea of golden stubble from horizon to horizon and not a patch of shadow, the baroque towns, the huge tunny-fish, the *cassate*, the puppets, the ancient weary families in their crumbling palaces, the edgy new men who try to look as if they were Milanese (and, so long as they keep their eyes shut, manage to: but their restless, lively eyes betray them), the resigned poor people, the wary ruthless view of life, the truths only Sicilians know, the heavy flavor of the wines, the proverbs, the dignified acceptance of death. I love these things, and many more about Sicily; so much so that I even defend them against the Sicilians themselves, who are quite capable of making accusations against their island and its inhabitants serious enough to en-danger any non-Sicilian Italian who repeated them—because, among other things, they are nearly all true.

I don't know why I love Sicily. Perhaps because of mysterious inner affinities, shown externally by the Sicilian face nature gave me. Or because as a boy I used to go to Palermo twice a year, during the summer, on my way to and from the United States, and it is full of memories of my adolescence. Or else because when I came back to Italy, escaping the frantic insipid life in America, I instinctively went to look for the most Italian part of Italy, almost as if I were a foreigner; for those places that were most unlike the industrial world I knew, least watered down, where the ancient way of life and thought of our people was still kept unaltered. Of course, like any foreigner, I am upset by the poverty of Sicily and wish it could be remedied. Yet, as an Italian, I still hope that Sicilians will manage to solve the problem that practically no one has managed to solve—the problem of how to become prosperous without at the same time becoming mindless and crude, of how to make life better materially without making it flavorless and characterless.

Whatever the reason, I have been to Sicily any number of times, far more often than some of the rich bachelors of Palermo I know have been to Paris. I have been there of course as a journalist, before the war, in the post-war years, and during regional elections, to study its problems—economic, political, or criminal. I have also often been there at my own expense, to do nothing, to wander about seeing things and listening to the terrifying and incredible true stories that all Sicilians seem to know. (One of the reasons for their literary success may be that they are simply telling quite homely tales, about things that have happened to people they know, and everyone else is dumbfounded and thinks them inventions.) For all these reasons I have Sicilian friends, or at least, I delude myself that I have, judging by the faultless hospitality and courtesy of my Sicilian acquaintances, who pity my foreigner's illusions about their country.

Among these friends I should like to have included Giuseppe Tomasi, Duke of Palma and Prince of Lampedusa.[1] The second feudal title, Lampedusa, would have struck me. Noblemen who have islands as fiefs are rare. I must certainly have met him, as I knew many of his relations and friends. People in Palermo say to me: "Well, yes, don't you remember, that evening at the club . . . He was there, tall and fat and pale, with slow gestures . . . He never spoke." Or else: "That afternoon, at So-and-so's. He listened to the talk. Laughed a bit. Never said a word. Looked sleepy. Then he went into the library. I'm almost

[1] Duke of Palma is the small, intimate family title, conferred by the kings of Spain on the Tomasi who founded the little town of Palma in Sicily, named Palma Montechiaro after 1863 to distinguish it from Palma Campania, near Naples, and avoid postal mistakes under the new Kingdom.

sure he was there." A journalist friend of mine said: "He joined the cine-club, the film society, and used to come with his wife—tall, stout, dressed in black. He never said a word, but watched the films and left. A couple of times I think you were there as well."

Very likely I met him in a bookshop, Flaccovio's, which is one of the best in Italy, where he used to go nearly every day to browse among the books and where journalists from outside go to hear news and gossip. We must surely have met there—we could hardly have failed to. But honestly, I don't remember. Giuseppe Tomasi di Lampedusa lived (everyone said) unnoticed; he merged with the background, and hardly spoke, lost in his own thoughts, shy, modest, or else too proud, irritated by other people's superficial chatter. He said of his grandfather (the Prince of Salinas of *The Leopard*), and certainly meant it of himself as well: "His mind [was] conditioned by long periods of solitude and abstract thought . . . The air was turbid with commonplaces. Among these men Don Fabrizio was considered an 'eccentric'; his interest in mathematics was taken almost as sinful perversion . . . They did not say much to him, for his cold blue eyes, glimpsed under the heavy lids, put would-be talkers off, and he often found himself isolated, not, as he thought, from respect, but from fear."

And this is one of the many regrets that *The Leopard*, the book he wrote shortly before his death, has left behind it. We all read it too late to be able to tell him how important it was, this book that made all us Italians understand our life and history to the depths. (Only Sicilians think they are different from the rest of their fellow-countrymen. We in the rest of Italy know that the island is like one of those concave shaving mirrors, in which we see our image pitilessly enlarged, both faults and virtues.) We read it too late to be able to visit him, with the excuse of writing an article, as just occasionally one does after reading a new book; too late to get him to tell us what he hadn't written, and why he wrote what he wrote in that particular way, seeking to continue in conversation the restless pleasure of reading.

If only someone had told me that that stout silent man was

writing a very fine book, perhaps one of the masterpieces of
Italian literature . . . Very likely I should not have believed
it, for I have been made cautious by the many undeserved
reputations, optimistic praises and indulgent forecasts I have
met when traveling in the provinces. But no one knew or could
imagine it. To tell the truth, he did not allow himself to suspect
it. When his uncle, the old senator, Marchese Pietro Tomasi
della Torretta, who had been the King's Ambassador to the
Court of the Tzar at St. Petersburg, asked him what he was
doing, filling exercise books one after another, he replied:
"Enjoying myself . . ." To his wife (who was his uncle the
ambassador's step-daughter) he said the same thing: "*Je fais ça
pour m'amuser* . . ." But she knew that he had had it in mind for
the past twenty-five years to write a book about his grandfather,
in which he described the transition from the old patriarchal
world to an almost modern one.

*        *        *

I WENT TO SEE the Princess of Lampedusa soon after I had read
*The Leopard*. She lives in a small house in Via Butera, the little
street behind the splendid buildings facing on to the sea, on the
great tree-lined avenue. The street looks like those back entran-
ces you approach on foot to the famous palaces on the Grand
Canal: full of peddlers and stray dogs, rubbish heaps, washing
hanging out, half-naked children and mothers calling them, and
craftsmen at work. (I hope the street is named after Prince
Butera, a great Sicilian gentleman who, when he saw Mussolini
in 1923, said: "Too many spats, too many spats!") The fact that
princely families in their grand houses live side by side with the
ordinary people is one of the old traditions of Italy, a symbol of
our people's ancient unity. The idea of shutting rich and poor
up in their respective ghettos of reinforced concrete is a modern
imported one.

    The house in which the widow lives is one of the old Lampe-
dusa residences. The main family seat was the palazzo the
Prince described in *The Leopard*, where the ball took place.

The ballroom was all golden; smooth on cornices, thick on door-frames, and repeated in a pale almost silvery damask-like design on door-panels and on the shutters which covered and annulled the windows, conferring on the room the look of some superb jewel-case shut off from an unworthy world. It was not the flashy gilding which decorators slap on nowadays, but a faded gold, pale as the hair of nordic children, determinedly hiding its value under a muted use of precious materials intended to let beauty be seen and cost forgotten. Here and there on the panels were knots of rococo flowers in a color so faint as to seem just an ephemeral pink reflected from the chandeliers.

Further on the Prince says: "From the ceiling the gods, re-clining on gilded couches, gazed down smiling and inexorable as a summer sky. They thought themselves eternal; but a bomb manufactured in Pittsburgh, Penn., was to prove the contrary in 1943." This was in fact what happened to the palazzo Lampedusa, in the narrow crowded streets of the old part of Palermo, in 1943. It was destroyed by a bomb.

After the war the Prince, like many other people, could have bought himself one of the new apartments financed by the region and built in the new districts, where regional deputies and councillors live to give themselves the feeling that they are living in the Parioli section of Rome. Instead, he bought the little house in Via Butera, which in fact is really half a house because the building was divided into two in the last century and sold to two owners. For a man who was quite unbusiness-like and absorbed in his own thoughts, buying the house was a long and painful affair, which worried and tormented him for years before it was settled. But Tomasi di Lampedusa could not live elsewhere. The house was the one his great-grandfather Giulio, the astronomer, the main character in *The Leopard*, had bought just to have lunch in during the summer. "I have a seaside house, facing the sea," the Prince of Salina says in the novel, "with a terrace on the roof from which you can see the whole ring of hills around the city." And later, when they have to decide where to take the dying Prince from the railway station: "'Then let's go to our place by the sea, that's even nearer.' But that wasn't possible; the house was not in order, as he knew well; it was only used for occasional luncheons by the sea; there wasn't even a bed in it."

The enormous front door opened up on to a narrow courtyard, enclosed by the gray dividing wall built by the new owners, with windows of the old working-class type cut in it. A cold north light, like that of a painter's studio, poured down from the sky. The main staircase opened up on the right. A decrepit portress, her curly white hair parted in the middle, was sitting on a rough wooden kitchen chair; she made me a sign to go up and told me to climb to the top, where I would find a door. She looked as if she was expecting me, as if she had been warned about me and knew who I was. She got up and pulled a bell chain at the foot of the stairs, twice. This was the way things used to be in the old palaces of Palermo. The doors were always open, no one even stopped you. I went up in silence leaving the confused cries of the crowded little street behind me.

What I had gone to find at the widowed Princess's old palace in Palermo were answers to questions she could not give me. I wanted her to explain the miracle of *The Leopard* to me, I wanted her to tell me what her husband had been like, what he thought he was writing while he was writing it, and if he had foreseen, expected, hoped for or feared a great success. These were all answers which probably not even the Prince could have given me. The explanations a writer gives are always notoriously artificial and contrived, often elegant, even if they are almost always sincere. Few of them really know how a work of art is born within them. Moravia says, quite honestly: "I start by following a musical idea, a vague wordless feeling. Then I go ahead and unravel it, working every morning because, basically, I'm bored. What else is there to do?"

In reality, such works germinate in darkness and in secret, like mushrooms, putting roots down into the past; and they write themselves, feeding on childhood memories, landscapes glimpsed and perhaps forgotten, beloved faces, loves lost in the past, distant feelings, the emotions of others, stories told by strangers in trains. All this in the tormented effort to make and unmake, to co-ordinate and refurbish, to keep faith with the still almost imperceptible voice that dictates intermittently, raving, in some hidden cave of one's own being. Works thought out in a straightforward craftsman-like way, engineered like tower clocks, with characters that pop out when the hour strikes, every detail carefully studied, born at the level of conscious intelligence, that is, remain dead, good for nothing but to be made into second-rate films. Sometimes the work in progress suddenly comes to life, and is transformed as it proceeds, with an arrogant strength of its own that is quite outside the writer's own will. At the end the author knows what he has written, and why he wrote it, no better than the rare attentive reader or perceptive critic. As he reads it over he discovers that he had feelings he has forgotten, that he believed firmly in things he has rarely thought about, or else that he was sensitive to detail he believed had scarcely concerned him.

\* \* \*

AT THE TOP of the dark dusty staircase was a door, opened by a stooping, elderly man-servant in an immaculate white jacket newly taken out of a drawer. He led me to a library that opened straight off the hall. The room was dark, as for a séance, the closed shutters cutting out the dazzling light of Palermo and the deafening cries of the little street. On three walls were large plain bookshelves, probably only recently put up, full of tidily arranged books. In the middle of the room was a large sofa, and on it, surrounded by albums and newspaper cuttings on the success of *The Leopold*, sat the Princess, dressed entirely in black. A black cloche hat covered her fair hair and ears, a black veil her eyes, and she wore a black light woollen coat to her ankles, with a mink stole over her shoulders. She remained seated when I appeared and shook hands charmingly. When she rose, later on, I saw that she was very tall, almost taller than I was. Crouched at her feet was a subdued-looking old fox terrier, which did not even come over to sniff at my trousers. I thought of the dog Bendicò in the novel, one of its main characters, which perhaps, years ago, had borrowed from this one, when it was young, not its breed, but its affectionate lively nature and curiosity for garden smells.

Bendicò, incidentally, really existed. He was called Bendicò and was stuffed after his death, as Tomasi di Lampedusa tells, though he never saw him, just as he never saw his great-grandfather, Giulio the astronomer. The man who remembered them both was his uncle, the Marchese ambassador. Born in 1873—head of the cabinet of Foreign Minister San Giuliano, Italian ambassador to the main capital cities, Senator of the Kingdom before the First World War, liberal opponent of the Fascist régime—he died after his nephew and after the book's success. He remembered his grandfather Giulio, who died in an hotel at the end of a long railway journey, as in the novel, but not in Palermo, in Florence, where the family had fled to escape the cholera raging in Sicily. He died of typhus, contracted before he left home. The Marchese della Torretta also remembered the dog Bendicò both alive and stuffed, and the Jesuit domestic chaplain his nephew called Father Pirrone. "He taught me to read and write," the old ambassador once told me. At the end of a brilliant career (so distinguished that the *Enciclopedia Italiana*, even under the Fascist dictatorship, could not avoid mentioning him) Pietro Tomasi della Torretta could hardly have imagined that he would acquire a new claim to fame, in his last years, as uncle of a great Italian writer and witness of some of the events and people described in a famous novel.

On a low table beside the Princess's elbow stood refreshments, two glasses of cold coffee, some biscuits, and a cocktail shaker rather unusually immersed in a bowl of ice and water. There was no doubt that she meant to be nice to me. She is the daughter of a high dignitary at the court of Nicholas II, Baron Wolf-Stomersee, a very learned Baltic baron, who among other things was headmaster of the Imperial High School in St. Petersburg, where aristocratic boys were prepared for responsible positions in the Empire. Her mother, when she was widowed, married the Marchese della Torretta and took her adolescent daughter from capital to capital. This is one reason why the Princess of Lampedusa speaks and writes five or six languages perfectly. Her love of intellectual work, inherited from her father, led her deep into the study of psychoanalysis, about which little was known in Italy until a few years ago. (She was elected president of the Italian Psychoanalytical Society, and vice-president of the international society.) She met the Prince di Lampedusa in London when he was visiting his uncle the ambassador there, after the First World War. This all explains why, although her love for her husband and for the study of literature and science absorbed her whole life, and almost made her forget the existence of a world outside, she still remembered the old-fashioned frivolous graces symbolized in the cocktail-shaker. Perhaps she thought I was a globe-trotting cosmopolitan journalist, a Paul Morand of thirty or forty years ago, longing for the exotic drinks of the time, and had kindly done her best. What was in the shaker I have no idea. I was glad to have some homely coffee, to which the Princess added a spoonful of cream taken from the loose wrapping paper in which it had come from the shop; and we chatted.

\*    \*    \*

THE MAN, first of all. I wanted to know what her husband was like. She told me very little, perhaps because of the modesty of a well bred person who dislikes having details of her private life in the newspapers, and perhaps also because the Prince of Lampedusa's life had not been full of anecdotes and outward excitement. She had met him in London, as I said, after 1919, when he had first come on a visit. During the war he had been an artillery officer (in his book he always spoke very accurately about horses); captured by the Austrians, he was imprisoned in Hungary, from where he managed to escape and to reach the Swiss frontier. There, only a few yards from freedom, he was recaptured at the very last minute and sent back to the prison camp. He escaped a second time, near the end of the war, and managed to cross the front, passing through the disintegrating Austro-Hungarian army. [2]

[2] I remember a showcase, in an aristocratic house in Syracuse which I saw recently, where family decorations were kept which the Prince of Salina

Lampedusa traveled a great deal. He studied in a number of places (including Turin) and read in many languages—Italian, French, German, and English at first, and later Russian, with his wife. All his life he bought books. As a child in Paris, on holiday with his family, he used to rush out to the *bouquinistes* along the river, not far from his hotel, clutching his pocket money, to buy an old volume or two. History interested him more than anything. About some of his favorite periods (Italy in 1860, for instance) he knew practically everything, day by day. Public and private details in *The Leopard*, even the most trivial, are exact. (I have caught him napping only once. The sabers of two Italian officer friends, the *lanciere* Tancredi Falconieri and the *bersagliere* Cavriaghi, from Milan, are described as being "curved". Only the *bersagliere*'s was curved. The other was straight, as all cavalry sabers were, and an artillery officer ought to have known it.) After history, he was most interested in literature. He read and re-read the ancients, the classics, old writers, nineteenth-century writers, and followed the new ones, good or bad. Husband and wife exchanged the books they had read and discussed them endlessly, speaking to each other always in French. He smoked heavily. (Smoking undoubtedly gave him the lung cancer that killed him.) He was shy and avoided meeting new people, always lost in his own thoughts and fantasies, but courteous, "very courteous". In spite of his international education, his Russian wife, and his love of other literatures, he felt he was Sicilian, a Sicilian patrician, and, like all Sicilians, he loved and hated his island, its ordinary people and its patricians like himself, his first second and third cousins and all the Princes of Palermo.

"He had subtle, delicate feelings," the Princess said, "a very

---

would have liked: the Holy Spirit, the Golden Fleece, and the ribbons and badges of St. Gennaro, of the Bourbon Kings of Naples; the Iron Crown of the Austrians in Italy; the cross of Malta; and, of the kingdom of Italy, only some medals for bravery won in the trenches during the First World War. Rewards and honors are not accepted from new usurping rulers. But a gentleman never refuses risks, sacrifices, and duties for the good of his country.

special sensibility." In a few words, which she quickly cut short, she described the emptiness left in her life after so many years by the loss of a man who sensed and defined emotions whose existence practically all other men die without having suspected. He disliked being photographed. There are only a few amateur snapshots of him, taken with a cheap camera by his adopted son, the young Giovacchino Lanza di Mazarino, the present Duke of Palma, who is the prototype of Tancredi. They show Tomasi as tall and fat, with a face vaguely resembling that of T. S. Eliot. There is only a single important photograph of him, a head, taken after the First World War, when pain, deprivation and hunger had made him very slender. His face in it is lined, the lips are thin and suffering, the nose is sharp, and the hair straight and black over a wide forehead. The expression is that of an ironic mystic, with great black eyes in a pale face and a disturbing look.

Then we talked about the writer.

\*     \*     \*

ALL YOU CAN DISCOVER about Giuseppe Tomasi, Duke of Palma and Prince of Lampedusa, all his widow and relations and friends and the youngsters he advised in their reading can tell you does not, of course, explain the miracle. The fact that he had *The Leopard* in mind for twenty-five years and the talent to write it means nothing. Plenty of people carry the seed of ambitious works in the mind for a lifetime, and never write them. Some, bored with provincial life and old age, actually manage to finish a manuscript: learned men, literary men, academics, gentlemen, churchmen, fill exercise books in secret with crabbed illegible prose which they hand down to their heirs. Some of them actually complete the work, polishing, improving, rewriting, revising. Mostly these are pathetic transparent works, full of unused good intentions in which the author's hopes and wishes are all too clearly, too embarrassingly apparent. Provincial learning and provincial taste often hamstring these amateur writers. They are worried about words, which they cannot control, just as unskillful jugglers worry about the balls they are trying to keep in the air. Some still cling to their memories of d'Annunzio and to old-fashioned elegance. Others fling themselves into arbitrary, way-out and almost incomprehensible writing, moved not so much by inspiration as by the fear of appearing out of date. They always lack skill with language, the unconscious and forgotten technique that makes the wall between writer and reader transparent, the art of concealing art, in fact.

The idea of *The Leopard*, some might say, made a masterpiece of it. But the idea of studying the transition from the patriarchal and *seigneurial* life to that of bourgeois society has been used by any number of writers for over a hundred years, and is so tired and trite that it should make even the boldest quail; from Georges Ohnet's *Le Maître de Forges* to *The Cherry Orchard*, to mention well-established prototypes outside Italy; from Fogazzaro's *Piccolo Mondo Antico* to Giacosa's *Come le Foglie* in Italy; and, in Sicily, from Verga's *Mastro don Gesualdo* and *I Malavoglia* to de Roberto's *The Viceroys*. Is it, then, that the point of view was not that of a bourgeois writer, but had the age-old keen-sightedness of a defeated aristocrat? Nobly born writers are not rare. Palermo even boasts a king of Sicily and holy Roman emperor, Frederick II of Hohenstaufen, who wrote poems as well as most of his sons and courtiers. In the rest of Italy the nobles included (to mention the most obvious) the Tuscan Lorenzo Medici, called "The Magnificent", Count Torquato Tasso, Count Algarotti, Count Gozzi, Count Vittorio Alfieri, Marchese Cesare Beccaria, the nobleman Don Alessandro Manzoni, Count Giacomo Leopardi, Marchese Massimo d'Azeglio, and so on, many more until modern times, when there was the late Duke Tomaso Gallarati Scotti, Prince of Molfetta, grandee of Spain, and Count Giudo Piovene. In other countries, too, they are plentiful: Chateaubriand, Lamartine, de Vigny, Byron, and Leo Tolstoy.

I talked about this to the widowed Princess, because a French correspondent in Rome had written in his paper that *The Leopard*'s success was owed to two things—the fact that Sicily was fashionable, and the fact that the author was a prince. Things like this might launch a new sea-side hotel in café society, but not a book among readers in their anonymous thousands. This Frenchman failed to realize that such arguments carry little weight in Italy, that the nobleman outside his traditional field—the army, farming, and diplomacy—has a harder time of it than the bourgeois. No one, in fact, votes for a political candidate who belongs to an aristocratic family, no one now trusts an aristocrat in public life; indeed a great many people have hidden or hide their titles. No one I know of gets a surgeon who is a marchese to operate on him because he is a marchese; no one lightly appoints a duke to conduct a symphony orchestra.

\*     \*     \*

YET THERE WAS something special to say. The subject Tomasi chose was notoriously overworked. He knew it himself, but was not afraid of that because he was the last person who tried to deal with it. (Of *The Viceroys* he said to his wife: "It wasn't like that. That isn't Sicily.") He meant, after a century of polemics that have always been unanswered to say what no one knew because no one had expressed it. The other aristocratic writers I mentioned were first of all writers. Whereas he was something else; he described, as an authoritative witness, the transition from one world to another, as it had been seen and as it was secretly remembered by the great families, and he was free to do it because it was now too late and their greatness, power, and prestige had vanished with their land and palaces. He had shown, among other things, that the old world had been destroyed, with its shortcomings and its virtues, but that it had left emptiness behind it, because no one had seriously built a brave new one. And this dreary emptiness, full of sharp practices and phony improvisations, is still one of the curses of Italy.

It is something that affects our whole life. The old towns had been disfigured, despoiled, filled with lights, noise, advertisements and violent traffic, in an effort to make them function as the centers of modern cities. But today's cities, built for today's life, have not been built. The old schools for an élite have been

ruined in an effort to adapt them hastily for hordes of unwilling students. But schools for the masses, which will really
prepare them for the needs of contemporary society, have not
been set up. Ever since the unification of Italy, codes and statu-
tes have always been brought in from abroad, and foreign ways
copied; take, for instance, the way in which German-style
overcoats and the goose step were used in an army still equipped
with bayonets and decrepit cannon. But the substance was no
longer the same. Its old-fashioned values and limitations might
have gone, but so had its loyalty and its honesty, and, except in
appearance, the new was not really modern.

All this (in which lie the troubles of contemporary Italians,
who are faced with terrible problems that a century's history
and official rhetoric can neither justify nor explain) he said
after a lifetime's reflection, with the same standards of modesty,
moderation, disinterestedness, courage, sensitivity and courtesy
that the proper man used in war towards his enemies and in life
towards his friends, without regrets for what no longer existed
and had been swept away, not arbitrarily, by the march of
history. His uncle, the ambassador, told me: "My nephew
described the acceptance of the new life in Italy without ran-
cor, without fuss, without nostalgic regrets, like a . . ." He
stopped, embarrassed. Then he said what he was going to say,
but first apologized thus: "I want to use an unsuitable word,
the kind of word that ought never to be spoken, an ugly word,
an improper word . . ." What terrible word could the venerable diplomatist want to use, in this age when the most hair-
raising things are printed in books and newspapers? He said:
"My nephew described these things like . . . a gentleman." A
gentleman never calls himself a gentleman, as we all know, and
this was why no one had ever spoken in public about the things
that concerned gentlemen. The Marchese recalled that in his
family, the family of *The Leopard*, which had once faithfully
supported the throne of the Two Sicilies, no one ever spoke of
Ferdinando and Francesco, the last two Bourbon kings, and
the old days. Living, that was what mattered.

Even this is not enough. It is not enough to write a fine book from a prince's point of view and set down authentic, forgotten truths. Something else is needed. Giuseppe Tomasi worked, as he said, "to amuse himself." He did not know for certain whether he was writing a good book, or even what kind of book it would be, and he sheltered behind those words. Not even his wife imagined what it would be like. "After reading the first chapter, I told him there was talent there." (Talent is of course an inadequate, almost worldly word.) The fact was that he was forced to write a masterpiece, dominated by his characters and by the material he had been turning over in his mind for years. The chapter on the death of the Prince of Salina (a death so much like his own) was conceived and written in a number of ways, many months before illness struck him, long before the doctors condemned him. Like Mozart in his final compositions, like other great artists who foresee what is to happen to them later, he had been compelled by some secret force to describe his own destiny.

The book he really thought he was writing was a mere shadow of *The Leopard*. "None of what has been said about the writers that were his models is true," his widow said. "His favorite book, the one he thought he was imitating, is never mentioned because it is so far removed from his work. He thought he was using its plan, its tone, its humor. It is Dickens's *Pickwick Papers*. He had a copy on the bedside table at night, he took it with him when he traveled, he kept re-reading it . . . He wanted to write a long story, in separate episodes, around a main character, without any connection between them or any continuity." The episodic form was to jump twenty-five years twice. The beginning took place in 1860; then came the Prince's death in 1885 (through an error, the date in the book is given as 1883); and finally there are the last chapters, in 1910, when the victory of the ruthless new men pushes the family into an unimportant position and the old virtues of the now powerless aristocracy become the lonely manias of crazy old women, meaningless caricatures. This was what Giuseppe Tomasi did. The sense of incompleteness which the second part of the novel gives one is not a result of the illness which hastened and at his death cut short his work on the book, but is owed to the fact that he kept filling out the earlier part, which was his favorite, episode after episode, almost without meaning to. The rest remained how it had been planned.

The other writer who inspired him was Tolstoy, the whole of Tolstoy. (The Princess perferred Dostoievski, among the Russians, and they argued over which was the greater for the whole of their life together.) In *The Leopard* one hears, in fact, a faint echo of *War and Peace*. Among French writers his favorite was Racine, whom he considered outstanding for his understanding of the subtlest ripples in the human heart, and never tired of studying. But the writer he loved best was Shakespeare. He had several editions of him, some of them were pocketable, and these he took with him on his walks or to the club; others were large volumes to read during sleepless nights, one in his study, one in the country. Was there, perhaps, a trace of Hamlet in the Prince of Salina? Finally there were all the nineteenth-century Russian poets, whom he read in the original, helped by his wife. The Princess said that in the choice of certain words, in certain touches, in the texture of some sentences, she could feel the influence of Pushkin.

*        *        *

SOME PEOPLE in Palermo try to explain the miracle of *The Leopard* by recalling its author's blood, as people do for Derby winners. These are scientific explanations which are valid only after a win, as those who bet on horses know. However, there is no doubt that restless, adventurous, unpredictable blood flowed in the veins of the Duke of Palma and Prince of Lampedusa. His mother was born a Tasca di Cutò and was a beautiful, lively, whimsical and intelligent woman, who got herself talked about. The Tasca di Cutò princes are the ennobled branch of the old middle-class Tasca family. The nickname Tasca (pocket) comes, it is said, from the love which one of its members, perhaps the founder of the family, had for pockets— his own and other people's. The Tascas were extremely rich. One of them married the last princess of Cuto and, in the

Spanish manner, their first son took on her titles—more than thirty of them.

One of the last of the middle-class Tascas, without a title, was Don Lucio, a distant cousin of Giuseppe Tomasi di Lampedusa; he was the first angry farmer on the island after the Second World War, a man who was "respected" and "listened to" even in the Sicilian sense of the words, which means that the Mafia was awed by him. A few years ago the elderly Don Lucio was kidnapped—together with a grandson of nine—by ordinary criminals. They took him out of Palermo by car, with wads of cotton wool under the lenses of his dark glasses, as is usually done, to prevent him knowing where he was. But the old man kept a note in his mind of the number of minutes that had passed, the number of times the car went round corners, the hills it went up and the slopes it went down. During a pause when his captors made him hide in a cornfield, he picked an ear of corn, which was less ripe than those in his own fields on the plain, and therefore grown higher up, at a height he calculated roughly and which confirmed his own deductions.

When they reached their destination, the bandits said loudly: "Isn't Catania nice?" He knew they were actually at Partinico, but he said nothing, to avoid being done in. When, later on, they made him change house, still with cotton wool under his dark glasses and led along by the arm in short steps, he counted footsteps, turns, and steps taken up or down, so that when he was eventually freed by the police in the second house he found the first without hesitating and had his captors arrested. He accused them, but paid their defending counsel, because they had treated him with respect and spared his life. The behavior of his little grandson was equally exemplary. He showed no emotion, and said nothing, and treated his kidnappers with dignified reserve, as a grown man and a Sicilian.

The writer's uncle was Alessandro Tasca, Prince of Cutò and socialist deputy. It is worth remembering that half a century ago in Italy the word "socialist" brought horror to the hearts of respectable people; it was then a terrible, revolutionary word, not the weak, almost ambiguous one it is today. Tasca was a man of paradoxical mind, disorganized and impetuous. At the age of 20 he founded a violent inflammatory newspaper, *La Battaglia* (The Battle), most of which he wrote himself. He lost his entire fortune, down to the very last lira, "in one of the catastrophes," his nephew wrote, "in which even the silver braid on the servants' liveries was melted down."[3]

The revolutionary prince, who preached the abolition of other people's property and in doing so squandered his own, had several sisters, the novelist's aunts. One of them, Giulia Trigona, lady-in-waiting to Queen Elena, was stabbed to death by her lover, an elegant cavalry officer who was blackmailing her, at a lovers' meeting at the Rebecchino hotel in Rome, with tremendous scandal. ("She was born and died di Cutò," (*di 'couteau'*), as a Cutò, the wags of Caffè Aragno said.) Another sister, Teresa, married Baron Piccolo, of Capo d'Orlando, and is mother of one of the best contemporary Italian poets, Lucio. The Piccolo family lived isolated (not having been to Palermo for many years), discussing philosophy and literature, watched by a pack of dozens of suspicious dogs. All the Piccolos knew four or five languages. This story is told about the Baroness: once she sent for a relation who lived a long way off and said she "wanted to see him" urgently. He made a long journey, traipsing over half Sicily, and wondering what she could want. When he appeared at the villa, she made a sign to him to stop where he was, in the garden. Then she looked at him through a ship's telescope for a long time, and dismissed him with a wave of her hand. That was all she wanted.

Alessandro Tasca's son, whose name was Sandro, ran away to the United States some thirty years ago (almost like the son of the Prince of Salina, in *The Leopard*), to escape the disorder and decay of his family. He departed with his grandmother, his mother's mother, a Polish lady. Arriving in New York without

---

[3] The palace of Donnafugata, which dominates part of *The Leopard* like a character, was in real life that of Santa Margherita Belice, which belonged to the Tasca di Cutò family. It was destroyed in the earthquake on 1968. Tomasi remembered it from his adolescence, and chose the name Donnafugata without appearing to worry that there was a small town near Ragusa actually called that, though not the last bit like it.

a cent, he worked at night as an electrician with a group doing emergency repairs, and by day delivered the heavy recharged batteries, which in those days worked radio sets, in working-class districts, often climbing up four flights of stairs with them. Later he became an office boy, a page boy on the Wall Street stock exchange, a journalist, and a number of other things, keeping his grandmother comfortably and taking a correspondence course in accountancy in the evenings. Occasionally, in the Italian neighborhoods, immigrants from Santa Margherita Belice invited him to a meal, kissed his hand and asked if he had any tiresome enemies who needed wiping out. At last he achieved a respectable, anonymous middle-class position as Mr. Tasca, chief accountant of a shipping company in Baltimore. Today he is the efficient chief of production for English and American film companies working in Rome. Even this tenacious desire to vanish into earnest anonymous work and receive a regular salary, while it is normal in a middle-class man, may be called unusual and extravagant in a Sicilian prince.

*     *     *

BLOOD EXPAINS NOTHING, of course; neither the victories of a race horse, nor the sudden emergence of a great novelist. At the most, his many relations gave Tomasi facts and odd incidents of decaying aristocratic life, and the capacity to see things from the inside with resignation. (Many aristocratic old ladies in Palermo said, after reading the book: "I don't see what people see in it. These are all old things we know already, well-known facts best left alone . . .") Some distant relations, who presume they are descended from Tancredi and Angelica, think *The Leopard* a betrayal. Physically, Tancredi is a portrait of Tomasi's adopted son, the young Gio Lanza di Mazarino, today Duke of Palma, as I have said. But the historical character can only be Corrado Niscemi ("It can only be he," people tell you, "He was the only one to join Garibaldi."), who married a rich woman of humble origin, although she was highly cultured and had regal manners. However, Angelica is not the real Princess of Miscemi: everything in her is artistically made harsher, to point the antithesis between liberal Italy and the patriarchal and *seigneurial* world. Duke Fulco della Verdura, painter and designer of jewelry in Paris, London and New York, and a man of exquisite taste, thinks he is Angelica's grandson but has "not yet" read the novel; he says he will, though. Then there are the angry Sicilians, jealous of their country's good name, who hate the book in particular for the chapter in which the Prince of Salina cruelly explains the soul of Sicily to the Piedmontese nobleman who offers to nominate him as senator of the new kingdom. These same people, however, strongly defend Tomasi di Lampedusa, his genius and his vision of things, as soon as a non-Sicilian Italian makes any timid suggestion of criticizing him.

*     *     *

TO CONCLUDE: *The Leopard* is a mixture of all kinds of things—the man, his blood, his talent, his culture, his thoughts over the years, Sicily, the historical present; a miraculous mixture that even Giuseppe Tomasi di Lampedusa did not foresee while he was writing. Even those who first read the manuscript did not realize what it was. It is well known that it was sent anonymously to Elena Craveri Croce, Benedetto Croce's daughter, in Rome, and that for a couple of years she forgot it. Then it was sent to a publisher in Milan who gave it to the Sicilian novelist Elio Vittorini to read. Meantime Tomasi was dying of lung cancer in a nursing home in Rome. Before he died, he got Vittorini's letter returning the typescript. It was clear that Vittorini had read it, and he turned it down, he said, because it was "essayish". As everyone knows, all good novels—including Vittorini's—are essays. Perhaps he merely wanted to say that the Prince's ideas, which were so far from those of the tranquil literary good taste, from all official conformity or phony non-conformity, annoyed him.

Giuseppe Tomasi read and re-read the letter and said: "It was kind of him to take so much trouble. You can see he read it carefully. It's a pity." (Only two dialogues in the novel are strictly "essayish", in fact, the one I mentioned already, with the nobleman from Piedmont, about Sicilian virtues and vices, and another between Father Pirrone and the "herbalist". This latter dialogue worried Tomasi himself, and he did not want it published, fearing that it expressed his ideas too openly, not through the characters' actions and psychology.) It is also well known that the novelist Giorgio Bassani, then editorial chief of Feltrinelli, after reading the typescript which Elena Croce sent him after the author's death, rushed to Palermo, and at Tomasi's home discovered another manuscript, in his own hand-writing, with important additions, among them the chapter on the ball and the episode with Father Pirrone, and published it just as it was.

"What would my husband have written, had he lived?" the Princess of Lampedusa asked me, at the end of our talk.

I had come to ask questions, not to give answers. I was non-plussed. What, indeed? *The Leopard* had been in his mind all his life, into it were woven all the things that were most dear to him, all his most intimate feelings. He himself was the main charac-ter, his great-grandfather's study of astronomy having taken the place of his own reading and meditation. Its theme was one of those that haunt a man like Giuseppe Tomasi all his life, the inevitable decline, which cannot be halted, of the old virtues and graces that have grown useless but made life human even for humble people; the triumph of other qualities, rougher but essential in the modern world, which do not correct the old injustices but often merely show them up, make them unbear-able, and replace them with others that are sometimes crueler and worse. What else could he have written but *Il Gattopardo*?— just as Manzoni really wrote only one book, *I Promessi Sposi*, in all his life. Could Giuseppe Tomasi have written another? The Princess said she had often asked herself the same question, but without finding an answer; then she said good-bye.

# 15

# A PERSONAL AFFAIR

THE FORTUNATE JOURNALIST is sometimes able to tell how he survived some appalling catastrophe, escaped some desperate danger, or how he came close to death. It has happened to many. To give the examples I know best, it happened to my father and to me. In 1907, driving in the Peking–Paris car race, my father was pinned under the ruins of a bridge of rotten wood, somewhere in Siberia, the car, an Itala, crushing his kidneys; he also crashed in a Zeppelin in the Black Forest and was rescued from the branches of a tree; and he narrowly missed being shot as a spy by the Germans, in Belgium in 1914. I disappeared in the Danakil desert during the Abyssinian War, with an adventurous small column that was practically wiped out in an ambush, and for days I was thought to be dead. Another time, having been refused permission to go at the very last minute, I was unable to fly in a military plane that was going to take over a distant Ethiopian province which was said to be ready to submit, indeed well disposed towards us. Those who set off in it were all slaughtered on arrival. The most senior of them, a young air force general, and a dear friend of mine, is now a street name in Palermo. The following year I was sunk on the Yangtze on board the *Panay*, an American gunboat bombed by the Japanese. Sandro Sandri, a journalist, who was with me, is now also a street name in Milan.

It happens. Survivors' stories are always dramatic, picturesque, fascinating: distant lands, terrible climates, ice, deserts, forests, smoking ruins, brutal uniformed foreigners, wounded men groaning, interrogations, small-arms fire, desperate escapes. Without meaning to, the man writing takes on the magical airs of an indestructible hero, merely because the man who writes is the one who got away and the man who didn't get away never puts pen to paper again. The fact is, though, that while the adventure is on and you are living through it, you are neither bold nor heroic nor amused. You doubt your own indestructibility, you curse softly, or pray, or do both at once, because you don't know where or how you are going to end, writing it all up or being written up yourself. "The best of us is no more . . . Still do we seem to hear his footsteps in the corridor, to see his face before us, at his desk . . . He was so full of life." Journalists' obituaries are all alike.

\*      \*      \*

THIS LAST TIME, though, this last desperate adventure of mine, my last trip to the edge of life, was something quite different. It was a plain, monochrome, almost flat-footed affair. Death appeared to me with no dignity, unpretentious, banal, almost colorless, perhaps suited to the middle-class times we live in. The very place in which it happened could not have been quieter or more domestic: my own study, my own work-desk. It was the afternoon of September 30th, 1960. It was neither hot nor cold. There was a stormy wind, *scirocco* or *libeccio*, that swept black clouds across the sky, whipped angrily at the trees and moaned gloomily down the chimneys; a wind to make you nervous and on edge. My secretary was typing some manuscript or other. I was sitting in my usual place, and listening to the polite peaceable words of a visitor sitting in front of me. He was a well bred man, possibly a former naval officer, who was putting before me the point of view of various film producers in connection with the restrictions of a forthcoming law. I was on a small parliamentary sub-committee that was to study it. I listened.

It was purely a courtesy call and our conversation was almost pointless. Film producers are not particularly keen to keep me up to date with their plans and ideas. Colleagues on my sub-committee, parliamentary deputies from a number of parties, both left and right, spoke up for them. Most of these had been

elected by backward country districts in the South, places given
to sheep-farming; they were obscure young men who had practically nothing to do with the cinema or with cultural matters
and, perhaps for this very reason, were more easily swayed by
other peoples' ideas. It was a simple matter to recognize them
because they repeated more or less the same arguments and
proposed similar or exactly identical amendments, obviously
thought up and typed out in the same offices. I was not deemed
useful. I have the tiresome knack of wanting to see things in at
least some clarity and of refusing to commit myself until I am
completely persuaded. Kind people say of me, as if apologizing
for a fault: "What can you expect? He's a liberal . . ."

I must say this to make it clear that there was nothing at all
exciting about our conversation. I listened calmly to the cogent,
almost convincing and sometimes valid points he put forward. I
made no objections. On the other hand, my views were not
asked for. Occasionally my attention wandered, and I smoked.
At one point I was distracted because I felt a strange discomfort
gradually coming over me. It was a vague general sensation that
spread all over my body, from head to chest, from belly to limbs;
a gradual dulling of consciousness, a vague sense of nausea. It
was, I thought, the sort of sickness you sometimes feel on a small
ship, when a swell is running high astern, and first raises it very,
very slowly and then lets it drop, in a broad, spiral movement.

I might have been poisoned, I thought. But, a few hours
earlier, I had only eaten some homely food: no mushrooms, no
oysters. What then? There was no doubt about it, I had contracted some illness, which would soon break out. Which? I had
no temperature, not even the shivery feeling that meant I was
working up to one. My visitor went on talking. I barely listened.
I was attending to my own inside, with some anxiety. What the
devil was going on? My secretary looked up and saw that I was
pale, very pale. She looked as if she was going to say something;
but seeing that I was calm and apparently listening, she said
nothing and went on typing.

The general uneasiness grew worse and at the same time
became concentrated on the left side of my chest, in an intense

knot of pain. It wasn't a sharp, alarming pain, either—quite the opposite. It was a dull ache in the ribs as if I had fallen against something hard, the not unbearable sensation you feel when you are thrown from a horse and hurt your back and chest. This local pain then began moving slowly, spreading in various directions, while the sea-sickness grew worse. From my chest it went to my left arm-pit, then down the arm and through the wrist, a painful, thread-like feeling that ran like fire along a powder-train, rather like that which a slight attack of sciatica gives you in the legs. Then—or perhaps at the same time—it went on towards my neck, squeezing it gently and painfully, and finally higher up to my face, and to my teeth which suddenly started to ache for no apparent reason.

I followed all these sensations, worried but not yet alarmed, because the pain was not dramatic, no worse than ordinary feelings I already knew and have mentioned—a fall from a horse, the beginnings of neuralgia. My visitor said, as I remember: "You do understand our difficulty, don't you, sir? . . . Before we make plans we must know quite definitely what is going to happen to us . . . How can we possibly work if we don't know what's coming, from one day to the next?" Quite right, I thought. We all need to know quite definitely what's coming before we make any plan at all. All of us. Me, for instance, at this very moment, I thought. Here I am talking about future legislation, but do I know where I shall be in a day, maybe in an hour?

My discomfort was increasing, and so was the pain; besides which I felt strangely uneasy, almost restless. My visitor's talk was beginning to annoy me. It was nothing but meaningless words, vague mutterings. Suddenly, unable to keep still, I rose and said I wasn't well, that he must excuse me, that we would talk again another time. He rose politely as well. I took him to the door, said good-bye and went upstairs to my bedroom. I felt the need we all feel, the need animals sense when they are wounded or seriously ill, to shut myself up somewhere, to hide and curl up alone, in silence, to control the pain and wait for what was going to come.

Because at this point I was beginning to realize what it probably was. Over the past few years and months I had lost several friends, dear friends and brotherly colleagues with whom I had started working over thirty years before, nearly all of them the same age as I was (and nearly all in the same way, with a small pain in the ribs or back or left arm), vigorous, clear-sighted, active men whose heads were full of plans and things to do, whose desks were piled high with papers, manuscripts to finish, letters to answer. All of them said, smiling: "It's nothing, it'll pass, it's a trifle," to their worried families. All of them knocked out like stags by gamekeepers from a distance, with a single shot, to thin out the herd.

What about me? I went slowly and thoughtfully up the stairs. In my bedroom there was no glass in the windows; as it happened, that very morning the frames had been removed for painting. The wind came howling in from all sides, flapping the curtains frantically. I felt I was on the deck of a torpedo-boat in a storm. No peace there. I went to another room, belonging to one of the children, trying to keep calm, to relax my nerves, yet almost uncontrollably restless. My wife came to help me almost at once, made the painters put back the windows, fixed my room and took me to it.

She sensed something. But we said nothing. Maybe we should have exchanged solemn concepts, or else small, simple, familiar words, dimmed by emotion; perhaps we should have recalled some of our most intimate moments. But instead we talked about other things, smiling as if nothing was wrong, I to reassure her, she to reassure me, and both of us knowing we were deceiving nobody. We were afraid of being moved, afraid of betraying ourselves, of doing or saying anything that might show it was an important moment, a moment unlike so many others. My wife kept busy, gave orders, made a lot of telephone calls, searched for a heart specialist and found one. He was coming "as soon as possible," she said.

While we were waiting she asked me, as if I were really struck by some mild indisposition: "Shall I make you some camomile tea?" Do, I said, thanks, go and make some. Camomile's always good for one. It calms down at once the person who drinks it and the person who gets busy making it. Then, while I was waiting, I remembered that practically all my friends had died while someone, a wife no doubt, was in the kitchen making camomile tea. Had I been rash to accept?

\* \* \*

THE EMINENT HEART SPECIALIST could not come at once; he was very busy. He promised to send an assistant as soon as possible, but the assistant was busy as well. He came, in fact, after an hour and a half. In the meantime I hadn't quite died. I was no better and no worse. I lay still in bed, crouched up in silence and darkness, controlling as best I could the dull pain in my chest and left arm, in my neck and teeth, and the nauseating sickness that had taken over my whole body. Perhaps I was better? Or perhaps keeping still had deadened all feeling? I wasn't sure.

The assistant was an extremely healthy young man, vigorous, thin, athletic, chic, casual and amusing. He was smartly dressed in light grey, with a milk-white pullover, like a habitué of the Café Rosati on the Via Veneto. Possibly anyone would have irritated me at that particular moment, but certainly the sight of someone as aggressively robust, as bursting with energy, as elegant in a way I thought frivolous, was particularly offensive; it was almost as if he were determined not to accord me proper respect. I should certainly have preferred a wan, bald, short-sighted doctor, thick-spectacled and shabbily dressed, visibly worn with work and experiments. How could I die (if I was going to die) in the hands of a young man who looked like a film actor or a pop singer?

He put on a serious air, as was proper, and questioned me about what I was feeling. He nodded at everything I said, and assumed the slightly bored, smug expression of a man who finds his suspicions confirmed. All I was telling him (he allowed me to see) was perfectly in order, all of it foreseeable, textbook stuff. Nothing surprised him, it was all old hat. Occasionally he suggested an adjective or a verb, used a more exact, more technical and more relevant term for some generic expression of mine, or even completed a sentence or two for me. He seemed unwilling to leave me with any illusions.

Then he arranged his electric gear on a table, hung wires round the room, tied them to various parts of my body, and tied one of them to the radiator. I watched his movements carefully: they were the quick, relaxed and unconscious movements a professional makes when he is doing what he is used to, with occasional casual flourishes, like a conjuror preparing a new trick. When everything was ready, he first tried out the apparatus to see that it was working properly: he unrolled a strip of squared paper that came out with a visceral rumble. Everything was in order. Then he started recording what was happening inside me.

He let the paper run between his fingers, slowly perusing the data, his stance just like that of the Wall Street speculator as he follows the market prices on the ticker-tape. I watched his face, of course, to read there what he was reading on the paper. He was frowning slightly as he concentrated on it, pretending to look puzzled and cool. He pressed some more buttons, studied a particular part of the cardiogram for a moment, slowing it up between his fingers, then let it run on or fall on the floor, almost without looking at it, as if he had understood it all too well and there was no need to confirm. Although he pretended there was nothing to it, I could feel a certain controlled emotion in him. His eyes glittered.

At last, as if freeing himself from some weight, he said: "I prefer to speak plainly . . . It's better . . . I can't hide it from you that I can see something . . . There is something . . ." What exactly did he see? "Well, I can see an attack in progress." Perhaps registering an attack while it is taking place is a rare experience, appreciated by experts, or perhaps something quite common; I don't know. In any case he looked pleased. "A slight attack," he said, comfortingly. But what else could he say? He put down his instruments, wrote down the names of four or five medicines I should take at various times, and injections I should be given, told me above all not to move, left telephone

numbers at which he could be reached in case of need and
promised to come round early next morning. Then he was off
like the wind, with all his gear.

I stayed motionless in bed, waiting. Waiting for what? If I
had been the kind of man who tries to deceive himself, and if I
still had any doubts, I could no longer have them; I was no
longer allowed them. The doctor had told me "the attack was
in progress." That is, it wasn't over. A small part of my heart
was still dying for lack of blood. When would the progress stop?
How big would the hole be? The size of a five-lire piece? Or a
fifty-lire piece? Would it be fatal? Nobody knew.

How could one tell? I had to wait for time to pass before I
was given any answers. In an hour, or two, or three, or four,
before midnight or at least before morning, I would know. Or
my family would. I would be alive or else dead. I would also
have to wait to find out if I were to have another attack, for that
was possible too: the definitive one, the *coup de grâce*. Or else (if
all went well) I should have to wait a month to know what sort
of man I should be once the danger was over, and what sort of
life I would be leading.

So I waited, motionless, the way you wait in an air-raid,
crouched in a hole that is lit by explosive flashes and floating
flares, knowing there's nothing, absolutely nothing to be done
but wait, and that in a few hours you will either be a corpse
under the ruins or else go up into the clear and get on with
things. Waiting as I once had to, after the war, in a dilapidated
plane with Matteo Matteotti, when one of the engines caught
fire in flight between Rome and Milan.

\*       \*       \*

I TRIED TO COLLECT my thoughts. I tried to see my past life
again, as I had read that people in my condition did, trying to
find some meaning. I tried to see in my mind the faces of those I
had known who had died, and whom I might perhaps see again
soon. I tried to remove myself spiritually from those I loved
who were still alive, my wife, my grown-up daughters, my small

children whom I could hear playing quietly, scarcely making a noise at all, somewhere in the house. I tried as best I could to imagine the tearing of this intricate texture that bound us together with its innumerable threads, my family and myself; bound us so closely that we were no longer separate but now almost part of the same fabric, figures on a tapestry. I tried to imagine their life without me. Finally I tried to do what I had been taught as a boy, and that is to prepare myself as a man should when he is close to death.

I confess that I managed to think of these things only in fits and starts. My feelings, my reflections and my thoughts all wandered about on their own, as if they were abstracted and disembodied. Only with an effort did I bring them back, occasionally, on to suitable subjects. One thing above all irritated, hurt, and distracted me from meditation: death was approaching without the dignity and solemnity of great physical pain, of pain that was in proportion to its final result.

I was ill, of course, very ill. But I had been worse before, with ordinary, unimportant complaints; lost in feverish delirium, or suffering after accidents and incidents that could be cured in a fortnight—fractured arms or broken legs or eating oysters in Naples . . . What sort of death was this that failed to proclaim its approach with fiery trumpet blasts, blaring brass, thunderous drums and timpani, furious strings? What sort of a death was this that crept feebly up on me, announced by an illness not much worse than a mild flu?

I was also distracted from the kind of thoughts I should have had just then because I was too angry. I mean that the strongest feeling, the one that overwhelmed nearly all the others, was devouring rage. I was angry the way a man is when he has missed an important train or a steamer that sails once a month, enraged the way a man is who had suffered a serious injustice, or had been put in prison through a case of mistaken identity. Why did it have to be me? I asked. Out of all the people on earth—decrepit old things who scarcely had the strength to draw breath, criminals who stained the air around them, useless, childless persons, tramps with nothing to do—out of all of them this ridiculous thing had to happen to me of all people, dying of a hole in the heart.

To me of all people, and today of all times. I thought of all the things I still had to do in life: my arrangements for my grown-up daughters; the education of my small sons; the finances that I had to straighten out; the work plans I had in mind or already set out on paper on my desk, the books I wanted to write, the play I was planning. What annoyed me most, though, was not so much the many things I still had to do, for surely whenever I had to die I would still have as many, unlike these or similar to them. What irritated me was the absentminded, meaningless choice of day. Why Friday, September 30th? My life had reached no significant point. The various threads that made it up had not been tied into a single knot. Everything seemed to be ending by chance, as in a film that has been torn, when the characters are left on the screen waving a leg, raising an arm, open-mouthed, in the middle of a shout.

Perhaps the real explanation is that this was not to be my last day, nor my last night. My illness seemed weak, faint and ordinary just because in fact it was only a slight illness—weak, faint and ordinary. Everything seemed inconclusive, perhaps, and unlinked with the rest of my life, because I was not in point of fact going to die. People used to say that death nearly always comes as it is deserved, as a comment on our own life, a sometimes ironic symbol of what we have done, even when it seems to have come quite by chance and is least expected. And that inconclusive death I was awaiting motionless in my bed was not yet to be mine.

\*     \*     \*

EVERY tiny insignificant thing, every thought, every sound, every sensation and every word becomes precious when you are about to die, or when you think you are going to die at any moment, which is the same thing. Every detail seems to be full of vital, indecipherable meaning.

I remember once in Africa, under small-arms and rifle fire at a few yards' range, flinging myself down behind a rock and gazing greedily at the small patch of ground under my eyes, which was as large and important to me as a view of the Alps. The small stones were as big as mountains. Their curves and color in a few minutes became lovingly familiar. Stalks looked like tree-trunks, tufts of grass like woods. Fascinated, I watched the painful progress of unknown insects dragging themselves across my landscape like antediluvian monsters. I recall trying to understand why they, and nothing else, were the last things I should see in my life, as important as my mother's face; why that small patch of ground and none other should soon be soaked with my blood and why I had traveled so far, in years and in miles, from my childhood, to end up in that of all places, among those rocks and in that grass, and not elsewhere.

So I stayed motionless in bed in the darkness, listening to my heartbeats and the moaning of the wind down the chimney that fell and then rose with unexpected fury, and with my wife breathing audibly on a camp bed, pretending to sleep. Everything seemed to me an oracle, a sign, an omen from which to foretell the future. I went over every movement, every word and expression of the doctor's a few hours earlier, reading in it my own condemnation or my own salvation. "You fool," I said to myself, "not to have realized right away . . ." His levity and casualness might in fact have confirmed the slightness of my attack or else the opposite.

At the same time I was assailed by a thousand little worries, some of them quite unimportant; things I should have done which had seemed to be absolutely urgent. I was thinking hardly at all of my work—the things I had to write, my book, my play, an urgent article, all the things I suppose I should have been thinking about. No. My mind was all taken up with thoughts of my wife, left alone with the enormous and unknown responsibilities of bringing up the little boys and steering them towards the future. I thought of my daughters, regretting that I hadn't seen them married and settled, and perhaps my regret was partly the selfish one of someone reading a fascinating novel and having to stop half-way through. A deep distress overtook me.

What could I say now (I thought in the darkness) that would

really help, that would go with my children all through the years ahead and save them from any possible trouble, from snares and weakness or temptation? What advice could I give them, what few words could I now say or write containing all I had learned from life, all I might have said, more or less, in their future years, the few words that would keep them on course in any storm, like an automatic pilot? What could I say, when I myself had really understood nothing, or practically nothing? What could I say when I was merely a slightly older creature than they were, almost the same boy I had been so many years before when I had left the university and first faced life; puzzled and bewildered, to be sure, disguised as a mature, knowledgeable greyheaded man, but still little more than an inexperienced boy inside. What more did I know than they did, except for the tiny, wretched, stupid cunning tricks of the prisoner who has been in jail a bit longer than the rest and learned ways and means of avoiding troubles, retaliations, punishments, and corvées, and getting the odd extra bowl of soup?

Had I (I wondered in the darkness) understood the first thing, why I had been put here on earth? To do what? Why had I been made to undergo this complex, difficult test? I had tried to find my way, tried to do my duty, had not consciously harmed anyone. I didn't think I would leave the world worse than I found it. Or at least so I felt. Possibly everyone feels this, even the criminal; maybe even Hitler felt it. And was this what I ought to have done? Perhaps. Yet this final reason for all the tribulations and joys, the satisfactions and disappointments, the displeasure and the mistakes—this, quite honestly, I had not understood. What use had I been except perhaps to continue this endless chain of being and mystery, this inexplicable chain letter, this snowball with no apparent meaning that has lasted since humanity began and continues to grow from generation to generation?

What should I say to the children? On my own, I had discovered a few things which I thought true, important. Did I really discover them, or were they the things my family vainly tried to teach me as a boy? Things I took from the teacher of literature; from the liberal, patriotic *bersagliere*; from Alice; from the good Barnabite priest at Moncalieri, and my puritan teachers in America? And if I had known what to say to my children would they have understood it? Or would they have understood only later, each one in his own time? Perhaps the things I should say now, even if they were perfect, the quintessence of wisdom, would seem quite meaningless to them, things said by grown-ups and old people, empty noises, little notions to write in autograph books, quotations from dusty poets, chocolate-box mottoes. Each man learns on his own. Learns? Or does he grow old and one morning wake up to find he knew things he didn't know the previous evening?

As I suffered impotently, I consoled myself by thinking that possibly the memory of their dead father might help my children more than words; their father as they imagined him, disapproving of some things, cheered or pained by others. Perhaps my face in photographs would be more eloquent than my living self. I thought how often an imaginary father, full of the virtues created by the reverence and love of those who have survived him, may serve as an example and a warning in any eventuality, even in future, unimaginable contingencies, rather more than a real live father with all his faults, old and querulous, embittered and petulant, weak and resigned. The dead, after all, never age. But memories slowly fade, like photographs. My face as a living man would become more and more that of an imaginary being. The clothes worn by my image would become more and more unfashionable and absurd and my character more remote and unreal.

What should I say to my wife? We had always understood each other without speaking. What could I offer her to take the place of my presence? What recommendations that she would not formulate herself, within herself, suffering as I was in that very moment? All I was thinking she was no doubt thinking herself, in silence, a few yards from me, while she pretended to sleep. Then there were a few practical things I had to say to my elder daughter, unimportant things having to do with the ordering of my affairs, which could not be left unsaid. My elder daughter, who was eighteen, was also awake in the rooms next door, and occasionally when I tossed about and softly asked for something, she was at my pillow too and helped as much as she could, her face pale (my face when I was a boy), her eyes red, and she tried to smile, as if it were a night like any other, as if she was used to not sleeping, to listening for every sound, to getting up at any minute. Once, when I had her near me and alone, I pulled her head towards me, embarrassed, and started saying, as if it was quite unimportant:

"Listen carefully . . . It's probably nothing and I'll get over it and work better than ever . . . These things are like that. Either you die or else you come out of it healthy and vigorous. But it might go wrong . . ."

I had little breath and it was an effort. Every word was important. But this preamble was necessary. I had to prepare things ahead. Above all, I was afraid of appearing foolish, later on. If I got well, I should be ashamed of having made our talk pointlessly solemn. Also, I didn't want to be interrupted. I didn't want her to reassure me, as people always reassure those who are seriously ill. In order to get in first, I was doing it all myself: reassuring and deceiving myself, or pretending to deceive myself. But she interrupted me all the same, white-faced.

"What nonsense you're talking, papa!" she exclaimed.

"It's not nonsense . . . Listen carefully . . ." I went on.

"You mustn't tire yourself," she said. "You must keep quiet. There's nothing wrong with you. The doctor said so. You'll soon be fine. Go to sleep."

Obstinately I insisted:

"Don't interrupt me. Let me speak!"

"I won't hear a word," she replied.

I was getting angry. I had no breath, no strength, and I even had to fight to be heard. What did she think she was doing, stopping her dying father (or at least her father who thought he was dying) from expressing some wishes and suggestions, from asking her for a promise? I remembered forgotten historical paintings of old men in their beds propped upon great piles of pillows, surrounded by children and grandchildren listening respectfully and feelingly to their last words, solemn, well-turned words, no doubt passed on to later generations. *Altri tempi*, those were the days! Whereas I had to fight to get myself heard, and get involved in pointless arguments about my state of health.

"You're stupid," I said imperiously. "For God's sake keep quiet and don't make me waste time. It's probably nothing, I know that. Everyone's told me so. I hope they're right. But if it's serious, I've got to tell you this. Listen!"

And I stopped, wearily. My daughter was weeping in silence.

*Part Three*

# PROBLEMS

# 16

# A FINE ITALIAN HAND

O N A SUMMER DAY before the First World War a slim and Roman-nosed European gentleman walked down a New York street, idly looking at the shop windows. His name was the same as mine, Luigi Barzini. He was my father, perhaps Italy's best known journalist and writer of his day, sent by the *Corriere della Sera* to write colorful but definitive articles about the outlandish, peculiar, and inexplicable life in the United States. He was then in his early thirties and had been almost everywhere, in Europe, the Far East, Latin America, to cover some of the biggest stories of the time and describe people and countries in lucid prose.

America frankly puzzled him. The people were human, hospitable, open; the women were often dazzlingly beautiful; New York was intoxicating. Still, he did not feel quite at home. There was something in the life around him, perhaps a too passive acceptance of pure economic motivations or a ruthless search for the practical and the utilitarian, which made him uncomfortable. This, however, he did not clearly know until that morning, when something happened which proved to him how vast was the chasm between him, an Italian of the last century, and contemporary Americans.

He stopped in front of an antique dealer's window. There, handsomely and respectfully laid on yards of red velvet, was a handsome brazier. It was old, made of copper; the handles were dimpled cupids cast in brass. There were dents here and there, carefully preserved, which proved it had been used a long time. My father entered the shop to price the article. The antique dealer rubbed his hands, pursed his lips, and said reverently that this particular charcoal-burning utensil was of Italian origin, possibly seventeenth century, obviously designed and made by a master artisan or a minor sculptor, probably Tuscan. It was, he said, a tasteful *objet d'art*, worthy to be placed in any elegant drawing room. He quoted the price, in a low voice. It was a high figure, much beyond the limitations of my father's expense account.

He walked out with infinite sadness in his eyes and stopped to say good-bye to that particular brazier forever. It had been in the kitchen of his childhood house in Orvieto ever since he could remember; it had been sold with everything else when his parents died and he and his brothers had been left penniless. He knew it as well as he knew his mother's face. Each of its dents, bumps, and scratches recalled some familiar incident. He also knew it wasn't ancient. It had been made by one of Orvieto's craftsmen in the 'seventies'.

In later years, my father would sometimes love to analyze this remote and insignificant incident, in an effort to unravel revealing deductions, valid for both Italy and the United States, as well as for the contemporary and future worlds. There it stood, he would say, this humble household appliance, so well known to him, in fact, that he could have drawn it from memory, incongruously and somewhat ludicrously displayed as if it were a crown jewel. And there, severely separated from it by the plate glass (and by the high price) was he, who, in the past, when warming his hands on it, had never given much attention to it. How come an ordinary kitchen utensil of his youth had become a precious and rare bibelot in a different world? What did all this mean?

Seventeenth century, the man had said. Clearly that was either a mistake or a lie, a proof of many Americans' approximate erudition or of an antique dealer's professional inaccuracies. In a way, however, my father reflected, the man had unknowingly not been far from wrong. To be sure, the brazier was relatively new, but an anachronism at the same time, because it had been made with the care, skill, the graces of other times. Times, my father would say, when men all over Europe (and the American colonies, for that matter) never had to have anonymous objects about them, things without character, identical to myriad other objects in other people's houses. Each was unique, well designed, made not only to do its work well but to embellish a room, to give pleasure to the eye and dignity to life.

Men of other times never gave this a thought, as they had no alternative. But contemporary men did. American millionaires like William Randolph Hearst who bought all sorts of European bric-à-brac for their many mansions, and the Italians at the beginning of the century. My grandparents in Orvieto, like many of their countrymen, could actually have purchased a wide variety of things made by machinery in Germany, England, or in Italy itself, but stubbornly preferred the old-fashioned hand-made articles. For some reason, people in Italy kept on buying gay earthenware pottery, shining copper pots, ornate braziers, elegantly carved furniture, wrought-iron grills, hunting guns with decorated barrels and carved stocks, just as some of them ordered automobiles of unique style.

That day in a New York store my father realized he and the brazier could be considered contemporaries, exiled from an imaginary and immobile seventeenth century, remnants of a way of life condemned by modern techniques and tastes. But were they really *démodés*? Was his inclination for handsome and unique things a sign of backwardness? Maybe the fact that his old brazier had been promoted to the class of expensive *objets d'art* was significant of a new trend. Maybe he and it belonged to the past but also to the future, to an approaching time when all men, not only the rich, would finally revolt against the leveling of taste.

\*　　\*　　\*

EVERYWHERE in Europe the new urban bourgeoisie had no doubts. For them the old ways were to be despised as well as the old ideas. Old objects were to be burned, old buildings demolished, old furniture discarded as fast as worn-out clothes. They drove straight boulevards through the hearts of medieval cities. The new for them was always best. They wanted the world around them to be *endimanché*, as bright as they themselves and their families on their way to church on Sunday morning, and crowded with brand new, machine-made, anonymous, and glittering objects. This confirmed to them that they lived indeed at the climax of civilization, in the most advanced and therefore best of all ages.

In Italy, however, in spite of the earnest efforts of the Milanese, the triumph of modernity was somewhat slower than elsewhere. With feeble results, La Scala put on a spectacular ballet, about 1906, called *Excelsior!* in which one saw the Alps being pierced by tunnels, electricity dispelling the darkness enveloping the world, etcetera, etcetera. The name, of course, as retrograde professors tirelessly pointed out, was a Latin mistake. It should have been *Excelsius!* But then was it not an illustrious American mistake, the title of a poem by Henry Wadsworth Longfellow? Was America not the undisputed champion of progress? Wasn't contempt for the niceties of Latin grammar also a sign of advanced thinking?

There were many reasons why the Italians lingered in the past. One was an affectionate acceptance of things as they had always been because these were more comfortable. My grandfather probably did not think twice before ordering a new brazier from the son of the man who had made an old brazier for my great-grandfather. Then there was the national passion to embellish everything. I remember examining an Isotta Fraschini motor many years ago, in New York, together with an eminent American automobile engineer. He looked at everything for a long time, then shook his head, looking very puzzled. He asked me: "Can you tell me why parts that do not work are as polished and well finished as those that work? This seems to me an irresponsible waste of labor and money."

I did not explain to him that one could not restrain Italian engineers, designers, and workers from beautifying everything they made. In fact, most Italians thought that a pleasant appearance was as important as (and often more important than) usefulness. "*L'occhio*," they always said, "*vuole la sua parte*." Neither did I tell the American automobile engineer the story of the Italian Renaissance armor, because he might not have understood.

It was universally considered the most elegant of its time. Each specimen was different from all others, each uniquely shaped and decorated, inlaid with gold and silver, the front and back adorned with mythological or allegorical scenes invented by famous artists. No military leader, *grand seigneur*, sovereign prince, or dandy could be without. Such armor was worn at parades, courtly jousts, ceremonies, *Te Deums*, and coronations. It was *di rigore* when posing for famous portrait painters. But when men went into battle (and that includes the Italians themselves) they wore German armor, which was ugly but safe, thick, and solid. This is perhaps why so many Italian master-pieces of armor are to be found, in contemporary museums, well oiled, undented, and impeccably preserved.

Neither did I tell the engineer about the immense sums the Italian Line spent to decorate their liners plying the Atlantic in the 1920s. Their engines were not particularly noted for ad-vanced design, their safety measures no better than what Lloyd's prescribed, their hulls not rigorously shaped according to the latest technology, but the public rooms could be compared with the best at the Hermitage, Versailles, Caserta, Palazzo Pitti, and the Quirinale. The Line's board of directors possibly spent more time choosing new patterns for silverware and stationery than deliberating over the adoption of newfangled scientific devices.

Obviously this inordinate passion for appearance and for the work of proud craftsmen was expensive and helped retard Italians in their efforts to transform their economy from a pre-dominantly agricultural, poor, and archaic one to an industrial-ized, affluent, and modern one. Connected and confused with this passion was another national characteristic which also helped slow Italy on the road to progress. This was the inhabi-tants' innate and ineradicable dislike of monotony.

An American friend of mine, the late Paul Bonner, novelist and diplomat, years ago ran identical textile factories in Italy and the United States. They were built from the same blue-prints, supplied with the same machinery, and functioned according to the same well-tested rules. In spite of the fact that wages in Italy were much lower, the product was more costly. My friend told me he had studied his baffling phenomenon and concluded it was probably due to the fact that the Italians became bored watching practically unaided machines endlessly produce uniform cloth for months or years on end.

Somewhat similar was the experience of Matteo d'Agostini, an energetic industrialist who produced bricks and tiles in Salerno. After the last war he had landed a big order from the United States for a small subsidiary factory of his which specialized in artistic pottery. He was to deliver hundreds of thousands of identical hand painted ashtrays.

His workers mutinied after a while. They sent a delegation to confer with him, explained that they could not go on making the same things day after day, week after week, month after month. They considered it an inhuman form of torture to which they refused to submit. They were even willing to take lower wages if the patterns could be varied, and finally asked him to persuade his American customer to cancel his stolid order and to accept ashtrays of many different designs.

\* \* \*

CLEARLY ALL THIS (the compulsion to beautify, reluctance to accept novelties, resistance to uniformity) obstructed the quick adoption of mass-production techniques, the only methods that could transform the economy and solve the problem of poverty. All this also inevitably provoked vast political repercussions, with which Italians are still coping. But there was something else. They could have fully employed their ancient skills in the modern world if they had abandoned another of their pet prejudices. They still admirably knew how to make use of all kinds of materials. They could still make armor as precious as the Renaissance models; they hammered copper, and hand-forged wrought iron, made splendid mosaics, knew the secrets of inlaid stone or woods; blew iridescent glass; wove tapestries and brocades; produced magnificent leather goods. Their coral and tortoise shell products were unique. They cut stones and marbles and molded artistic plaster bas reliefs as no one else. Yet only a small discriminating minority of the world appreciated their genius.

This was due to the fact that for a very long time they believed their skills could only be used to reproduce the ancient objects in the old styles. They thought their fathers had achieved perfections no modern man could surpass, that the greatness of Italy was in the past, that contemporary Italians could do no better than to go on imitating archaic models. This allowed them to produce impeccable false antiques, some of which are now exhibited as masterpieces in the best museums in the world, as well as a flood of imitation antiques.

This form of timidity was partly shared, at the time, by many other countries. (Munich is filled with eclectic imitations of ancient architecture.) It dominated and paralyzed Italians more than other people for deep psychological and political reasons unknown elsewhere. Carol L. V. Meeks, an authority on Italian architecture, wrote:

The dominant style of (United) Italy was derived primarily from the developed style of the high Renaissance, which had been perfected in Rome by Sangallo, Michelangelo, and Vignola. This was no sudden return to the past. In a sense the sixteenth century had never entirely died in Italy . . . United Italy was very conscious of its past, and used architecture, as all governments have done, to state its position.

The élite not only used architecture to demonstrate they were the worthy heirs of a glorious past, but also the every day *arts décoratifs* for the same purpose.

All Italian cities (Rome, naturally, more than others), in the seventy years between 1860 and 1930, were filled with diligent and talented reproductions of Renaissance *palazzi* and stately villas. They were built for the old rich and the newly rich, big corporations, banks, ministries, post offices, courts, universities. The affluent middle class built themselves numberless medieval castles with towers. One of the best known of these imitation buildings is the American Embassy in Rome. It was designed in 1886 for Prince Boncompagni di Piombino, as the grandest private residence of its time. The complete building was sold to the Queen Mother, Margherita, who occupied it until her death in 1926. The United States government bought it after the war. It is so handsomely designed and well built that many tourists are unaware it is not a venerable masterpiece of Italian period architecture.

Not all Italians, however, were ready to accept this passive admiration for the past. Ever since the end of the last century, young men, rebels of the right and the left, wanted their countrymen to plunge into the contemporary world, a world of industry, speed, wars, danger, revolts, machinery, and adventure. Poets began praising living men and their achievements, painters depicted roaring modern machines in motion, novelists described the pulsing life of modern cities, industry, and the daring of pioneer fliers and African explorers. This mood was successfully interpreted by a group of wild artists who called themselves "Futurists". The name, *Futuristi*, was a coined antithesis to a non-existent *Passatisti*, or lovers of bygone times.

The Futurists felt themselves and their country imprisoned and retarded by the passive submission to the past, and not even a real past but a usually imaginary one, reconstituted by romantic scholars and antiquarians. They considered this disproportionate attachment to and reverence for their ancestors an escape from the mediocrity of contemporary Italy, an excuse for laziness, a cowardly refusal to face hard tasks, and a consolation for their impotence. Futurists believed that modern Italians should try to emulate the most modern and powerful nations, France, England, Germany, and the United States, and try to surpass and forget once and for all their past glories.

They published a revolutionary *Manifesto*, in Milan, in 1909. It is composed of random unconnected words (the "destruction of syntax" was one of its proclaimed aims). It promoted, among other things:

Antimuseum. Anticulture. Antiacademy. Antilogic. Antiprettiness. Antisentimentality. Down with Dead Cities. Modernolatry . . . Aesthetics of machines. Heroism and clownism in life and art. Pure architecture (concrete).

The movement grew very slowly. It was considered at first to be a huge joke, a scandalous *fumisterie* invented by men in bad faith who only wanted to attract attention.

We now know these young rebels were prophetic souls. Some of their architects foresaw the shape of things to come, designed dream buildings which resembled those that were erected decades later. Painters and poets left their indelible mark. The movement contributed to the birth of dadaism, cubism, and surrealism, among others. It is now recognized as one of the many revolutionary rivulets which formed the mainstreams of contemporary art and taste.

*     *     *

IT TOOK ABOUT thirty years for the preposterous, ludicrous, and absurd revolt of a handful of deranged artists against the sacred ways and styles of their country's past to become respectable. Just before the last war the stodgiest bourgeois finely considered imitation Renaissance buildings, furniture, prose, and trappings with disgust and contempt. To be sure, by that time many of the lunatic Futurists had died. Most of them had volunteered for World War I and some of the best had been killed in action. War was one of the aspects of the modern world praised by the 1909 *Manifesto*; war was filled with violence, colored rockets, noise, and modern machines; it was feared by the timid traditionalists. Others had become solemn pillars of the establishment, like the founder F. T. Marinetti. A few more had forgotten their youth and became important writers or painters with sober styles of their own.

The defeat and the end of the Fascist régime made the new task definitive. Mussolini had found office space in a (real) sixteenth-century building, Palazzo Venezia, so called because it had been built as the embassy of the Republic of Venice to the Papal State, and had furnished it with a collection of period pieces. All Fascist chieftains imitated him. Their early offices resembled stage settings for plays in which Lorenzo il Magnifico,

Machiavelli, or Savonarola could have appeared. Most of the furniture was not old, to be sure, but the homage to the past was unmistakable.

The end of the last war also opened Italy for the first time in two decades to foreign influence. Furthermore foreigners began observing Italian artistic and industrial products with new interest and started to buy them. New techniques were imported. The economic boom which followed provoked a vast re-examination of accepted habits. Young men began experimenting with daring new shapes. They designed industrial products in a bright oriental style which surprised the world. The Olivetti typewriters, the Necchi sewing machines, and Pininfarina bodies looked so startlingly new that every similar product in the world, even the most recent models, seemed immediately archaic and stodgy. New buildings sprang up here and there in Italy, obviously influenced by American trends and by contemporary functional necessities but definitely Italian in conception and execution.

The following generation of designers and architects went even further and conquered more admirers, followers, and customers. An up-to-the-minute house or executive office anywhere in Europe or the United States had to have one or two of the latest Italian-designed *objets d'art*, or industrial products camouflaged as *objets d'art*. The world was flooded with attractive and original lamps, furniture, tapestries, pottery, sculpture, jewelry, household appliances. Italian fashion designers like Emilio Pucci invented new color combinations and new styles which had little relation to official fashions.

Even in the modern world fortunately there are still jobs which only a master craftsman can do, with the help of his loyal assistants. Prototypes of all industrial products, to begin with, have to be fabricated by hand. The love and skill with which these are made in Italy are reflected later in the mass-produced articles and are probably among the reasons for their success. Unique automobile bodies, racing or *gran turismo* models designed for particular sporting events or very different clients, are still hand-fashioned by the thousands.

Then there are sailing yachts, for racing or cruising. Three builders are left in Italy who can interpret contemporary design with the taste of a century-old tradition. British and Scandinavian architects often entrust their dreams to one of these Italians, as the last artisans of other parts of Europe who possessed the ability, patience, and contempt for gain necessary to give perfection to a boat, have died more than half a century ago. The three builders are Sangermani in Lavagna (near Genoa), Carlini of Rimini, and Gino d'Este at Fiumicino Porto (near Rome). They could all make infinitely more money if they produced series of identical power boats but they contemptuously refuse to.

Or saddlery. One of the greatest saddlers in the world is Antonio Pariani of Milan, or, to be exact, the heirs of the late Antonio Pariani who carry on the family tradition. They make saddles for the great riders of two continents. There are horse shows in Dublin, London, New York, or Rome, in which almost all the saddles used are Pariani's. Old Antonio became famous about fifty years ago; he was the first to adapt the traditional English saddle to the new forward-seat, invented in Italy by Federico Caprilli at the turn of the century.

Pariani also makes personal saddles to a man's exact measurements, and finishes each only after the customer tries it, to see that it fits not only the length and thickness of his thighs and the broadness of his bottom, but the precise angles at which he keeps body and legs when walking, trotting, cantering, or jumping. Pariani too refuses to increase his yearly output and his earnings. "If we made more saddles," says the firm's manager firmly, "they might not be as good." Buyers wait six months, a year, or more for their orders.

Success has been immense. The Italian designer obviously tried to solve practical production problems (to design things that could be manufactured easily) and to make a product so attractive at the same time that buyers could not resist the temptation to bring it home with them, as it was not only a utilitarian object but a decoration. What is the Italians' secret? Bruno Munari, a great designer who sometimes teaches his art to Harvard students, wrote:

The designer tries to build an object with the same spontaneous ease with which nature shapes things. He does not try to impress his personal taste on everything but tries to be objective; he helps the object, so to speak, to form itself with its own means; and thus a fan acquires the shape a fan should really have, just as the *fiasco* has the exact shape of blown glass, and the cat has the fur a cat ought to have. Every object acquires its contemporary shape, which is not, however, a definitive shape, because techniques change, new materials are invented all the time, and at every new invention or discovery the problem is born anew and the object must change its design.

He also wrote:

The designer is the artist of our time. This is not because he is a genius, but because his work connects once again the world of art with the public, as in older ages, when artists worked for, and were understood by, everybody. He faces with humility and competence whatever tasks society imposes on him, because he knows his trade, the techniques and the means most suitable to solve each problem. Finally, he responds to the human needs of the people around him, helps them satisfy their material and psychological needs independently from hoary style prejudices . . .

In other words, the Italian designer thinks he is carrying out a revolution (or so everybody tells him) and he does so only incidentally, because what he is really doing is what craftsmen, artisans, artists, architects have always done in his country, what the Orvieto metal worker did when my grandfather ordered a new brazier for his kitchen. For the first time, he is not only doing what his ancestors did but also making full use of his native skill and talents in the modern world. His success today is due to the fact that he finally realized that the real inheritance to preserve was not the outmoded ways-of-life and obsolete ornaments but the very spirit of past centuries, when artisans humbly designed and made things for everyday use (even the picture of Our Lady for a church and the portrait of an elderly statesman were considered utilitarian objects in their day), utilizing the best techniques and materials available.

It has been noted that Italian designers have not written

much. They have not tried to justify their ways and elucidate their intentions. They have not formulated abstract aesthetic codes. In reality, they theorize very little, because most of what they are doing could not be honestly justified. They have seen beautiful things all their lives, in their houses, in museums, in the streets. They could not give an object an ugly shape even if it were the most practical and functional one. They unconsciously follow a very old tradition, from which they cannot escape, that of the makers of Renaissance Italian armor, who had to make it beautiful first, and then possibly also practical. It seems strange now that such inclinations, which are part of the national character and have enriched the world, should have been forgotten for such a long time.

# 17

# GRAND HOTEL MONTECITORIO

---

NYONE WHO KNOWS anything about post-war Italy
cannot help but conclude that all her major and minor
ills—and God alone knows how many there are and how
serious they are—can be cured by Parliament. Every senator
and deputy (including the author) ought, then, to reflect on our
confusion and chaos and, pointing at the mirror, say *"Culpa
tua."* Not that Parliament recognizes the vices we have or what
the most efficacious remedies would be; moreover, it does not
always have men capable of applying the remedies. No. Nevertheless it admits that Parliament alone has the power to make
Italy, in a few years, a modern, civilized, just, law-abiding,
cultivated, prosperous and honest country.

Italy's ills are all closely related. An educated people that has
good elementary, intermediate, technical and professional
schools and universities on the European level would not long
tolerate being badly governed and would provide a better
political and administrative class. In a country where legislation is tortuously confused and "discretionary", the bureaucracy
easily comes to have the last word, laxity spreads and anyone who really wants to get something done must always violate
some law that he has never heard of or pretends not to have
heard of. In a country run like this, even honest and serious
citizens, many of whom see in anarchy and disorder the only
safeguard of their liberty, often unite against attempts to improve matters.

Parliament ought to remedy all this, and could remedy it if
it wanted to. A good first step would be for it to learn what it
can from its past for the sake of future generations. Everyone

knows what happens when a parliament loses all authority and does not fulfill its function. Dictatorial and authoritarian groups from Left and Right rush into the vacuum produced by its ineptitude. Not by chance do totalitarian parties begin their rise to power by paralyzing and discrediting parliaments. They are enthusiastically abetted in this preparatory phase by democratic parties incapable of defending the common good because they are absorbed in the sordid struggle for petty demagogic and electoral advantages.

In politics as in history, not facing up to one's duties must be considered a deliberate act of the will. The feeble democratic parties at Montecitorio and in the Reichstag were as responsible as the Fascist and Nazi parties for Mussolini's and Hitler's rise to power. The man strolling in the woods on a summer day who absent-mindedly forgets to put out his match before tossing it into dry grass is an incendiary. The doctor who forgets to give medicine to a patient is as guilty of murder as one who prescribes poison. Likewise the one organ of the State that could renovate Italian society and does not do so is guilty not only of the poverty, ignorance and backwardness of a large part of the people, but of an even graver crime: discrediting the only organ that can preserve liberty—Parliament itself.

*       *       *

WHY DOESN'T the Italian Parliament face up to its duties?

It is feeble first of all because it is peopled largely by mediocrities. Electoral laws, deteriorating customs, cynicism, party machines that prefer the docile helots to men of character, relatively low rewards and the fact that the generation now in power was brought up under Fascism—all this helps discourage first-rate men from political careers. Moreover, the galloping industrialization of Italy now absorbs most of the capable young men, offering them a status, security, and standard of living that Parliament cannot in the present state of things guarantee.

Many measures for dealing with these problems are under study and are being discussed in the press and in the cafés of provincial capitals. These measures include proposals for changing electoral laws, increasing the emolument of members of Parliament, changing the character of the senate by restoring to it, at least in part, its ancient function as the House of life peers, the Areopagus of worthy and reliable elderly Italians in every field, men not preoccupied with the worry of being constantly re-elected.

It is however difficult to resolve such problems simply by legal devices. Every time one ill is remedied a new loophole is found. Only the pressure of public opinion can in the long run really change the prevailing political customs and compel parties and members of Parliament always to put the interest of the people before their own. But even if the senators and deputies were all men of great ability, unselfish, honest, able, hard-working and independent, Parliament as it is now set up would always find it difficult to function. There are additional reasons for its decadence. The first and most obvious is material. It seems insignificant but in reality is important, perhaps sometimes decisively important. The buildings in which the business of legislation is pursued are not adapted to their function today.

As everyone knows, the new additions to Montecitorio palace look like an *art nouveau* Kursaal, or a hotel for people taking mineral waters in the Germany of Wilhelm II. Here you can find almost everything that a luxury hotel boasts: an immense hall where guests pace interminably to and fro, a barber, baths, a travel agent, a bank, reading and writing rooms, a post office, telephone booths, clusters of uniformed *commessi* ready at the slightest nod, a bar where you can grab a bite on the run, a good restaurant. The only things missing are a newspaper stand and a small orchestra for dinner music.

But it is a grand hotel without rooms, where one wanders about like a traveler to whom the desk clerk has promised a room as soon as one is free. An ordinary deputy has no private office, no secretary, no telephone by which he can be reached. He cannot receive visitors. Anyone looking for him waits hours while a page locates him—or fails to. Often deputies who wish to confer cannot find each other. There is no sure way of meeting anyone. Sometimes urgent messages arranging vague appointments are left in the letter boxes; then all one can do is hope.

You wander about, pockets stuffed with letters to be answered, your head crammed with things to be done, things to be said, various problems. You talk interminably and pointlessly in "the Transatlantic" (the lobby) or sit distractedly in the chamber listening to an unimportant speech. You waste hours. You can't leave. Who would send for you if you were suddenly needed?

This kind of organization might have suited our fathers and grandfathers. The deputies then had little to do. Sessions were shorter. There were relatively few bills and they were drafted seriously by bureaus and agencies and studied at length by committees. The tasks of Parliament were less burdensome. Neither directly nor indirectly did the State concern itself with all the picayune details of everyone's daily life. Talking, exchanging ideas, gathering and disseminating information, negotiating with other groups, exploring the opinions of others, were among the principal jobs of the politician. No one, or almost no one, used the telephone. What few letters there were, one wrote in longhand . . .

In Italy the only deputies who have secretaries are party leaders (whose secretaries are paid by the party), wealthy senators and deputies (who pay for their own), and those who agree to have them paid for by some institution, office, organization, power group, confederation, society which will furnish secretaries, automobiles, chauffeurs, ready-made legislative drafts of bills, complete studies on specific topics—in exchange, of course, for specific services that are not always inspired by concern for the welfare of the whole. Why shouldn't the poor but honest deputy have a clerk or a secretary?

There is considerable discussion of the urgent need for modern, functional buildings. They've been talking about this for years. Montecitorio has reserved a plot of land for this purpose in the piazza beside the main building. It is now a parking lot for the clerks and officials of the chamber, an elegant roofed parking lot. Why not open a competition among architects, approve plans, appropriate the necessary funds and let out the contracts? Why not solve the problem? Some say that the officials and clerks are holding things up in order not to lose their parking lot. Probably nothing is being done because too many people find it convenient to have a parliament that stumbles about without vigor, ideas, or effectiveness.

Even if Parliament had better men and they were accommodated in functional buildings, it would still need legal and technical experts before it could cope with the tasks of today. In fact, as it now is, it has neither eyes nor ears; it does not possess the organs to know exactly what is going on in Italy or to follow the workings of the various ministries and hence the workings of the government.

The errors, abuses, inefficiencies, waste, deviousness, stupidity and negligence of the State machine are pointed out haphazardly by newspapers and by letters from constituents. The deputy then puts a question to the minister or demands an explanation. The minister seldom replies. (The only questions ministers answer promptly are those they have a friend ask so that they can justify some public statement on a topic of deep personal concern.) If the minister happens to reply, the answer is often valueless. It is written by the very bureaucrats who were accused of the failing and denies that the failing exists, or justifies it.

*          *          *

WHAT IS NEEDED is an appropriate plant and personnel directly under Parliament to follow closely and objectively the various problems, the functioning of the entire State apparatus and especially the budget estimate and administrative expenses. As things stand today, the budget estimate is not examined and checked seriously enough. In general, it is not a political document which testifies to government's intentions, assigning money for various objectives, graduating the amounts allocated and scheduling priorities. It is simply a long patchwork list of the sums the administration needs, with often hopelessly confused and incomprehensible explanations. The greater part of it, however, no government can modify, for it is made up of the sums set aside for salaries, pensions, interest on loans, amortization, etc.

Discussion of the budget absorbs more than half the time of the sessions. What discussion? The budget is unalterable. You can take it or leave it. The Government supporters invariably vote for it; the Opposition, against. The budget is mysteriously worked out by the bureaucracy of government "A", is presented to Parliament by government "B", which accepts criticism and proposals for modifications for the following year, when, it is hoped, government "C" will put them into effect. Then why spend so many sessions discussing it and make so many interminable speeches that leave things just as they are?

Moreover, Parliament never learns exactly or quickly where the money has gone. Actual expenditures are seen only after long delay and are mysteriously compiled. Have the monies allocated really been used for the purposes for which they were intended? Frequently Parliament can find out only by reading the newspapers.

The number of draft bills that deputies and senators belonging to the governing majority can introduce should be limited. (Those in the opposition clearly do what they please, and it would be neither constitutional nor democratic to prevent them.) The flood of meaningless bills, which is today paralyzing every office and impeding the rapid flow of more serious business, should end. At the moment of writing, for example, over four thousand bills—a great number of which have to do with the economic improvement of restricted groups of government employees or which interest only a part of the population— await the action of the Chamber of Deputies.

Let us look at some. Draft Bill 4075: "Allotment to communal and provincial secretaries of a non-pensionable monthly payment of 70 lire for every civil service rating point." Draft 4064: "Extension to communal and provincial secretaries and to employees of local bureaus and agencies of the benefits provided in the law of April 19, 1962, 176." Draft 4027: "To increase the contribution to the National Assistance and Welfare Board for Painters and Sculptors," etc. etc.

Naturally, the wheels of the parliamentary machine are slowed by all these bills as by a sea of mud. Many, in fact, have no chance of becoming law. The deputies who drafted them sometimes don't even trouble to push them through regular channels or to urge the appropriate committees to examine them. For the most part they are empty gestures, vote-getting documents, declarations of affection for a town, a category of workers, a sector of industry, equivalent to a postcard showing that the Honorable Member has thought of them, his dear constituents. In fact, some are even entered the day before a session closes, when all drafts of necessity end up in the hopper.

A parliament fully aware of its historic duties could in a few weeks enact those changes that would enable it to function better. In a few years it could function perfectly. It could give itself the eyes and ears that it lacks, the specialized personnel and offices to study problems seriously, conduct research, prepare preliminary material. It could follow day by day the workings of the governmental machinery in which it has placed its trust and see if it is worthy of that trust. By its offices it could help draw up the budget, make it a serious political document and see to it that funds were spent as was intended.

But above all it could turn its attention to the most urgent matters, the reform of legislation and of the State apparatus. A clear, simple, brief, condensed, co-ordinated, efficient legislation administered by a modern and efficient bureaucracy ought to please everyone. Unfortunately, nothing like this is happening and there is no expectation that it will. The grounds for my reluctant yet persisting pessimism I will return to in a subsequent chapter.

# *18*

# IT'S DIFFERENT IN THE SOUTH

I N THE LIGHT *of its cost and results, the policy for the rebirth of the* Mezzogiorno *may be considered:* ***a great failure, a modest success, a great success, a triumph?*** (MARK YOUR CHOSEN SQUARE WITH A CROSS.)

I should not be surprised to be asked this question some day, by some institute specializing in public opinion polls. Above all I should not be surprised because, like nearly all questions of the kind, it is formulated in equivocal tendentious terms. What does "rebirth of the *Mezzogiorno*" actually mean? I know: it is the formula everyone uses—politicians, technicians, bureaucrats, journalists. But it is, all the same, a further proof of the confusion of language that corresponds to the confusion of ideas in Italy today.

A man is reborn who has been born once already, and, figuratively speaking, a man is reborn when, after a period of decline, he goes back to the thriving life he once knew. But when did the *Mezzogiorno* ever thrive, when was it ever more thriving than the center and North of Italy? When, in historical times, have the great majority of Southerners (not a picked minority) eaten twice a day, lived in decent houses, worn adequate clothes? And who ever stole prosperity from them? What diabolical plot by all-powerful villains has paralyzed the activity and enterprise of the South?

The question would not surprise me, either, because it is formulated in a way that makes it impossible to give a single honest answer to it. To measure the success of any undertaking, including the enormous efforts made to push the South into the twentieth century, one must compare the results obtained not just with the situation as it was before (like the "Before" and "After" pictures in the old advertisements for hair tonic), but with the hopes universally aroused, the promises solemnly announced, the targets publicly proclaimed.

Nor is this all, of course. Before giving a responsible answer it would be useful, though perhaps impossible, to have some further information. What would have been the result if the same amount of money had been spent in another way? And what has the vigorous economic development of the rest of Italy, of Western Europe, and the rest of the world, done to improve conditions in the *Mezzogiorno* from 1950 until today?—an economic development that has both encouraged the demand for products from the South and urged millions of Southern workers to emigrate. . . .

What, then was the object of pouring in lire by the thousand million, of all this unprecedented investment by the State and by private interests, of these ambitious plans for public works and these vast loans raised both inside and outside the country? Was it just to improve the lot of Southerners, simply to drag them out of their poverty and their age-old resignation and apathy? Was it merely to start up industries, to open mines, to bring in the tourists?

If this was the case, then the policy for the "rebirth" of the South may be considered a success; expensive, perhaps, with the results not always in proportion to the effort made, because billions have been wasted in plans that were unworkable (or else spectacular but unproductive), or have ended up in dishonest pockets or been used for purely electoral purposes; but a success all the same. No one can deny that the *Mezzogiorno* is no longer what is was only a few years ago. Its progress is visible and can be documented.

*          *          *

THE IMPRESSION that the superficial traveler gets is indeed rosy. Everywhere he sees new roads, new ports, new hotels, new factories, new schools, new modern districts in the towns; and the science-fiction air of a good deal of this, the prosperous appearance of the people (Southerners seem not just better dressed and better fed but actually taller, perhaps because they have taken on a new dignity), the large number of cars, all make one suppose the *Mezzogiorno* is a modern country, bursting with enterprise.

Of course, beyond the hedges of prickly pear bush, along the dusty country roads, behind the gleaming modern house-fronts, in the crumbling parts of the large towns and in small country towns, the ancient, desperate poverty *still* remains. In many villages only old people and children live—and wretchedly at that. The men have emigrated and the countryside is empty. People left behind talk with their century-old skepticism, but now embittered by terrible new disappointments, by the certainty that only the cunning and the dishonest can get on and then mostly by illegal means, which means that honest people get nowhere and that injustice in the South may change names, methods, and appearance but will never be eradicated.

All the same, even these people cannot deny that, as a whole, there is a great deal *less* poverty than there was. Whole provinces are unrecognizable, factories have been built, hundreds of thousands of workers have found decent work at home, others are helped by the fact that there is more money about, however it is spent, and even if it does not profit them directly. Illiteracy is decreasing, some powerful families have grown rich, and millions of emigrants have eased the burden of unemployment and send money home.

All this might lead one to conclude that, if the purpose was merely that of improving some of the things that were wrong and raising some of the people from the state to which they were once condemned, then the policy for the South over the past few years has, for all its faults, produced positive results.

\*     \*     \*

BUT WHAT SOME HAD HOPED FOR was not just to improve their own lot, a little or substantially, but to proceed towards the economic, social, and cultural level of the center and North of Italy and the rest of Europe, to close the gap between the "two Italies" and even, shortly, to have parts of the South, or some particular sector of production, overtake the North in efficiency, seriousness, and productivity. If these hopes are borne in mind then the same policy must be called a resounding, expensive failure (as could have been foreseen from the beginning), and, what is worse, an historical opportunity lost for ever.

The fact that politically, economically, and morally the whole thing has failed is of course now firmly believed (and denounced) by eminent experts of Southern problems; those who, twenty years ago, ingenuously thought that the only desirable aim was to "catch up with the North" or to overtake it; and that it could be easily reached.

The matter is important because the psychological and political repercussion of this failure will afflict Italians' lives for decades to come. Southerners, like everyone else, quickly forget what they have suffered for centuries, but angrily remember the recent promises which have not been kept; everyone resents the fact that the center and north of Italy is advancing at a faster rate than the *Mezzogiorno*, and that the gap between the two is every year becoming more impossible to bridge.

It is impossible to bridge, in fact, because Southern people are not comparing the South with what the North really is—a North that has faults which seem almost Southern, with its own squalid, depressed areas and its own shabby poverty. They are comparing their own part of the country to a marvellous North spun out of envy and imagination, where everyone is rich and punctual, everything works perfectly, everything is modern, and the girls are all blonde and beddable.

The failure of this policy, as well as the relative success of the more modest policy, can easily be documented through figures.

(1) In 1951, the South's net product was 1,825 thousand million lire; in 1963, at today's values, it was 5,847 thousand million. In the same period (i.e. from 1951 to 1963) the net product of the center and the North went up from 5,763 to 23,336 thousand million at today's values.

(2) Investments in the *Mezzogiorno* went up from 541 thousand million in 1951 to 2,019 in 1963; during the same

period in the center and North, they rose from 1,641 to 5,674. As far as new industrial plants are concerned, the gap between the two Italies is alarming. From 1966 to 1969 the increase in the North alone was 45 per cent; in the South, in spite of plans to force on development, it was 13 per cent.

(3) This difference of growth is reflected in the export figures. Between 1953 and 1967, Italian exports rose dizzily, from 942 thousand million to over 4,000; but the amount of agricultural products exported fell from 15·3 per cent to 8 per cent, and it was the agricultural exports of the South that fell in particular, while the figures for agricultural products grown or processed in the North actually rose.

(4) The figures giving workers' employment confirm the same trend. Between the census of 1951 and that of 1961 the number of non-agricultural workers in the South increased by 700,000 (2·3 per cent per annum), whereas in the center and the North it increased by 2,700,000, or 3·1 per cent per annum. The percentages for the decade are 16 per cent for the South as opposed to 36 per cent for the center and the North.

\*　　\*　　\*

WHO IS RESPONSIBLE for this state of affairs? What are its likely causes? It is hard to say. The fault lies mainly with the simplified diagnoses which have called for cures that were too simplistic and encouraged an excessive and dangerous optimism. These diagnoses are not, repeat not, often made by the most responsible experts of the *problema*, but are clumsy popular misconceptions taken up at second or third hand by men of action who have no time to study the matter. No one seems to have realized that the problem was not merely political and economic but above all sociological.

People started off on the presumption that Southerners were in reality for the most part Northerners frustrated by history and the wickedness of others; that is, men who had more or less the same ideals in life and the same capacities as Northerners and who merely needed money, suitable laws, incentives, and encouragement in order to turn into *entrepreneurs*, industrialists, financiers, managers, and technicians. This is unfortunately not true.

Southerners can, indeed, become at times excellent Northerners, first-class workers and capable executives, provided they get away from their own society. Often they not only fit happily into other societies but manage to get into positions of authority and to make a success of them. Where Southerners have to make enormous efforts to succeed (and seldom do) is in the South.

The reason is that Southern tradition, especially among the lower and middle bourgeoisie, encourages ideals that are not economic. They prefer to sacrifice wealth to positions of command, authority, and prestige. Northern Italians, on the other hand, prefer affluence, even in obscurity.

This attitude means that when Southern bourgeois emigrate to the center and north of Italy they are alarmingly good at getting to the top. Sometimes they also manage to get extremely well-paid jobs in industry, but as a rule these are jobs in which technical knowledge matters less than the technique of acquiring and defending power. An example of this is the huge success of Sicilian financiers and stock exchange speculators in Milan in recent years, who have dominated the market, bought, sold, and merged banks, holding companies, insurance companies, and firms of all sorts.

This lack of understanding of the Southern character is odd in politicians and experts who were mostly born and brought up in the South. It has made the problem seem easier than it is, to be solved practically with the opening of credits. It has also meant that the real quantities of Southerners have not been best used in their own and the national interest; it has slowed down or distorted a program of gradual social change.

Among the causes of the trouble is the fact that little notice has been taken of precedents in other countries. In many parts of the world, both Communist and non-Communist, similar experiments have been carried on for decades, to turn agricultural depressed areas into modern industrial areas. Many mistakes have been made by others, millions of dollars, rupees, dinars, and rubles wasted, but there have been many successes as well. The mistakes have shown that there are analogous inflexible rules to follow, in order to avoid waste, in both the free and the Communist countries.

\*     \*     \*

FIRST OF ALL, what already exists must be encouraged in every way; that is, whatever activities nature itself has created, because these have a better objective chance of prospering. To begin with, agriculture must be modernized and the most promising local crafts turned into proper industries. Larger industries can then be built, carefully, on this foundation; these will partly be linked to earlier activities, that is to those that can prosper without help, and then, gradually, increasingly important industries and their ancillary organizations will rise spontaneously. Public works programs must be launched at the same time to provide the necessary structures. Criteria for determining which investments will do well are more or less the same on either side of the ideological frontier. That is, it has been found that, generally speaking, what is economically best is also best, in the end, from a social point of view.

In particular it has been proved that, although nothing can be done without capital, capital alone is not enough. The right men are needed as well. Good workmen are necessary (and there are plenty in the South), but also good *entrepreneurs*, industrialists, executives, organizers, financiers, salesmen, economists and managers. In other words, a serious technical middle-class, educated for what it has to do, honest, responsible, active; one that can judge problems, pick men, make plans, and successfully carry out difficult operations in surroundings that are sometimes hostile.

To cultivate a class like this may not be impossible, but it is very difficult. It needs a wide-ranging plan involving education at all levels, and scholarships to send the best students abroad;

it means setting up apprenticeship schemes in the most indus-
trially developed areas, awards to encourage the best, and strict
rules of promotion through merit. All this cannot be set up
haphazardly. It takes years, possibly one or two generations
before its results are seen in practice. And, as everyone knows,
it is the lack of this kind of men that has held back the South in
the past and today makes its rapid development difficult.

To these deficiencies of the *Mezzogiorno* must be added the
faults that today bedevil the whole of Italy. The machinery of
State is decrepit; the simplest decisions wait years for Parliamentary decisions and agreement from the Ministries; sober
responsible men have no defense against party pressures; there is
a shortage of trained civil servants who know the problems and
their background; and the funds allocated often have to provide
a rake-off to parties in power and key-men before they reach
their destination.

Apart from all this the policy for the South has been formulated by a political class that was largely unready for it, and sometimes filled with the crudest prejudices. It includes many men
without experience, who know little of the practical problems
of the world today. They are suspicious of private enterprise,
without the help of which it is hard to industrialize a Western
country; on the other hand, they believe rather oddly in the
miraculous power of money alone. They pursue power for themselves and for their group as the most important object, which
means that they often tend to turn what could be a productive
investment into a sterile but colourful alms-giving for limited
electoral purposes.

They are always tempted to favor their friends and relations,
and often think of a factory not as a machine to produce goods
but as a monument to set up in their home town, without considering whether it is useful or suitable. Finally, they share the
simple hopes of the local people: that is, they believe it is
possible for the South to "catch up with the North and to overtake it. . . ."

*　　　　*　　　　*

THE RESULT is what we know has happened. Billions have been poured into the South from 1951 until today. It is hard to say exactly what the figures are, because they include ordinary funds, extraordinary funds, grants from the *Cassa del Mezzogiorno*, State contributions to interest charges on loans for new industries, expensive salvage operations to bolster up weak industries, loans from the various international organizations, private, national, and foreign investments, and so on.

Most of this money, after stopping off in the South, has eventually found its way to the Po valley, thus encouraging further the economic development of the North, which is the opposite of what it was meant to do! The salaries of the Northern technicians and managers, who often leave their families at home, went North; so did the money to buy nearly all the machinery (as happened in the case of the Alfa-Romeo automobile plant to be built in Naples); so did the eventual shareholders' dividends and profits of the parent company. The improvement in living standards naturally increased the demand for products which only the North could provide, cars, television sets, textiles, electric household appliances, and everything for the building and furnishing of houses. And the money which Southerners were increasingly depositing in banks and in post-office savings also went North, to be invested in an economic area free from political pressures.

Around the hand-outs from the *Cassa del Mezzogiorno*, which could so easily be influenced by politicians, there hung (and still hang) crowds of petitioners, most of them quite incapable of setting up and running an industry or indeed any serious enterprise, but extremely skillful at obtaining political favors. Some of them used part of the money received to build ghost-factories which could not produce goods at competitive prices, and were closed down the day they were completed because the company owning them went bankrupt straight away. The real business lay in building the plants, not in running them, which could only have been done at a loss.

\*        \*        \*

THERE ARE, TO BE SURE, also serious modern firms, running efficient factories, but most of them are too modern for the primitive conditions in which they are set. Signor Libertini, a Member of Parliament, recently said in a speech to the House:

As you go along the motorway from here to Naples you see all kinds of thriving industries and get the impression that you are passing through a prosperous district. But when you stop and ask how things are, you realize that there is less work than ever because half these industries have just failed, and the other half are just about to fail.

It is not just on the motorway to Naples that you can see this; it can be seen all over the South and the islands. The *Mezzogiorno*, which was known to our fathers as the "cemetery of public works", may now be turning into a "cemetery of industrial plants" as well.

There are Northern industrialists, too, who have realized how the hand-outs really work and used them ingeniously for their own purposes. They set up firms in the South, with powerful friends to back them, fill the workshops with the latest machines, that are sometimes imported duty-free and always bought at bargain prices and with subventions of every kind. Then, after the factory has been opened, they quietly send part of the machinery up North, dismiss most of their workers, and carry on with what is left of the place (if it is not closed down altogether) at a much slower rate.

There are, however, a few large, serious, and extremely modern firms that produce goods at competitive prices, export at an ever-increasing rate, and thrive in an enviable way. They are nearly always set up by large private firms from the North or by State-owned mother industries. But they too contribute relatively little to the prosperity of the South. Some of them are so modern that they need few hands, and those nearly all highly skilled. They provide work for a few technicians, a few accountants, and a small number of office staff and workmen.[1]

---

[1] An oil refinery in Sicily, run almost entirely by automation, some time ago decided to surround the works with large gardens, in order to employ a few hundred local men, who from a strictly productive point of view were completely superfluous.

Other outsize works arise in all their technical perfection, like the pyramids of Egypt in the desert, in districts that are still too backward to be able to make use of the advantages their presence might provide. The steel-works at Taranto (envied by the Americans and the Russians) have not produced any noticeable metal-works around them. The large chemical and oil works at Priolo in Sicily have not produced any medium and light industries locally, using the materials turned out on the spot.

Are these faults, which everyone recognizes and which have often been denounced in the press and in Parliament, being corrected? Dr Guido Carli, Governor of the Bank of Italy, explained in 1966:

The spread of easy credit means that those who ask for it think they have a right to credit; and the institutes that give credit are mainly influenced in their decisions by considerations of the social usefulness of investments. And, through a process of natural selection in reverse, among organizations and banks with varying traditions those with most experience—best equipped, that is, to examine critically the assets, financial and economic position, and organization of firms— are overtaken by others more likely to grant every application, certain that this will be approved by those that decide how things shall be shared out.

Easy credit is becoming more and more a matter of giving alms; and its extension increases the feeling that its principal purpose is to deal with local situations, which means that the giving of credit becomes increasingly subject to interference that threatens the objectivity of the bodies that give it. Collaboration with the political authorities, far from being confined to matters of general economic interest, is now sought in particular cases and uses credit to solve problems connected with them.

\* \* \*

IT IS CLEAR that if things go on as they are the problem will become worse instead of better, because every year the North will advance at an increasing rate, helped in this advance by the vast sums handed out to the South and the islands. This is an explosive problem that might endanger social stability, internal peace, and the very unity of Italy. Minister Taviani, for the

*Mezzogiorno*, rightly said at the last Christian Democrats' congress that it was not "a" problem but "the" Italian problem.

It is now clear from what has happened that it is not just a simple economic problem, the kind that can be solved by increasing the amount of money allotted. A systematic social transformation is needed to give people the outlook needed for the economic development of their country and to allow them to take advantage of their natural resources, which are few, and above all of their resources of industriousness and intelligence, which are plentiful.

As always in such cases one must start from the foundations, which have been neglected: agriculture and education. No place can thrive economically if its agriculture is primitive and choked. Everyone knows that the problem of agricultural production no longer exists. Everything can practically be produced anywhere. What does exist is the problem of marketing agricultural products. They must be sold when they can command the best price, and they must be of the quality and kind demanded by consumers. People are beginning to realize this in the South, but slowly. Enormous amounts of capital are needed to transform farms, educate agriculturalists, and bring in experts from more advanced countries than ours. Sicily must follow and overtake Israel before it can beat Milan.

*Education.* The problem is a national one, but the South could be out in front with large institutes to train specialists in organization, experts in all the difficult modern techniques, managers, marketing experts and so on, as well as schools to turn unskilled into skilled workers. Without trained personnel at every level economic progress today is unthinkable.

*Credit.* It should be given (as Carli suggests) severely and shrewdly, by banks protected from political pressures. It should go to industries and enterprises that show a natural likelihood of surviving and prospering. On a framework of medium-sized industries larger and then very large industries could later be built, and they would then find suitable surroundings and plenty of customers on the spot.

Above all, prestige-industries should be avoided, the kind

that Southerners think they must have to prove to themselves they are no longer underdeveloped, the kind that remind electors of the name of the Minister who set them up, but which have no chance of prospering. Among those to be avoided are duplicates of Northern industries already well established. What should be chosen at first are plants that process local agricultural products, and completely new activities based on recent inventions, which have had no chance, yet, of putting down roots elsewhere.

\*　　\*　　\*

IF ALL THIS WAS DONE, which seems highly unlikely, the South would become part of the great economic currents of the modern world, and would be dragged finally into twentieth-century Europe. But it would not reach, within the next few years, the level of life in the North, unless (as many people cautiously suggest) the progress of the North were slowed down.

Why is it so unlikely that the gap between North and South will soon start to grow smaller instead of growing steadily larger? Above all, because the North has an old technically-minded middle class, so serious that to Southerners it seems dreary, which proliferates in each generation like bacteria on a culture; a class that is tirelessly able to found new firms, run those already established, modernize old plants, invent new initiatives, and set up advertising campaigns and sales and export drives. These people, who are experienced with money and respect it, rarely bite off more than they can chew.

The hundreds of firms set up every day in the North are strictly planned from the point of view of costs, modernity of techniques, scarcity of the product on the market, political competitors, and foreseeable sales. These enterprises are hardly ever short of money. In today's world, money is one of the easiest materials to find, at least for anyone who has what it takes to reassure the international brokers of capital.

\*　　\*　　\*

THE "TWO ITALIES" finally are divided (as I have suggested) by their basic outlook. For centuries the South has, for historical and other reasons, been dreaming solely of alms handed out from above by the Prince; and this means that today it is always (or nearly always) still dreaming mainly of help from the State. State support has some important advantages, to be sure, and in some cases there can be no alternative to it. But by its nature it is slow, clumsy, timid, short-sighted, always late, and it takes a tiresome amount of political string-pulling.

In the same amount of time the Northern industrialist makes up his mind, draws up plans, finds money, builds and runs new plants, gets back what he spent, pays his debts, accumulates assets, and starts thinking about new enterprises, conceived according to more advanced techniques, more modern, more efficient, and more profitable.

For these reasons, if I were asked "Is the policy for the rebirth of the South a failure or a success?" I should, if I were to be candid, answer: "That depends. . . ."

# 19

# THE COMMUNISTS, AND THE LOCOMOTIVE OF HISTORY

W HY HAVE the Communists not yet come to power in Italy? Will they do so and, if they do, when (in the indeterminate future, after the next elections in 1973, next autumn, or next month, and how (violently, surreptitiously, or legally)? Is there any organization or institution left in the country powerful and respected enough to cope with them? What can still be tried, which has not been tried before, to ward off their final triumph, or possibly to attenuate its disagreeable consequences? These questions have once again become as pressing as they were twenty-odd years ago, just after the war and before the 1948 elections when the Party suffered a great if temporary setback.

This may be surprising to foreign observers, who know that so many things have happened which should have long ago exorcised the specter haunting Italy. Tito, who represented an armed threat on the Eastern border, is no longer a Moscow vassal but a friendly neutral; Stalin and Palmiro Togliatti have died; Marxist republics and Communist parties everywhere are torn by doubts and discontent; the class struggle has been attenuated into a mannered joust by affluence, a flood of home appliances, and cheap automobiles; Italy, which lay prostrate, ruined, starving, and hopeless, is now a prosperous industrialized country holding its own among the best. Why should a Communist victory still seem so probable and the danger so frightening?

The reasons, of course, are many and complex. Perhaps one

of the decisive ones is that for a quarter of a century, all vital
political decisions were distorted by the dramatic necessity to
prevent an imminent Communist takeover by all means available. This obsessed Italian voters, Roman party leaders, the
Catholic Church, the U.S. State Department, and it inevitably
justified a number of ambiguous and ingenious stratagems and
subterfuges, the launching of wasteful and demagogic projects,
the ruthless manipulation of news, the hushing up of all scandals
involving parties in power, the formation of unnatural and
inefficient coalitions. Parties pursued the public interest only
incidentally; most of the time they exerted themselves to build
up their own financial and political power, and their electoral
following, often by dubious means, in order to cope with the
Communist menace.

They necessarily postponed the solutions of many fundamental problems, which were not commonly judged of primary
importance in the struggle against the Marxist-Leninists.
Good things were done at the same time, to be sure, some of
them important; but many more were left undone. (The
country, to mention one, is *still* awkwardly ruled by the Fascist
penal code!) As a result, the political situation has deteriorated,
and the bitter discontent of the lower classes, which feeds the
expansive power of the Party, increased steadily as the years
went by, instead of diminishing. The economic boom, which
many thought would do the trick, did not help. It is commonplace that unrest often grows with industrial development, and
that the majority of workers entertain dreams of revolution not
when they suffer privations but when their living conditions
improve and their expectations rise.

\*     \*     \*

THE ITALIAN SITUATION is not, as many think, merely a
marginal and picturesque one. It may be worth paying some
attention to. The consequences of the deterioration and possible
failure of the liberal and democratic parties could be calamitous,
not only for the future of the country itself, but also for the

balance of power which is now precariously assuring the peace of the world. Italy has a unique geographic position that would be important even if it were uninhabited. The Po valley is a glacis between East and West; the rest of the peninsula a mole dominating vital communications in the Mediterranean. Most of the wars for the control of the world were decided by naval battles in this general area: Actium, Lepanto, Aboukir, Trafalgar, Navarrino, and Cape Matapan, among others.

That politics in Italy can be dangerous for all is a well known fact among specialists. It was "to prevent a Bolshevik victory" that young Italians marched on Rome in 1922. They thought that they too could save Italy not by seriously tackling all the problems but by the use of arbitrary power, intimidation, and subterfuges, more in the style of the Mafia than the rule of law; they set up an oppressive and inefficient régime buttressed by police and propaganda, and spread a smokescreen of rhetoric over their failings. In the end, they helped provoke the Second World War which left their country a mass of rubble. The Italian Communist Party emerged as the largest in Europe, outside the Soviet Union, and the wisest of all. One is tempted to conclude from past experience that, for the safety of the rest of the world, the only way the Italians should follow to defeat Communism is a simple one—to govern as well and honestly as possible, taking on all the real problems, and to placate the people's discontent by trying to give them the efficient institutions necessary in a modern land. This has never been tried. Everything else, no matter how alluring, is to be considered a dangerous panacea which makes matters worse: a charlatan's nostrum.

*　　*　　*

THAT "NOTHING" WILL PREVENT Italy from becoming a Marxist Republic one day soon, firmly ruled by a proletarian dictatorship, is an article of faith only among millions of Communist rank-and-file members and their associated voters. (Many hold expensive Party bond issues which will be "redeemed after the final victory over the forces of imperialism and reaction".) The cadres are more prudent and less sanguine. They soberly deduce from the reality surrounding them that a serious breakdown of the State machinery is to be expected sooner or later, and they believe that the parties in power are too weak, befuddled, demoralized, tired, and paralyzed by internal squabbles, to face the coming emergency. They concede that their Party will almost inevitably be entrusted with a vital role, whether it wants it or not, as it is the second largest party and the only coherent political force of the Left with the necessary discipline, doctrine, experience, and authority. They will not shirk their responsibilities, when the time comes, and will do their duty.

What will their role be exactly? Here they are in a quandary.

Will the Party come to *de facto* forms of collaboration with the government? Or, to save itself from the general wreckage, must it face the inevitability of armed revolution? Can a civil war be avoided? What will the Western Allies do? And, in case of victory, what shape will Marxism-Leninism *all'italiana* assume? Many expect to be truly unorthodox, as they have timidly proclaimed themselves in print, but are they "unorthodox" enough to forgo the advantages of a one-party police state once they are in charge? The old handbooks on how to make a revolution and establish the dictatorship of the proletariat are all obsolete. They became useless after the Soviet invasion of Czechoslovakia. All this is complicated by the fact that international Communism is tortured by a vast schismatic struggle, and by the sporadic warfare between the two greatest Marxist empires. The Italian Party itself is in a crisis: it has changed from the simple and ruthless organization of the Bolshevik fathers to the subtle, Machiavellian and Italianized (but just as ruthless) organization of the sons. Furthermore, the prodigious economic boom in Italy made the radical re-appraisal of traditional positions inevitable. Will today's well-fed workers obey as easily as the starving unemployed did? The old Stalinist élite is decrepit, and the young are uncertain. Many of them have become accustomed to (and some are also secretly fond of) the prestige and bourgeois liberties enjoyed by eloquent revolutionaries in

Western democracies. What will they do? Can they really take power?

\* \* \*

THE PARTY is still conditioned by the Togliatti inheritance. It was Togliatti himself who prevented the Communists from taking power in the years immediately following the liberation, when they could have done so by merely giving a few orders. The Allied armies had vanished; the government was disarmed and impotent; the middle class was terrorized and divided; the country was in turmoil; the economy in ruins; the people (accustomed to authoritarian rule) were desperate and hungry. The Party was rich, powerful, disciplined, and still controlled a secret and well-oiled military machine. It had an immense following of fanatic and impatient chiliasts. In the government until 1947, it infiltrated loyal men in key positions at all levels: in the bureaucracy, armed forces, railways, telegraphs, telephones, radio, and many vital industries. Even the switchboards of several Ministries were in its hands. The rank-and-file pleaded with Togliatti: *"Quando si smura?"* (or "When do we break down the walls behind which our weapons are stored?"). It was Togliatti alone who did not believe the moment had come. He once explained his point of view in these words:

The British and the Americans had no intention of allowing the Italians to decide their own future and could not allow a definitive blow to be struck against the old capitalistic system. We were all seriously engaged merely to secure a minimum of autonomy for Italy. The recognition of Italian independence would have been withdrawn at the first signs of an ascendancy of the workers' parties and, more especially, if the Communist Party appeared to triumph, ready to eliminate the reactionary classes. A period of enslavement could then be considered inevitable for the country, a semi-colonial period under foreign control, which would have driven the workers' movement underground. . . .[1]

Many now consider his fears excessive in retrospect, i.e. not thoroughly based on the sober valuation of realities which Marx

[1] *Conversando con Togliatti,* by Marcella and Maurizio Ferrara (Edizioni di Cultura Sociale, Rome, 1953), p. 361.

recommends. For one thing, he attributed to the British and Americans the kind of logic, clarity and iron determination which Marxists always attribute to their satanic class enemy. His thinking was possibly also distorted by a subconscious need to hide his personal temperament behind intricate political justifications. He was no hot-blooded revolutionary. He personally disliked violence, massacres, and mass deportations, although he had to tolerate such things all his life. They were a disagreeable aspect of his job. He was by nature a gentle philosopher, known in his old Comintern days as a man who could always write a subtle thesis proving anything at all or its contrary, whatever in fact the leaders needed to prove. His own personal inclinations, his compulsive love of tidiness and thrift, made him prefer a gradual and well directed transformation of society to convulsive, haphazard, and wasteful revolts, whose results could never be determined before hand. (He was suspected at one time of being a deviationist of the right, a "Bukharinist".) In the memorandum he wrote in the USSR a few days before his death at Yalta in 1964 (the document which is now officially considered his "political testament"), he clarified his preoccupations:

Deeply reflecting on the theme of the possibility of constructing socialism by peaceful means, we come to the necessity of defining exactly what we mean by democracy in a bourgeois State, determining how we can help to enlarge the frontiers of liberty and democratic institutions, and deciding what forms the participation of the working masses in the economic and political life of the country can take which will be most efficacious. The question arises whether it is possible to conquer positions of power within the constraints of a bourgeois State which has not changed its nature and to provoke progressive transformations of the institutions from the inside, so to speak. . . .

In other words he did not exclude the usefulness of a violent *coup d'état*, and could not easily reject the theoretical necessity of revolutions which would quickly eliminate the bourgeoisie both politically and physically from the scene. But he was tempted to believe (though he never said so officially) that "bourgeois liberties" could be considered a conquest of all men for all times and not of a single class, and that not only they could be made use of by the workers to take power painlessly, but should be respected and preserved by them. His last words contained a subversive charge (with delayed detonation devices) which endangered the orthodoxy and monolithism of the international Communist movement.

He worked to make his Party what he needed for the job as he saw it. He had to cope with Electoral Defeat (1948) and Cold War. First of all, he eliminated many illiterate fanatics and terrorists from responsible positions, men who had emerged from Fascist jails, the underground, and the resistance; and he disbanded all clandestine armed organizations, probably leading the police to discover many (though not all) caches of weapons. He built up an élite of intellectuals in his own image, pale men, Left Hegelians, Marxist–Leninist theologians, who usually wore glasses, thought intricately, studied history and sociology, and delivered speeches lasting half a day.

He revised the Party line, trying to hide (but not contradict) some of the harshest and most embarrassing Soviet theses under elegant euphemisms.[2] He stopped all anti-clerical propaganda (power cannot be achieved in Italy without coming to some understanding with the Church). Above all, he tried to pacify the bourgeoisie by attenuating the terrifying image of the blood-thirsty Communist, ready to deport and exterminate *en masse* all political opponents. (This aim, of course, he never fully managed to achieve, both because the hard core of the Party still cherished such hopes, and because the fear of Communism was indispensable to the Christian Democrats who would have seen their votes dwindle dangerously the moment the middle class stopped being frightened.)

He was accused of following strict orders from Moscow. This was only partly true. To be sure, in 1947–8, Moscow believed

---

[2] When I asked him once how one could believe improbable lies, like the charge that Beria was in the pay of Western Intelligence Services, he said: "Such things have to be interpreted like rhetorical figures. Beria behaved as if he was an agent of the Intelligence Service, did he not? Therefore one could say, for short, that he *was* an agent of the Intelligence Service."

that the world had been divided at Yalta once and for all between two spheres of influence; that the Americans would surely go to war to prevent any part of their sphere from slipping into the Marxist camp; and that this was a serious matter, as the U.S.A. then possessed the only atomic bombs in existence. Therefore his Party was allowed all kinds of subversive activities but one. It could not start a revolution and could not take advantage of historic circumstances, no matter how favorable, to take power illegally. Its main task was the defence of the interests of the Soviet Union. This he did, strenuously attacking UNRRA, the Marshall Plan, the Atlantic Alliance, and the European Economic Community among others.

He repeatedly promised the neutrality of the Communist Party in internal affairs and its active collaboration with a bourgeois government ("any bourgeois government", he daringly specified at one time) which would take Italy away from the imperialist camp. Serving as he did Soviet interests, he was not moved by vulgar servility. He could always find valid theoretical reasons for placing the interests of the USSR almost scandalously ahead of the prosperity and welfare of Italian workers. As Togliatti explained it, the USSR *was* the proletarian revolution; the Italian Party was strong, and able, eventually, to promote the progress of the workers and build an Italian Marxist State only if it acted for the time being as an *instrumentum* of Soviet power.

He could not be said to obey the orders from the Kremlin also because he himself wrote the Kremlin orders. He had long ago defined the need to collaborate with democratic parties; formulated, with Dimitrov, the "Popular Front" theory in 1934; applied it for years and especially during the war, when he worked together with Italian anti-Fascist bourgeois parties and King Victor Emmanuel. He disapproved of Tito, who had stubbornly followed a contrary policy and had exterminated the Monarchists who had fought the Germans in the underground. After the death of Stalin, Togliatti was one of a handful of survivors of the Comintern of the 1920s, the most authoritative non-Russian theoretician left, whose opinions determined the official line. He was the man who formulated the policy guiding all Parties in the West, including his own.

\*       \*       \*

THE TOGLIATTI FORMULA was successful. The Party became the most efficient and reliable workers' party in Italy, at an historical moment when the workers evidently needed one. It runs the important trade unions and helps promote a few reforms, not too effectively, of course, as its power depends on the workers' discontent. It worries the middle class, the industrialists, the landowners, the Church, and the State Department. It is the loving foster-mother of many intellectuals of all colors, who find peace, prizes, and protection in its embrace. As an autonomous Italian socialist party it cannot help disagreeing at times with the official Moscow line. It dislikes too strict control of the arts and sciences, disapproves outright excommunication of the Chinese, and now mildly objects to the theory that orthodox Marxist armies must invade Marxist countries whenever these try to liberalize their régimes (though it wholeheartedly approved of the intervention in Hungary in 1956).

On the whole, however, in almost fifty years, it has acted as a faithful tool of Soviet policy on all important occasions. This has never diminished its prestige. On the contrary, its power as an Italian workers' party is enhanced by the fact that it is supported by Moscow. At the same time, it could not be supported by Moscow (and render Moscow effective services in Italy) if it were not, first of all, the best socialist party in Italy, with deep roots in the century-old local history, attuned to the national character and prejudices, able to express a few rare dissenting opinions.

Three sociological strata can be distinguished in it. The *élite* is a self-perpetuating group of able and pliant philosophers. Under them are the organizers, the Party members, the hardcore militants, many of whom are still waiting for the revolution. Below these are the voters, millions of them, who know practically nothing of Marxism but are vaguely attracted by what they know as the poor people's natural party. The structure is centralized but, within the limitations of a Marxist-Leninist-Stalinist party, relatively liberal. Opponents and critics of the official line, men who represent the diverging tendencies of the revolutionaries (left) and of the voters (right), are allowed to voice mildly dissenting views, mostly on matters of tactics rather than principle, as long as they are solidly backed by sacred texts. Dissidents are not permitted, however, to found movements or *"correnti"* of their own and print their own publications. In the end everybody always does with discipline what the leaders decide, according to the rules of so-called "democratic centralism".

Dissatisfied Communists point out that the Togliatti formula has allowed the card-holding militants to dwindle from 2½ million after the war to 1½ million now. But the leaders are satisfied with the steady increase in voting strength. The Party, allied to the Socialists, elected 183 deputies in 1948 (30.97 per cent of the total); alone, it won 143 seats in 1953 (22.7 per cent); 140 in 1958 (22.68 per cent); 166 in 1963 (25.2 per cent); and 177 in 1968 (26.9 per cent). In other words the revolutionary stratum is getting thinner while the local workers' party has been growing steadily since 1948. The massive presence of representatives in both Chambers, aided by their extreme Left allies, is not unimportant. It has always allowed them to influence one way or another all political decisions. Timid government coalitions, frightened by possible disorders in the streets and the factories as well as stubborn opposition in Parliament, steer clear of excessively controversial measures which might provoke the extreme Left's bristling opposition.

This has aided some of the ruling parties in their reluctance to tackle really fundamental problems. The increase in voting strength is pursued also for precise strategic reasons. Antonio Gramsci pointed out long ago that the Communists could not hope to take power in Italy by themselves, except in very exceptional circumstances, as the revolutionary Left is always sociologically limited to a few intellectuals and a small fringe of fanatical followers. They usually manage to instigate violent counter-reactions, coalesce disparate and contrasting forces against them, and at best succeed in provoking the formation of "strong governments" in the "defense of national interests". Therefore revolutionaries must try to attract moderate allies by pursuing moderate but intelligently graduated aims. Among the moderate allies not to be irritated for the time being in Italy are the left wing of the revolutionary socialists, the social democrats, the more democratic bourgeois and the left-wing of the Catholic movement.

*      *      *

THOUGHTFUL OBSERVERS of the Italian scene began to believe in the 1950s that the only easy way to enfeeble the Communists was to free their principal ally, the Socialist Party led by Pietro Nenni, from their embrace. In 1958 it had won 4,206,726 votes (or 14.3 per cent of the total) and eighty-four seats in the Chamber of Deputies. The Nenni Socialists had been disciplined and reliable vassals for years (even before the War), and this not entirely for reasons of convenience and prudence, as many insinuated, but also because they feared that "a split in the working-class parties" might once again confer a decisive advantage to the Right. After the war they duly signed all the Communist manifestos, took part in all demonstrations, riots, and strikes, served as auxiliaries in the Communists' trade unions, and voted with them on all important issues. They represented a conspicuous, if not decisive, arithmetical component of Left opposition.

As the war paled in men's memories, the country was reconstructed, the economy somehow managed to become one of the most modern, vigorous, competitive, and fastest expanding in the West, and the menace of an imminent Communist apocalypse waned, the Nenni men began to have misgivings. Many remembered they had always been democrats and fighters for liberty and that they had never entirely shared the authoritarian concepts of the Stalinist Communist Party. They found themselves in 1956 on the side of the Hungarian rebels against the Soviet tanks. Pietro Nenni was among them.

These men tended to agree more and more with the views of

the Social Democrats who, led by Giuseppe Saragat, had broken away from the mother party in 1947 on the Communist issue. They had not wanted to be accomplices in the formation of another totalitarian dictatorship, no matter how nobly justified. The Social Democrats were part of the coalition with the Liberals, the Republicans, and the Christian Democrats, with a majority of but a few votes, which helped govern the country in the twelve years in which Italy emerged from her ashes, signed and ratified the Atlantic Pact, and helped form the European Economic Community. A reunification of the two Socialist Parties was looked upon with favor by the two aging leaders, both of whom wanted to be at rest with their consciences. Nenni refused to be any longer a brother-in-arms of the Communists; Saragat had never got over the remorse of having "divided the working-class", an unforgivable sin (to which, incidentally, Italian Socialists are prone and have succumbed to numberless times in the past eighty years).

The reunification of the two splinters was considered by all the really crucial move. It would give the new Center-Left government a large and stable majority in Parliament, and make the coalition truly irreversible, as there was no longer a spare majority for the Christian Democrats to turn to in case of failure. This gave confidence to the Socialists, who thought they would be able to impose their will on the Christian Democrats, under the threat of the only alternative: new elections. The reunification, however, did not last long.

It was not an easy operation to unify the Socialists for a time and lead them to a coalition with the Catholics. Nenni feared that too many of his followers, many of whom were primitive and emotional socialists, would not understand it and would once again split the Party. In spite of his precautions, many in fact broke away and founded a splinter formation, the PSIUP (or *Partito Socialista di Unità Proletaria*), which adequately filled the empty space at the side of the Communists.

The Republicans, led by Ugo La Malfa, a tiny middle-class formation with a glorious past, believed that a Center-Left coalition would have the power and the clear ideas necessary to tackle the one problem whose solution was, as we know, the only effective anti-Communist operation: the reconstruction, modernization, and moral reform of the State machinery. La Malfa hoped that the new government would follow his advice and bridge the abyss between the industrialized *pays réel* and the archaic and decaying *pays officiel*. Like many others, he thought the preceding governments' reluctance to improve the efficiency of the administration was the fault of the Liberals alone.

The Christian Democrats, who even if they deny it, undoubtedly are the secular arm of the Church, had more complex ideas. The Center-Left coalition was promoted by the Vatican partly for the hopes shared by Saragat, Nenni, and La Malfa, but also for reasons of its own. It was thought that an alliance with a proletarian party would help free the Church from the stigma of being a staunch supporter of Cold-War anti-Communism, the defender of private property and a capitalist market economy, charges which had weakened its hold on Italian and other Western workers and had made relations with the régimes in Eastern Europe extremely difficult. In other words, the Church was not solely thinking in terms of the welfare of Italy (which is only incidentally its preoccupation), but of millions of Catholics beyond the Adriatic and the Elbe, in Yugoslavia, Hungary, Poland, Lithuania, Ukraine, who urgently needed aid and protection. It knew that without the tolerance of local governments, Eastern Catholics would be driven underground and, before long, reduced to a heroic minority of saints and martyrs. To be sure, the new orientation would have to be carried out in agreement and with the consent of the American Catholics who were the main source of financial and political power for the Church.

The design, of course, met with enthusiastic transatlantic approval. It was supported by "enlightened" Italians the Americans trusted for reasons that were almost too easy to understand. It was irresistible as it looked on paper to be the definitive, simple, clear-cut surgical operation that would settle the matter once and for all. The State Department saw it as the local application of a formula they had encouraged (or were intending to encourage) in other countries: the formation of an alliance between progressive Catholics and anti-Communist (or non-Communist) parties of the Left. The men in charge unfortunately overlooked two elements which made the Italian situation dissimilar from that in other countries. (*1*) There is no Italian Catholic Church led by an Italian Primate. (*2*) Italian Socialists are different from Socialists almost anywhere else in Europe.

\*      \*      \*

NATIONAL CHURCHES exist, of course, in all Catholic countries. Often, in times of trouble, they face foreign oppressors or internal menaces, heroically identifying themselves with the soul of their nation. Local Primates have been known proudly to defy the Vatican itself, when the ultramontane views appeared to endanger the moral and spiritual well-being of their flock. The only Church existing in Italy is the Universal Church. Its primary duty is—rightly, I think—the defense and promotion of its universal mission. The Primate of Italy is the Pope. This has always made the Church more vulnerable to hostile mass movements which endanger social peace in Italy, and often more eager than necessary to come to an agreement with them.

The peculiar quality of Italian Socialists is due to the fact that they are nineteenth-century Romantics. They have always been agitating wildly in the opposition, have practically no experience of administration or government, and tend to lose the support of their voters (and break up) whenever they try to collaborate with the Church or the class enemies. To be sure, some leaders are as contemporary, well-read, and able as other European Socialists, but they have no decisive weight in their Party. The best are seldom re-elected.

In spite of these points, the State Department (and other US organizations) worked hard to bring about the desired coalition. How hard, how long, how subtly, by what visible and invisible means, they did it, will be known for sure years from now when the relevant documents are published. A few pages in recent books of memoirs, scraps of information published in remote magazines, a few leaks and unreliable rumors only allow us to have a vague idea of the extent and the cost of the operation (doubtless one of the most ambitious ever carried out outside Latin America). Among its results is surely not an increase of American popularity among Italians, a few of whom remember that their country was kept in subjection for centuries, after the Counter-Reformation, by a comparable alliance of Church and Empire.

The operation was naturally welcomed and aided by the British Labour Party and by big business, privately owned big business in Italy and the West, and Italy's large nationalized concerns. It pleased the technocrats everywhere. It was strongly supported by *The New York Times*, the *Financial Times*, the *Economist*, the *Observer*, among others, and (obviously) the *Osservatore Romano*. In Italy it was vigorously promoted by *La Stampa* (owned by Fiat) and *Il Giorno* (owned, at the time, by ENI, the State petroleum concern). Foreign observers could not be blamed for thinking there was no other easy alternative. The lay Italian parties were too small and too weak to play a decisive role. It would have taken many years to build them up. Was the operation not designed to weaken the Communists, these foreigners asked themselves, acquire the goodwill of a substantial part of the proletariat, assure the solid majority necessary to pass much overdue legislation, guarantee social stability for the time being, promote further economic and social development, encourage foreign investments? Could anything else be tried that would produce such results?

\*     \*     \*

ALMOST NONE OF THESE THINGS turned out as hoped. The newly formed *Partito Socialista di Unità Proletaria* became, as Nenni feared, an important and energetic ally of the Communists, and a handy receptacle for all kinds of Left-wing deviationists who could disturb the harmony and discipline of the orthodox Communist Party. The PSIUP won twenty-three seats in the 1968 elections and shows signs of gaining more. The Communist Party itself does not seem to be withering away. It gains approximately one million more votes every time the Italians go to the polls, and sees its power and influence grow in every field, in spite of its own internal crisis and that of the world Communist movement. The unified Socialist Party in the government coalition lost votes in the 1968 elections and was tortured by dissensions and polemics.

Little of the urgently needed legislation was proposed or passed. Schools, courts, hospitals, public housing, and the State social security organizations went on deteriorating at a quicker rate than before. Social stability was not assured. Unrest grew. Workers, students, professors, doctors, State employees, housewives, old people living on miserable pensions, took part in continuous demonstrations, strikes, the occupation of public buildings, asking for higher wages, pensions, better living conditions, reorganization of offices, modern laws, or the end of the Viet Nam war. Everybody knew the government tackles only those problems whose urgency is advertised by means of riots. The abyss between the industrialized *pays réel* and the archaic *pays officiel* grew deeper and more unbridgeable.

There are, to be sure, many bright spots. Industrial production rises steadily; the lira is stable; exports to the Common Market and elsewhere in the world are growing. Millions of tourists leave millions of dollars behind them every year. The people are lively, energetic, industrious.

On closer examination, however, even in the economy there are a few disquieting features. The growth in industrial production is not matched by a proportionate increase in employment. The number of employed workers decreased by 190,000 in 1968 (and went on decreasing the following years). New investments are lagging. The stock exchanges are deserted. Capital seeks more secure and remunerative prospects abroad, and couriers cross the Swiss border carrying valises filled with banknotes.

People who still save money are intimidated by imprudent speeches made by Cabinet ministers, ill-conceived laws (many of which, like the nationalization of electric industry, would have been extremely useful to the country's economy if more carefully thought out), or the threat of future punitive laws which may never be passed. Local consumption is still low, lower than the economy should permit or encourage. Industries seek American partners, to acquire new capital, to be sure, and to modernize their plants with transatlantic know-how, but also to find some protection from their own government under the Stars and Stripes. In other words, private Italy is still progressing vigorously (for the time being) in spite of public Italy, but not as vigorously as in the 'fifties.

That the Italians flourish in spite of bad governments has always been true, to some extent, in a country where the inhabitants, under foreign oppressors and inefficient rulers, had to develop private virtues and public vices to defend themselves. Business men instinctively prefer a paralytic government to one that would effectively promote immature and dangerous reforms. The grand hope always was that the national habits would gradually dissolve the moment a more modern and farther-looking government would for once try to help the people instead of hindering them.

The causes of the government's paralysis are not lack of ideas, goodwill, or good men in the Cabinet. Neglected problems have by now become so entangled that they can no longer be solved simply by a few ingenious laws (even if such laws could be agreed upon, formulated, passed by Parliament, and enforced); other causes are built-in in the Center-Left coalition itself. Most important reforms are bogged down, because the Christian Democrats cannot agree with the Socialists and the Socialists cannot always agree with themselves. The fundamental point is that the State administration is too inefficient (and the laws governing it too obsolete) for *any* political action to produce any desirable effect.

The State cannot be reformed because the parties in power have too divergent views of what a modern State organization should look like. The Socialists dream of a vast variety of ideal prototypes, ranging from extremist, utopian, left-of-Lenin models, to moderate British-type or Scandinavian models. They are, however, embarrassed in their decisions by the aggressive competition of the Communists, who take voters away from

them by accusing them consistently of "selling out the proletariat" to the bourgeoisie. They therefore have to support
vociferously the most drastic punitive solutions, to carry on the
class-war, even when the majority would be ready quietly to
accept realistic proposals. On the other hand, their persistent
extremism spreads fear among the middle-class who vote increasingly for the Christian Democrats, in order to give them the
necessary force to cope with such uncomfortable allies. The
Socialists, therefore, are bound to go on losing one way or the
other, whatever they do.

The Christian Democrats should profit by the Socialists'
weakness and successfully promote the particular reforms dear
to their hearts: the reforms needed for the gradual construction
of a model Christian Democracy. Unfortunately, there is no
such model. They cannot agree among themselves what it should
look like because theirs is not a "European", or ideologically
homogeneous, party, but a patchwork coalition of practically all
the principal social, cultural, economic and political ideas
existing in Italy. The membership ranges from the extreme
Right (the authoritarian champions of archaic privileges, the
enemies of a civil divorce law), to the Center (the *Dorotei*, who
promote a society maneuvred from above by technocrats and
the extreme Left fringe (quasi-Communist Catholics). All these
men are kept together not by a political idea but by the exercise
of power, ecclesiastical interests, and religious faith. The only
orthodoxy enforced among them, the only set of beliefs they all
uniformly must share without deviations, is the Athanasian
Creed.

Most of them were formed by Catholic schools and universities during the decades when the State was the opponent of the
Vatican's temporal pretensions. They were imbued not only with
the Church's century-old mistrust of lay laws and authorities but
by its bitter defiance of the Italian State. Almost all of them, Right,
Center, Left, think any State, even one created *ex novo* and run by
them, can but be a frail human construction, reflecting transient
ideals, beset by temptation and doomed to decay. They therefore watch the administration break down without surprise—

and without doing much to repair the damage and retard its final collapse. They think nothing can really be done, man is what he is (and the Italian man is more man than others), the country has always known bad governments, and perfection is only to be found in Heaven. In fact the Christian Democratic Party flourishes in the prevailing disorder and corruption. It is indirectly financed out of public funds, finds jobs for its *clientes* in the bureaucracy, awards public-works contracts to its loyal friends and entrusts nationalized industries solely to its own men. In sum, the best of them cannot shed their old prejudices, even now that they are in power, and cannot remember that the institutions are now also the defense of their own and the Church's liberties.

The situation is so bad that the Communists themselves are upset. Communist Deputy Ugo Bartesaghi expressed their misgivings in a recent speech in Parliament:

The country will revolt on account of the things you are not capable of doing, all the problems you cannot solve. . . . There is no other alternative to your impotence than rebellion, a rebellion which will take place whether we [the Communists] want it or not, a chaotic, disorderly, violent revolution, for which you alone will be responsible!

\*     \*     \*

A GROWING NUMBER of Christian Democrats and Socialists are beginning to think that (according to the old political rule) the only way out and the only hope is an agreement with the Communists. Ambiguous speeches are being made more and more often by authoritative leaders of both government parties, cautiously exploring this possibility. One of them, the best known, Christian Democrat Aldo Moro, ex-Prime Minister, is now officially considered the future leader of a pro-Communist (or non-anti-Communist) government. Another, Luigi Bertoldi, deputy secretary of the Socialist Party, recently said: "We do not consider including the Communists in a government coalition. This they would refuse as a bad bargain. We aim, instead, to accept the reality of their existence and their power in the country and in Parliament." The deputy Prime Minister, Francesco de Martino (a socialist), does not hide his desire to collaborate with the Communists in all those projects in which the Christian Democrats might drag their feet.

To be sure, the citizens who voted for the Christian Democrats and the Socialists, thinking these two parties would defend them from revolution and a Communist take-over, would be astounded and frightened by a sudden and radical reversal. The State Department and the NATO powers would equally look dimly upon a change of fronts; the Catholic masses in the United States would consider it a betrayal of their trust in the Vatican. The operation will have to be done (if at all) very very gently, *con garbo*. In the beginning the Communists will have to keep their place in the Opposition and play their part. Harsh polemics, violent accusations, and endless controversies should go on as if everything was normal. But, at the same time, under-the-counter *ad hoc* deals could be arranged (as de Martino suggested) on specific problems for the time being and, later on, more important general questions.

Obviously, the men who want to come to an understanding with the Communist Party, and to govern the country with its help and connivance, are following a logical line. If an alliance between the Socialists and the Christian Democrats was considered necessary for various reasons, an eventual alliance with the Communists would be even more so for all the same reasons (except one, the defence against Communism). In fact, most of the promises of the Centre-Left could only be fulfilled by the Communist Party. It alone has the power to give stability to a government; ensure peace and order in the streets, the factories, and Parliament; keep the students studying quietly; keep the workers contented with reasonable wages; and help to transform Italy eventually into a quasi-socialist State, where the Church would find ample protection for her activities, Italians keep their big mouths shut, and nationalized industries develop without hindrance, or excessive controls.

\* \* \*

THE DIFFICULTY, of course, is in the price to be paid. Obviously, the Communists would want what they have always

demanded: a gradual neutralization of Italy, its eventual with-
drawal from the Atlantic Pact, the departure from Italian soil
of all foreign armed forces, air and naval bases, and atomic
weaponry. But this is not an imminent matter. For the time
being what is envisaged is the temporary purchase of benevolence and a relaxation of tension. The price can be fixed on each
occasion: the passing of laws which the Communists might want,
for reasons of their own, like the division of Italy into autonomous regions (some of the key ones will be dominated by them);
the election of Communists to the European Parliament in
Strasbourg; or disarming the police. Some of these things are
already being done, anyway. More will follow gradually.

The Communists are clearly fascinated by all this, but are
apprehensive and nervous. To be sure, they are willing to
collaborate now and again on particular reforms, chosen by
them, which would facilitate their activities. They know that
the repeated appeals to them by majority leaders enfeeble the
government and strengthen the Party; but they also know that
any form of open collaboration or connivance with the Christian Democrats and the Socialists is looked upon with horror by
the rank-and-file. The leaders know they thrived, like the
Christian Democrats, for more than two decades, on anti-
Communism. It was precisely the fact that it was feared and
opposed by the Church, the bourgeoisie, and the Americans,
that made millions of poor Italians cast their vote for the Party.
Furthermore, collaboration would not be a solution but a pallia-
tive, a subterfuge to gain time. The important point is what will
happen later. The Communists agree that the situation is
deteriorating rapidly, things are moving towards a final crisis,
and there is a power vacuum at the top. They know (as Ugo
La Malfa has repeatedly affirmed) that this is "the last of the
Center-Left governments". They know they will have a great
role to play when the present coalition collapses, a role for which
they have prepared themselves since 1921.

A reading of modern history suggests that similarly weak
Center-Left alliances, which tried unsuccessfully in the past to
govern troubled and defeated countries, were almost always

followed by reactionary and authoritarian régimes or dictator-ships. Communists know that this was facilitated whenever a premature revolution was staged. The fact that no such reactionary forces exist in Italy today does not matter. Marxists *know* that "history" will generate the parties and leaders necessary for a particular situation when the times are "ripe". It is therefore probable that the men capable of engineering an authoritarian *coup d'état* will emerge at the proper moment. Clearly a day will come when the industrialized *pays réel* (which has looked indifferently in the past on the decay of the administration and the institutions because it believed that a little disorder was good for business) will discover that a reasonably efficient state is preferable. A day will come when the people will be afraid of bloody riots and disorders in the streets. Furthermore, on that day, the Communists believe, the "law and order" forces in Italy will find support from abroad, from Atlantic allies frightened by the danger of an imminent Communist take-over.

*　　*　　*

WHAT MUST THE PARTY DO? Only a vigilant, well-disciplined and organized Party with clear ideas, aware of the dangers of the situation, capable of getting millions of workers in the streets at a moment's notice, paralyzing the life of the country, can confront enemy machinations and annul any attempt to enforce the law, and theoretically (though this is not the case of contemporary Italy) prevent a Right Wing *coup d'état*. On the other hand, it is the duty of the Communists to become the reluctant praetorian guard of the Center-Left government, to see to it that it is not toppled by the wrong people. They should, however, not go so far as to help the government solve problems and live more vigorously. This is a difficult tight-rope act. To keep the Party mobilized, they must intensify agitation in the country, increase strikes and riots, fan discontent. Yet all this will not strengthen the government but inevitably enfeeble it further, fan anti-Communist feelings, encourage Right Wing plots, and facilitate the formation of an anti-Communist bloc.

There are other pitfalls. The "vanguard of the proletariat" is often tempted at times to march too fast, too decisively and violently, and thereby to lose contact with the frightened masses. This has happened to Communist leaders in the past in several European countries and was the cause of their most conspicuous débâcles. On the other hand, if the Party is too timid, it will encourage the rise of revolutionary movements to the left of it. Furthermore, the Italian Communists know they and their vassals represent roughly one-third of the electorate, not enought to conquer power without outside aid. They need allies. They need Left Wing, democratic, progressive allies. They need the help of the very parties which form the government coalition, against which a revolution would be staged, a government coalition which is being discredited daily by the Communists themselves. They therefore talk of finding allies not among the government parties but among the "Left Wing sectors" of those parties, to form a new coalition. But this elegant compromise is considered improbable even by the leaders who propose it.

They prepare themselves for troubled times ahead with very mixed views. What they would like is to keep things more or less as they are: the country in turmoil, the government losing more and more authority, the Communists gaining more and more votes at every election. But a day will come when they will have reached a percentage high enough to have power thrust upon them or when the country will be so tied up by strikes, riots and agitations that people will ask the Communists to take over, out of sheer desperation. They will then have to make up their minds. Even these seemingly placid hypotheses would be very dangerous. Their victory (or their approach to victory) would threaten profound international repercussions, provoke a realignment of the balance of forces between the two blocs, and surely increase the risk of a European conflict. Obviously, the Soviet Union has more vital and urgent problems elsewhere than to encourage a Communist government, let alone a proletarian revolution, in Italy. Will the Kremlin leaders allow the Italian Communists a free hand when the time comes? But does the Party still have the revolutionary impetus it had at the end of the war, before Togliatti began reforming it? Is it not now, as some believe, merely a large and soft electoral force of moderate labor voters? In other words, will it disobey Soviet orders and carry out its revolutionary mission—or will it find it convenient to accept them as a good and convenient alibi for its own deficiencies? There are Italian Communists who, now that victory is almost within their grasp, are afraid of themselves. One of them said to me: "I only hope we shall never be left alone in power, because you know what always happens when we are left to our own devices . . ."

The most important of all questions is this: Will the paralysis of the government, the rapid decay of the public administration, the accumulation of unsolved problems, the spread of unrest allow the Communists to choose what role they prefer or to postpone the time for decision? What a spectacle for the dialectical philosopher—Marxists being carried forward by their locomotive of History and worrying whether to stay on or get off.

# 20

# THE ANATOMY OF EXPERTISE

IT IS NOW just about becoming worthwhile even for the people born and living in the countries concerned to read the "whither" and "inside" books, the data-studded résumés of current history and future prospects in foreign lands written by American experts (or by foreigners for American readers, which comes to about the same thing). Only a few years ago such surveys could be easily overlooked. They were literary trapeze acts, too risky for reputable authors to undertake: while the manuscript was being printed venerable régimes toppled, seemingly insoluble problems vanished, and robust personages in the prime of life suddenly passed away. Only devil-may-care journalists attempted such *tours de force*, working as fast as they could, hoping their intuition, experience, and luck would save them from disgrace. They wrote fast but lightheartedly; there was a good chance their books would be forgotten within a few months anyway; and nobody, except perhaps grandchildren and some compiler of a PhD thesis, would one day care to check the accuracy of their diagnoses and prophecies.

Responsible authors understandably preferred to dedicate themselves to the immutable past. They could contemplate *faits* which were definitely *accomplis* and personages who were irrevocably dead; they could safely rake the cold ashes of old controversies and determine who took what wrong turn, at what time, and for what reasons, without fear of being contradicted. Only in the last few years have the men venturing to describe events even before *rigor mortis* sets in become more and more authoritative and qualified. Has this kind of work become safer? Are they no longer afraid of being made fools of by future developments? They seem undaunted. They appear to have more time, access to more authentic and verifiable data than the old journalists. They sprinkle reassuring footnotes everywhere, with learned quotations in several languages, carefully omit the amusing anecdotes, character sketches, and eyewitness accounts of the superficial observer, but pay a great deal of attention to all-embracing bibliographies.

*     *     *

THERE ARE OBVIOUS REASONS for this innovation. Times change and we change with them; rule-of-thumb empiricism is losing ground to the scientific approach in every field; events move at more and more breakneck speed from the present to the remote past; the interval necessary to turn palpitating headlines into inert historical facts is becoming shorter every year. More important is, perhaps, the new anxiety in contemporary society which craves a special and continuous reassurance. The intellectuals have somehow become the augurs who read omens in the entrails of economic, sociological, and statistical compendia, the oracles without whose nod statesmen do not go into battle. The universities, foundations, and occasionally the secret services have unprecedented funds to finance erudite research. Only academic studies, couched in reassuring professional prose and supported by an impressive scholarly apparatus, seem to have the power to placate frightened men.

In a way, the impatient can no longer bear to wait for the future to determine who was right and who was wrong. They expect specialists to provide instant-posterity, and these men do what they can. Their books, of course, rarely achieve the magic tranquilizing powers required. They are about as infallible as— and always less readable, and less perceptive than—the best work of the old-time journalists. Yet they are extremely useful. They are obviously indispensable to enlighten the great numbers of young correspondents, diplomats, and technical experts parachuted daily into incomprehensible and explosive situations in alien countries, as indispensable as the synopsis of past installments to the man who starts reading a serial novel at midway. No praise is sufficient for the tidy summaries and chronologies of past events, the reliable statistical tables, the thumb-nail sketches of principal problems. These probably are preventing at this very moment many beginners from committing a number of minor and even a few catastrophic errors.

\*          \*          \*

IT IS MY CONTENTION that these books, properly read and interpreted, can now be even more useful to the native of the country described, the man who knows the facts at first hand and possibly took part in the events described. He naturally finds there are discrepancies between what he knows and what he reads, but he learns to disregard them. All people are resigned to the occasional differences between what they have seen and what the newspapers print the next day. Everything, he discovers, has been touched-up and simplified, often as unrecognizable to him as the picture taken from a plane of an intricate jungle, filled with wild beasts, colorful birds, and monstrous flowers, is to the traveler on foot. This, too, must be overlooked: everybody knows all books are over-simplifications of sorts, otherwise they could not be contained within two covers. The real benefit one gets from reading these surveys is not the confirmation of known facts or the discovery of minor errors and differences of opinion. One realizes soon enough that the most eloquent passages are the omissions, the vast empty spaces left here and there in the story.

Most of them, of course, are invisible to foreigners, but to the native reader they are as evident as the large white spots in ancient maps where the cartographer wrote: *Hic Sunt Leones*. They are not as easy to explain away. They surely cannot be due to ignorance or neglect: unlike the map-makers of old, the contemporary expert knows practically everything knowable and has an array of all-embracing authoritative sources to draw from. He is fully aware of historical precedents, geo-political factors, or meteorological imperatives, and the conditioning national characteristics. What, then, made such a thorough and diligent man omit data without which the picture is incomplete or meaningless? Is his negligence deliberate or unconscious? Is it a compulsive attachment to symmetry and coherence, the fear to see contradictions destroy the formal garden-like arrangements he has patiently composed? Or is the author a weakling, unable to force himself to look disagreeable or frightening truths in the face?

In a way, these omissions, whether conscious or unconscious, manage to reveal the author's mind more plainly than the printed pages. The empty space is where one can catch the scrupulously objective scholar off guard. One discovers that he uses silences not only to hide unsavory realities for himself and his readers, but also to give vent to prejudices and preferences. One discovers that one is not only looking at a cold, reliable, business-like survey, but also at a subtly distorted image, a passionate portrait of a land the writer wished to believe existed or would have liked to see emerge, often the dream country he would fashion if he were granted the powers of a demiurge. The last point is of extreme importance today, because most of these scholars belong to the American foreign affairs establishment and either have the powers of demiurges or could unleash demiurges with little difficulty. It is well known that Americans not only have the moral, political, technical and military might, but also the will, the philanthropic, experimental and missionary spirit to change foreign nations according to an ideal pattern, designed possibly to suit the wishes of the local population but always the interests of the United States.

*　　*　　*

TO BE SURE, THIS MAY NOT be a bad thing if it succeeds. It succeeds rarely. Even the United States has not entirely managed to make themselves into the kind of country their best experts prefer. The feat is infinitely more difficult abroad. Primitive countries in distant continents find it impossible to mold themselves into the prescribed shape; they not only lack the embryo of a dependable middle class but also have little in their religious beliefs, ways of thinking, habits, wants, and inclinations to help them become affluent bourgeois democracies. There are societies which are sometimes tempted to enact Potemkin-like representations of the prescribed model, and hide their old shabby reality behind the façade. This, too, can be a good thing, better than nothing, to be sure, but only in the short run. The trouble is, both the Americans and the natives often delude themselves that obstinate century-old afflictions have been cured, that everything is definitely changed for the better, and stop worrying. The old ills fester in secret and get worse. Such make-believe constructions are necessarily flimsy, good only in fair weather, and collapse in historical hurricanes. At such critical times, the Americans, faced by reactions they had not foreseen from a people they do not recognize, are baffled, embittered, and utterly unprepared to meet the emergency. As Chesterton puts it: "What really produces trouble between peoples is when one is quite certain it understands the other—and in fact doesn't. . . ."

\*     \*     \*

FOR MANY REASONS ALL, or almost all, the surveys dedicated to contemporary Italy by American experts land sooner or later on my desk. There are two at the present moment.[1] The first is addressed to a virgin public which may want to acquire quick superficial knowledge without effort; the second to more sophisticated but not particularly well informed readers; both books are clearly and economically written, well ordered, and well edited. There are few misspelled Italian words and practically no mistakes.[2]

[1] *Italy After Fascism, A Political History, 1943–1965*, by Giuseppe Mammarella (University of Notre Dame Press). *A Political History of Post-war Italy*, by Norman Kogan (Frederick A. Praeger, New York; Pall Mall Press, London).

[2] Kogan thinks (p. 9) that General Cadorna's first name is Giuseppe. Cadorna, the military commander of the resistance, was named after his grandfather Raffaele, the general who entered Rome at the head of the Italian troops in 1870, and not his father Luigi, the general who commanded the Italian Army at the beginning of World War I. This is one of the few minor errors of fact to be found in either book.

Both books are definitely inspired by left wing views, or, more precisely, what pass for left wing views in Italy. This is by no means a controversial stand. It is the natural position for foreigners who believe Italy to be backward, her progress slowed down by reactionary capitalists, her liberty threatened only by the Communists Party, and know that the cure for such ills is almost everywhere a good stiff left-wing non-Communist government. Mammarella does not think it necessary to define his standpoint, though he does not hide it. For instance, in his book all important Italian privately-owned concerns, which at best have provincial dimensions when compared with their European market competitors, are called, in Lenin's polemical language, "monopolies". Kogan bravely admits "I am constitutionally incapable of withholding my opinions. . . . The basic orientation could be characterized in Italy as falling within the democratic lay Left." (It is definitely within what the Italian political commentators call Left but scarcely within what they call "lay", if by "lay" one means a tendency to separate Church and State with a sharp line of demarcation.)

For the sake of clarity, both authors classify the principal parties into two Manichaean camps. The good, as it should be in a well-ordered world, are all in the government, and all the bad in the opposition. The Fascists and the Communists are bad, for analogous though opposite reasons; the Communists a little less bad, as their intentions are praiseworthy but the means of achieving them deplorable. Only the Liberals are very bad. They are accused of being "in the pay of the industrialists" (all parties in Italy, including the Communists, have at one time or another accepted contributions from the industrialists, the Christian Democrats more than all others). The Christian Democrats and the Socialists are good, but the very best are the left wing Christian Democrats and the right wing Socialists. The exemplary citizens, therefore, are implicitly either those who vote Socialist but believe in the democratic process and the recent Papal encyclicals, or the Christian Democrats who believe in the class struggle and the gradual nationalization of the means of production.

*       *       *

POLITICAL LIFE, ONE LEARNS from these books, has been extremely difficult from the end of the war until the early 1960s, but in what parliamentary democracy has it been easy? Nevertheless the Italian people can proudly look back to some significant achievements. They established a democratic republic, which assured the people fundamental liberties; they have amazingly reconstructed their economy and developed it beyond all expectations. "In the ten years between 1952–1962", Mammarella accurately notes, "Italy has made more progress in the economic field than in the entire preceding span of the twentieth century." (The governments of that decade were *Center* coalitions formed by Liberals, Christian Democrats, Social Democrats, and the Republicans.) The *Problema del Mezzogiorno* was tackled energetically in those years, if not without some difficulties, delays, and waste. New industries were built in the southern provinces, old ones were enlarged and modernized, the cities spruced up and developed; ports widened and deepened; many roads built. The people as a whole achieved a moderately fair standard of living, not much higher than that of Great Britain in the early 'twenties, but still better than they had in the preceding millennia, and all this was made possible by government interventions on an unprecedented scale.

Now, of course, the situation is still difficult, in some respect more difficult than before, but the road is finally open for vast future improvements. The Center-Left coalition was formed to tackle the fundamental problems once and for all, and it did not come about easily. Even at the last minute, Kogan recalls, there was a danger that the more conservative Christian Democrats would vote against the government (as the Left-splinter Socialists did):

They [the conservative Christian Democrats] controlled approximately thirty deputies. In justifying their insubordination, they claimed that too many reforms had been conceded to the Socialists without any guarantees that the Socialists would split from the Communists. . . . On December 16, however, a sharp editorial in *L'Osservatore Romano* condemned any breach of Catholic party discipline and unity. The potential dissidents retreated immediately.

Obviously Kogan's "lay" preferences are stronger when the Vatican supports non-Left governments.

The blueprint for the future is contained in a vast program agreed upon by the allied parties before the formation of the Government. A loose plan was drawn up, containing all the desiderata, which would take several generations to be translated into law. It is designed to furnish the authorities with a guide-line for action and the powers necessary to assure a more orderly economic growth, regulate the proportion between public and private expenditures and investments, spread investments more thickly in the South than in the Center and North, and encourage government ownership. The plan has now been submitted to Parliament for approval. Regions will be established as soon as possible, each with its own tiny capital, little Parliament, minute Government, and all the bureaucracy necessary, in order to end the hegemony of Rome. All this is designed to transform the State that was formed in the nineteenth century. It is well known that the Catholic masses and the proletariat were hostile to the *Risorgimento* (and the liberal democratic revolution it represented at the time). It is a tidy and satisfactory picture, but not quite accurate.

*          *          *

WHY SHOULDN'T FOREIGN political observers be confused by Italy, when the vast majority of Italians are too? Strangers often fall in love with the country and its inhabitants (they would not spend so much time traveling and studying if they did not) and see everything through a sentimental mist. Almost all are mesmerized by the abundance, or the apparent abundance, and multiformity of the problems. Italy, in fact, can boast of practically every problem associated both with the archaic and the ultra-modern industrial worlds; most of those typical of backward underdeveloped countries, plus a vast number of her own, like the costly preservations of ancient archives, *palazzi*, art treasures, whole cities and the defense of world-famous landscapes.

Cold-hearted and clear-minded scholars, on the other hand, know that almost all Italian afflictions can be considered the infinite effects of one single pathological condition, a monstrous and frightening one. This is the discrepancy between the energy, vigor, feverish activity, zest for life, adaptability, resourcefulness of the people, most of whom refuse the miserable living conditions they had resignedly accepted for centuries, and the growing paralysis of a decrepit and decaying State machinery. The Italians are visibly transforming their country, by hook if possible, and by crook if there is no other way, into what looks like from the outside a modern country not very dissimilar from the *Mitteleuropa* model, namely, Belgium, Switzerland, Western Germany, or Eastern France. They are trying to move away from the pastoral, patriarchal and archaic Mediterranean on a generally northwest course. At the same time, the public administration is sleepily dragging itself in almost the opposite direction, with Byzantium as its ideal resting-place.

Obviously this contradiction cannot go on for much longer without provoking the complete collapse of organized collective living. Something will have to give, the State or the people. As the people cannot be dissuaded from their enthusiastic activities, it is hoped the State will sooner or later be brought into line. Nobody in Italy expects utopian perfection but everybody, or almost everybody, agrees that it should not be difficult to set up, in a short time and without much trouble, a relatively business-like and responsible administration, government departments which do not wage incessant wars against each other like feudal barons, offices manned by reasonably competent and honest civil servants, adequately trained and paid, ably led by selected officials, to administer streamlined laws according to simplified legal procedures. It should not be impossible to equip this with what it needs, which does not mean science-fiction gadgets and wonder computers, but chairs, tables, filing-cabinets, telephones, typewriters, all of which are at present very scarce, and capable secretaries.

Superficial observers think all this simply cannot happen in Italy. On the contrary, nothing could be easier. Many Italians have a natural inclination for State employment and enjoy the security and the authority connected with it. They like nothing better, in fact. And they can be satisfactory, if not always exemplary, bureaucrats whenever the system requires it. They were impartial and efficient under Giovanni Giolitti before World War I, and perhaps better than that under the Austrians in Trent and Trieste at about the same time. They are expert administrators today in the Canton Ticino and the Swiss Federal bureaucracy. They have successfully created and run for about twenty centuries the greatest bureaucratic masterpiece of all, the most subtle and complex organization devised by man, bigger and more far-reaching than the Standard Oil Company of New Jersey, the Roman Church. There are a few sectors of the Italian State which still function impeccably, even today, the *Banca d'Italia* and the *Carabinieri* among them.

Of course, government responsibilities were less exacting and less specialized in the old days, and distinctly more suitable to the Italians' native qualities. But they have also proved themselves resourceful and skillful in the intricate organizations of the contemporary industrialized and scientific world: they are doing well, for instance, in the European market, Euratom and the coal and steel bureaucracies. In other words, they love the jobs, possess the necessary qualities, and are good whenever they are enclosed within well-defined rules and entrusted with precise powers and duties. For these reasons many believe the Italian State could be made to function in an adequate manner within a short time with substantially the same men already employed, give and take a few thousand, and at approximately the same cost.

\* \* \*

SHOULD ITALY ACQUIRE a relatively efficient administration, nobody doubts she would be able to advance more speedily and with less impediments on the road to progress, and manage to cure most of, if not all, her ancient ills. They can be reduced to three main ones, the first results of the State's impotence (and first causes of all other problems), namely illiteracy, poverty, and the "Communist Menace". The first, illiteracy, should not be difficult to liquidate in a country in which practically the entire school system is run by a Ministry of Public Instruction. Additional teachers could be recruited or trained, the necessary funds obtained by the use of various devices: e.g. a part of the six hundred billion lire spent yearly for the dubious advantage of running railways at a loss could be saved, or money collected from tax evaders by more resolute offices and the abolition of superfluous exemptions and discriminations. Within a few years a better instructed citizenry could decidedly find it easier to achieve a durable affluence.

A prosperous and reasonably educated electorate, in a country served by an adequately modern public administration, could then more easily resist the fascination of Communist promises. At present, it is well known that one-fourth of the voters, or about eight million, vote for the Party, and their number grows steadily at every election. Many Italians, being hopelessly destitute, dream of turning the tables on the rich; being illiterate they cannot fit into an increasingly technological world and do not have the elementary knowledge to protect themselves from demagogy. As only the smart and well-connected now manage to be served by the State, or to obtain favors from it, many of the others live in the hope of establishing an impossible utopia, a workers' paradise, organized solely for their comfort and welfare.

\*     \*     \*

I WANT TO NOTE, at this point, that a radical modernization of the State should be the aim of both the Right and the Left. Conservatives in Italy as elsewhere pine for law and order, the protection of life and property, and the certainty of well-defined rights and duties; they enjoy seeing crooks and grafters end in jail and public affairs smoothly and economically managed. The Left, however, should want an energetic, refurbished bureaucracy and stream-lined legal procedures even more. Their avowed policy is "the intervention of the State in the economy for the advantage of the collectivity". (To be sure, they did not invent the formula. Every Italian government since the days of Cavour did just that. Only the ideas of what constituted the advantage of the collectivity varied with the times.)

In order to intervene effectively one must have suitable instruments, i.e. bureaus manned by trained experts who gather the necessary information, watch the diastole and systole of the economy, and try to formulate effective measures to produce predetermined results and avoid unwanted side effects. As most of the laws passed by the Left encounter obstinate resistance from powerful groups, the need for impartial and energetic enforcement agencies is particularly evident. If, some day, the country should be divided into regions, a well-run administration will be found indispensable to harmonize local initiatives into a coherent system, and avoid chaos. Finally, the many impatient nationalizers among the Socialists must know that only a good central administration can keep powerful State-owned monopolies (as well as private industries) working for the common good and not (as they are tempted to do) in their own interest and for their own aggrandizement. Nobody forgot the time when Enrico Mattei, the president of ENI, mainly to serve the interests of his organizations, dragged reluctant and protesting governments into compromising foreign combinations.

That the State should be modernized without delay is universally recognized. It is admitted by the first victims of the administration's disorder, paralysis and decay—the civil servants. For the last twenty years, their unions have been putting an anguished request for a total overhaul of the system at the head of their lists of demands, when negotiating with the government, even before higher wages and more tolerable living conditions. The minor parties—the Liberals, the Republicans, and the Social Democrats—considered reform a preliminary to all other political action. The Liberals, who insist that the "rule of law" is a prerequisite of liberty in a country which has

always been tempted by dogmatic paternalism, made the renovation of the State machinery their principal electoral issue since
1946. Many Socialists have now come around to the same idea.
Pietro Nenni (Vice-Chairman of the Council of Ministers) has
lately pointed out to journalists what he should have said to
Cabinet ministers, that "one cannot entrust more and more
intricate, technical, and delicate new tasks to offices so disorganized they cannot even face their old ones. . . ." In short,
the *aggiornamento* of the public administration is the first and
most vital task. If it is not faced, the Italian people will probably
survive, as they have done through centuries of decay, disorder,
and calamities; they may occasionally manage to have good times
and prosperity; but the Italian State will fatally wither away.

*     *     *

ONLY THE LARGEST PARTIES, the Communists and the
Christian Democrats, appear to be apathetic. The Communists
understandably watch with dry eyes the growing ineffectiveness
of the bourgeois liberal State and impatiently look forward to its
final collapse. The Christian Democrats, who have governed
the country practically singlehanded since 1947, never thought
the problem urgent. They made feeble efforts, from time to
time, to tackle it, more to humor their occasional allies and to
silence the opposition than to change things. About twenty years
ago they set up a special office, in charge of an Under-Secretary.
Later they made it a Ministry, headed by a full-fledged
Cabinet Minister, *Ministro per la Riforma della Pubblica Amministra-
zione*, and even allowed Social Democrats to run it at times.
Almost twenty such Ministers followed each other, immense
quantities of data were gathered, intricate problems were
eviscerated, experts consulted, bottlenecks identified, suggestions
sifted, and, a few years ago, complete and realistic plans made
ready, which everybody, including the opposition, agreed were
what the country needed. The plans were never presented to
Parliament for debate and approval. Somehow they were never
awarded a high enough priority.

*     *     *

IT WOULD BE pointless for me to dwell at length upon an obvious and self-evident topic were it not for the fact that most foreigners, especially Americans, writing the "whither Italy" books, scarcely consider it worthy of attention. Like honest Dr Watson, they seem unaware of what almost everybody else knows is the revealing clue. Professor Mammarella, for instance, seems to accept the chaos in the public administration as an irremediable family disgrace which polite people do not mention. Professor Kogan skims lightly over the matter when he must explain why the many ambitious projects dear to him seldom produce anything resembling the desired results. He sadly writes, for instance, that a "cause of the ineffectiveness (of the *Cassa del Mezzogiorno*) lay in the behavior and action of the traditional government departments". To justify the fact that one of the early Center-Left Governments could find no way to resuscitate the building industry it had inadvertently caused to collapse, he explains:

The delays and inefficiencies of the public bureaucracy, the complicated procedures and systems of review, the legal requirements of codes that were a half century to a century out of date, all served to slow down the actual application of policy decisions made at the top.

This forgetfulness, the curious disregard for what others think, is the most significant fact of all, the most glaring of all omissions, the largest of the large white spots where the biggest lions dwell. The experts' blindness is difficult to explain. It cannot be due to ignorance: everybody knows that the best-laid economic plans can only be as good as the offices that must apply them, and that it would be madness to entrust the destiny of fifty-three million people in the heart of Europe to the least responsible organization among them. Clearly the Center-Left programs, which are presented to Parliament from time to time, interminable lists of all possible problems and their proposed legislative solutions, which would take at least two generations to pass, could be compared to a vast menu, containing everything from *antipasto* to *zabaglione*, presented to customers in an *osteria* without cooks and without kitchen. Such plans obviously must not be taken literally. They are rhetorical devices, the pathetic lists of *desiderata* the poor sometimes draw up for their consolation, *trompe l'oeil* decoys designed to attract and reassure innocent people and those who badly want to deceive themselves.

This, of course, is the heart of the matter. Why is nothing ever done for the renovation of the public administration? One must deduce there are forces in Italy which, consciously or unconsciously, consider even a moderately efficient State with fear and deep hostility, and are strong enough to prevent the mildest reform plans from being adopted. These forces probably find it convenient not to fight what they probably think is unrealistic and abstract legislation (as they did not oppose the manner in which the electricity industry was nationalized in 1962, which everybody now agrees was the most expensive and politically ruinous possible), but merely see to it that the machinery necessary to enforce it, in the attempt to make Italy a quasi-modern country, is left in its Byzantine condition. At the risk of disturbing the neat Manichaean arrangements dear to foreign experts on Italian affairs, those forces should be called reactionary eve when they use left-wing rhetoric and slogans.

\*          \*          \*

WHAT ARE THEY? Who works for the perpetuation of confusion, chaos, corruption, anarchy, the waste of public money in insensate electoral projects, the preservation of obsolete laws and the proliferation of inapplicable new ones? Obviously it is not a diabolical conspiracy. There are powerful men, groups, organizations, institutions that encourage and exploit a favorable situation, a condition they did not create but which is the spontaneous product of recent and remote history, national inclinations and propensities. One vainly looks for a clear identification of these forces in Italian publications. The local Marxists simply accuse private *entrepreneurs* of blocking progress. These might want to do so, as they always found a little confusion in the public administration good for business, but are not strong and resolute enough to promote it. The State controls the most important 50 per cent of the national economy and can easily intimidate the private industrialists. Most of them now support the Center-Left Government anyway.

Wisdom from foreign observers is no more illuminating. I am afraid English and American correspondents do not dig very deep. They reflect official views and report the glittering surface of things. The scholars, who not only have leisure, money, confidential sources of information, but also the detachment from local prejudices and passions, practically ignore the subject. They unquestioningly classify parties in power according to what they say and print, and parties in the opposition according to what the Government says they are. What stops the experts from going deeper?

\*　　\*　　\*

I WOULD BE THE first to admit that confusion is not difficult to promote in Italy today. The times are propitious: even in virtuous countries, where the civil service has always been an impersonal and well-oiled machine, inefficiency and corruption are beginning to spread. The Italian administration has been further dislocated by a series of appalling catastrophies. World War I caused the first erosion; then the Fascists disrupted what was left of the only good bureaucracy united Italy ever had; they imposed strictly partisan criteria for recruiting and promoting personnel. Then came the ravages of World War II, the defeat, the collapse of the old structures, the tumultuous reconstruction which swept everything before it, the inevitable errors of an experimental and inexperienced democracy.

Parties in power for the first time had little respect for the laws passed by their predecessors and did not resist the temptation to use the power of the State for their private ends. They financed party machines and electoral campaigns; they filled Ministries, municipalities, and publicly-owned enterprises, including social security organizations, with herds of impecunious and incompetent followers. Civil servants could no longer be sure of quick promotion by joining the right party and wearing the right uniform. Now they had to guess to which party the next Minister would belong, to which faction in his party, to which clique in his faction. I must admit, furthermore, that there are many cautious Italians who prefer confusion to the rule of law as a safeguard of their liberty. The law can be unjust and cruel. In the past it was imposed by foreigners to serve their interests, and later by compatriots who often preferred the triumph of their ideologies and the humiliation of their opponents to the public good.

Why should confusion not triumph, these people ask, when it is well known that the national genius thrives in it? Discipline, they say, paralyzes Italians who, when left to their own initiative in utter chaos, function at their best. Political scientists have proved that if all laws on the books were firmly applied, Italy would come to a stand-still and the people would theoretically starve to death; this is probably why they achieved the highest standard of living at the moment when their public administration was at its lowest level.

In confusion, it is true, the native navigates with circumspection and usually gets what he wants with the help of powerful relatives, accomplices, and friends. But it would be misleading to think love of anarchy is a permanent twist in the national character. It is not. To be sure, the Italians enjoy the exciting hazards of an orderless world in which anybody can win the jackpot, at any time, but they do not have an inborn taste for risk. If they did they would now be happy. They are not. They are among the most wretched, desperate, and frightened people in the Western world. Confusion breeds injustice. They watch the cunning and unscrupulous, the friends of powerful people, gain their ends with ease: the vast majority of citizens is unprotected, hopeless, often robbed of its rights; the gap between persons, classes, and regions increases every year. Fundamental problems are neglected and become almost insoluble. Even superficial observers should notice some of the most visible signs of this: the unprecedented floods, for instance, which each year dramatically submerge larger and larger parts of Italy, including famous cities, are encouraged by the long neglect of the most elementary measures for soil conservation and river control.

\*      \*      \*

CONFUSION, FOR MOST ITALIANS, is by no means a deliberate choice. It is a *pis aller* at best, accepted with resignation or bitterness, a subterfuge devised to survive somehow under bad governments in difficult times. In reality, the people's preference has always been for a well-ordered, static, decorous, paternalistic society, as tidy and symmetrical as one of their baroque regulations. This is why they have always pined for *"il buon governo"*.[3] They always dreamed of a *"Principe"*, from Dante's Veltro to Cola di Rienzo and Mussolini. This is why today, as well as in centuries past, there is little social stability. A large part of the lower classes are in an endemic state of revolt, and vote Communist (Gramsci believed the contemporary impersonation of Machiavelli's *Principe* was the Communist Party). The upper classes are wary, suspicious, and haunted by fears.

\*      \*      \*

UNFORTUNATELY, any Italian government dominated by a Catholic party must find almost insurmountable difficulties in fighting anarchy and confusion for well-known century-old reasons. Non-Italian Catholics have occasionally been efficient and honest rulers; where schismatics, heretics, materialists, or atheists prevail, the local clergy with their flocks have fought, often heroically, in the defense of liberty and for a clean-cut separation of Church and State. In each country the faithful form the National Church, led by its Bishops, almost always headed by a Primate, who stands up against an overbearing Prince or an arbitrary government, and respectfully defends national views even against the Holy See when there is a difference. History is filled with such conflicts. Nothing like this happened in the old Papal States or can happen in contemporary Italy. The people do not have a Church of their own. There is only one Church in the country, the Universal Church. The Primate of Italy, Bishop of Rome, is the Holy Pontiff,

[3] *Il Buon Governo* is the title of a famous fourteenth-century fresco by Lorenzetti at Siena, and also the title of a well-known book by Luigi Einaudi, the economist who was the first president of the Republic.

whose only divine duty is to promote the welfare of Catholics in all parts of the world. Where there is a conflict with the aspirations of the Italian flock, it is obvious that the interests of the international flock must take precedence.

To be sure, this difficulty is purely theoretical most of the time. It can, however, become a serious hindrance to the conduct of affairs at critical periods. In 1848, for instance, when Pius IX gave a constitution to his subjects, he granted liberal institutions, an almost modern bureaucracy, a government responsible to an elected Parliament, but could not make any concessions on one essential point: he could not allow the creation of a lay Foreign Ministry. No way could be found to distinguish between the interests of the citizens of the Papal States and those of the Holy See; the conduct of foreign affairs had to be left in charge of the Cardinal Secretary of State.

The difficulty re-emerged one hundred years later in 1948, when the Christian Democratic party took over the national government with an absolute majority. It owed its overwhelming electoral victory to the parish priests, the lay and clerical organizations of the Church, and the powerful help of the hierarchy. It timidly struggled at first to defend its autonomy but without much success. Its deputies, chosen (or approved) by the Bishops, knew they had to be pliant and understanding. They were resigned to accept orders in matters pertaining to particularly sensitive sectors, like censorship, the divorce law, birth-control propaganda, the financing of Catholic schools, etc.—in which their opinions did not differ from the Vatican's anyway. But they soon discovered they had to harmonize most other policies with those of the Church, particularly foreign affairs.

Under Pius XII, Italy became the stalwart of the Atlantic Alliance and the stern enemy of Communism. Under John XXIII and Paul VI, as the international situation gradually changed, the official Italian stand was attenuated. Some commentators believe the Communist Party will soon enough be persuaded to participate, directly or indirectly, in the Government with the Christian Democrats, and Italy will gradually establish more and more intimate relations with the Soviet

Union and the Communist countries. This may turn out to be in the interest of the Italian State; but it certainly is in the interest of the Holy See, which must defend millions of Catholics across the "Iron Curtain" from persecution and obliteration. Inevitably, the Vatican is tempted to use Italy as a demonstration model. Just as what is good for General Motors might not always be good for the United States, what is good for the Holy See might not always be good for the Republic of Italy.

\*    \*    \*

ANOTHER REASON WHY the Christian Democrats find it difficult to increase the authority of the State lies in the very nature of the Church. Churchmen admit States run by the Church have never been efficient (just as Churches run by Princes have always lacked vigor). The government of Papal Domains in the nineteenth century was notoriously among the least efficient in Europe. Finances were in a confused state; nepotism was rampant; the laws were innumerable and irksome but universally disregarded; the few roads infested by bandits; public services practically non-existent, or entrusted to the benevolence of religious orders and good people; industry and commerce were discouraged; arts and culture kept under strict surveillance. It could not be otherwise: priests were not educated to run worldly affairs; the Church did not really believe in the possibility, or necessity, of improving material conditions.

The Church always knew man is naturally inclined to sin and it is pointless as well as almost impossible to prevent him from committing crimes. Other countries were proud of their modern sciences, industries, railways, telegraphs, and inventions. The Roman clergy looked upon such things with amused diffidence: they deluded man, made him think of worldly things, and distracted him from his spiritual life. Likewise, the priests lacked enthusiasm for the many political improvements of the century, and ignored economic trends, liberal institutions, democracy. They knew injustice could not be defeated easily. After all, only patience, hope, and charity could really alleviate man's earthly sufferings: alms, free soup at the doors of convents, the sheltering of the destitute and old in suitable homes. For the rest the foremost duty of the Church was to defend and increase its power for the greater glory of God.

Of course, the Church has changed greatly in the last century, since it was liberated from the burden of governing the Papal States. It has gained in authority. It has learned to make use, for its purposes, of many contemporary inventions and techniques. Churchmen have become admirable experts in practically all mundane activities, active in all kinds of pursuits their predecessors thought were the inventions of the Devil. Priests no longer seem to think the improvement of man's lot on earth as a secondary task, and have developed up-to-date political and social theories of their own, to counteract the iniquitous teachings of materialists, atheists, and agnostics. Nevertheless, in spite of all this, the Church has definitely not become a worldly institution. Its very nature makes it still consider mere human organizations and man-made laws with detachment. It prefers political régimes run by good Catholics, naturally, but any other can be equally acceptable, of the Right or of the Left, on condition that men are treated with reasonable justice and the Church is left free to carry on its work unimpeded. Finally, it pursues its own fundamental aim, which, now as in the past, is the consolidation and expansion of its own institutions.

How could this be otherwise? Should it stop one day considering Heaven its real home, stop believing in the *au-de-là* as infinitely more important than the *ici-bas*, and stop working for the salvation of souls, it would evidently cease being the Catholic Church. It has lasted two thousand years because it was always stubbornly faithful to its fundamental creeds. If it modified them, it would probably become a worthy, benevolent, ethical organization, respected, rich, and powerful, but would slowly fade away. Therefore, it is still not the best institution in the world to run a State. Why should it use its powers for purposes it does not understand, e.g. promoting the efficiency of the public administration and prosecuting corrupt officials? Why should it fortify the authority of the State when it knows that in a weak State the Church flourishes best and in a strong State it must continually be ready to defend its rights and privileges? Which, after all, is the higher aim: a well-fed, well-read, well-administered citizenry, or a holy one?

\*　　\*　　\*

THE CHRISTIAN DEMOCRATS are the heirs of several Italian Catholic movements, formed after the unification of the country, at the end of the century. The Church had strongly disapproved of both unification and the way it was achieved. It would have preferred the gradual and bloodless formation of a God-fearing and submissive League of the existing principalities, headed by the Pope (just as it championed the division of Italy into regions). It could not help being horrified by the many acts of banditry and the violations of international law perpetrated by the patriots, shocked by the unprovoked aggression on the Papal Domains, or angered by the occupation of Rome by force. It considered the leaders of the *Risorgimento* impious, sacrilegious, blasphemous men, and excommunicated them all. Catholics furthermore disliked the new unified Italian State because it was up-to-date and secular; it confiscated the land of some religious orders and made the life of all Church organizations difficult; tried to monopolize the education of young people, and embraced all the errors of the century, summed up by Pius IX in his *Syllabus*.

Many Catholics at first were in favor of a return to the *status quo ante* and allied themselves to legitimists; later they occasionally joined forces with all the enemies of the new kingdom, both reactionary and revolutionary. The State, *voilà l'ennemi!* Many of them (and their fathers) had besieged the new centralized administration for so long that, when they finally conquered it, they could not easily shed their old mentality. The older Christian Democrats never could remember that the hated walls, moats, ramparts, and bastions should be kept in good repair and reinforced if possible, as they were now also their own defenses.[4]

---

[4] It is significant to point out that Alcide de Gasperi was not among these men; but he was a Catholic of a different breed, brought up in the Austrian Empire.

This hostile sentiment is still strong among the rank and file. Even among the bright young men who are now trying to run the country, some of whom show exceptional qualities of leadership, there is still a vague feeling that the *Rechtstaat* ideal is impious. The weakness of the public administration, to be sure, is not the fruit of a deliberate plan, but the result of that vague and incredulous mistrust all good Catholics have for worldly legal mechanisms.

MANY OTHER FORCES, of course, collaborate consciously or unconsciously to keep the State as impotent as possible. The job is not difficult, as most of the time it merely requires inaction. Big business concerns (both private and State-owned) find a loose and flexible administration, manned by timid and frightened bureaucrats, helpful for the conduct of big business. Powerful trade unions, which have succeeded in preventing the passage of legislation regulating their status, the right to strike, and other related matters, would equally be hindered by efficient offices applying modern laws. Medium and small concerns, the middle classes, the poor and disinherited people, and the South should all want to see their rights defended by the law. But the mass parties to which most people give their votes also find a weak State advantageous to their interests. For one thing, some of them would probably lose a substantial part of their financial backing if all the laws were applied impartially and it were suddenly impossible to persuade responsible officials to close their eyes to irregularities. Modern mass parties are extremely expensive organizations. The list of forces co-operating to keep the State weak could easily be continued.

*          *          *

WHY IS IT, then, that this vital point is so rarely raised? Why is it the experts do not dedicate a few extra days and a few extra paragraphs to it? All the facts rapidly summarized in the preceding pages are accessible to newspaper readers, or to anyone listening to the conversation going on at the next table in any café. Anybody who has an Italian friend (and what foreigner does not acquire one after a few days?) cannot help hearing endless lamentations, backed by case histories, of the injustice prevailing and the disorder in the administration. The Church's hostility to the State is nothing new; it is studied in the schools; Machiavelli and Guicciardini wrote eloquently about it, in terms which could almost be applied to contemporary events. The conflict between the Liberal and Catholic conceptions of the *Risorgimento*, the State, and Society is well known, part of the living memory of older Italians. There are whole libraries dedicated to it. The fact that all political parties, whatever their real aims may be, use vast social programs as noble fronts is true in many other parts of the world and should not deceive shrewd observers.

In reality, Western and especially American experts often seem frightened not to take things at their face value. They believe official handouts and Government statements, that are no more reliable in Italy than in many other countries. This curious propensity to think the surface of things is good enough, which is in contrast with their academic and scientific pretensions, is revelatory. Obviously these people are not as interested as they believe in the welfare of the Italian people, their economic, social, political, and cultural progress. What really interests them is to prove to themselves and their readers that the Italian problem has now been settled once and for all and that no surprises are expected or will be tolerated. This is what they want to believe: Italy is now a stable country, reasonably well run by a seemly coalition of parties with quotable programs; the American establishment, which is backing this formula and has definitely financed its victory, has therefore not made a mistake; the Communists are definitely on their way out; nobody will henceforth raise uncomfortable new issues and really try to improve conditions.

The most significant aspect of this view (and the proof of its fragility) is the irascibility with which these experts consider all kinds of dissenting opinions. To maintain their own tranquility and to pacify their readers, they even abandon a long-held enlightened belief, that no champion of democracy can be worthy of his name if he does not respect the opposition, believe in its utility, and uphold its rights.

# 21

# THE MAFIA

I T WOULD SEEM that this generation of Italians was in a unique position to do away with the Mafia once and for all. We can determine its historic origins and social causes, define the conditions in which it flourishes, and should therefore be able at last not merely to prune a few branches but to strike at its roots. And at the present time all Italian political parties, both in power and in the opposition, consider the Mafia a national shame and are vociferously determined to do what is necessary—conduct investigations, vote *ad hoc* laws and special appropriations—to exterminate it.

We are only the latest in a long line of defeated Mafia fighters. Our forefathers, fathers, and older brothers tried to cure it according to whatever diagnosis was fashionable at the time. These remedies were by no means wrong; but in so far as they were only partially right they produced only partial results. The Mafia was intimidated at times, once in a while driven underground, but never conquered. In fact it always bounced back more powerful and arrogant than before. One hundred and more years of wrong approaches should therefore have made it easy for our generation to determine exactly what is to be done. For some reason, this has not yet happened. At the moment of writing, the Mafia, though hampered and embittered by national and international initiatives, is flourishing more than it ever did in the past.

Our generation should be helped, for one thing, by the vast number of good books now available on the subject. There used to be a few standard authorities that everybody quoted. The best (still the fundamental text) was written in 1876 by Leopoldo Franchetti, called *Condizioni politiche e amministrative della*

*Sicilia.* Franchetti was the descendant of a distinguished Jewish family from Venice, a man of means, a patriot, a *Liberale*, who was made a baron by King Umberto I for his many civic merits. He wrote his book on the basis of only one visit to Sicily, but described the phenomenon more or less as we know it today. Every year since World War II more books have appeared, a few written by foreigners, many of them based on painstaking research or field surveys. There are the famous works of Danilo Dolci (*Report from Palermo, Outlaws, Waste*) which contain a mine of facts gathered at the source. A former judge, Giuseppe Guido Loschiavo, is the author of a learned historic and juridical study called *Cento anni di Mafia.* The feeling of life under the leaden oppression of the society was described by one of Italy's greatest living novelists, a Sicilian school teacher named Leonardo Sciascia, in two novels, *Il giorno della civetta* and *A ciascuno il suo.* There are works by journalists, some of them hurried compilations with lurid covers, and one superior piece of reportage, Michele Pantaleone's *The Mafia and Politics*, with a preface by Carlo Levi, now translated into English.

Pantaleone was born in the town of Villalba, one of the most important Mafia nerve centers, the birthplace and headquarters of Don Calò Vizzini, the highly respected *Numero Uno* until his death a few years ago. Pantaleone learned all about the Mafia in his infancy. It was everywhere around him, in the fear, servility, and resignation of many, the eternal mourning black of the women's dresses. He learned to hate the Mafia and wanted to do something to free his people from the bloody oppression and degrading protection. He began writing a scholarly treatise, with a dissertation on the probable origins of the phenomenon, but when he got around to current events he could no longer hold his passionate indignation in check. He describes intrigues, complicities, bribes, shady business deals, threats, murders; he names every man who benefited by each killing, and every man who did the actual shooting. As a result, the book is a somewhat disorderly accumulation of terrifying stories, some government-shaking disclosures, others little more than Sicilian *faits-divers.* The author excuses himself in the preface: "I have put together various writings . . . adding only a few essential passages to help co-ordinate them . . . Perhaps the results may still be uneven and fragmentary: if so, the blame must be attributed to the several parts of the book having different origins, its original nucleus having been completed with pieces conceived as journalistic reportages." An anonymous reviewer of *The Mafia and Politics* in the London *Economist* complained peevishly: "Surely a book worth printing is also worth writing." This is, however, a pedantic objection. In fact, the confusion adds a dramatic and urgent quality to the book; the disorganized and breathless list of crimes and their complicated explanations reaches at times the cumulative effect of an avalanche. The defect of the book is a different one.

Nobody can deny the author's courage. He denounces the complicity between Christian Democratic leaders and organizers in Sicily and the Mafia, backing his assertions with well-documented examples. He is not even intimidated by the power of the United States. He endeavors to prove that the American Army landings in 1943 had been prepared and aided by the Mafia in contact with American criminals of Sicilian origin, and that Americans are at the back of the Society's current renaissance. He points his accusing finger at the predominant economic forces, the monopolists, the owners of vast land-holdings, the North Italian holding companies, the Banco di Sicilia, all partly responsible for the prevailing state of things in the island and the preservation of the conditions favorable to the Mafia. The book should have created a scandal and should have forced all concerned to take decisive action. Nothing much happened when it first came out in 1962. Not only was Pantaleone not killed by a shotgun blast of the thick lead pellets usually used for hunting *lupi* (wolves), called *lupara*, the efficient weapon employed by the Mafia; he was not even sued for libel. Nobody bothered to issue a denial. No magistrate used the newly published facts to start a new chain of investigations, which might have brought a few of the responsible leaders to justice. Even the anti-Mafia committee of the Italian Parliament filed the book away among its many documents and went on with its own work.

In this particular case, the impact of the revelations was deadened also because the author's Marxist views are too simple-minded. His secondhand, optimistic, and adolescent ideas often prevented him from seeing the whole picture and building up a convincing case. For instance, he tells the story of the aid given by the Mafia to the landing of the American Army in 1943; he does not clearly explain, however, that the Mafia aided every successful revolution and landing of foreigners in Sicily, including that of Garibaldi in 1860, because the Mafia cannot afford not to be on the side of the winner in any historic conflict. At the present moment, it is working hand in hand with the Christian Democrats, who now govern the island. The *Mafiosi* deliver the vote in their districts and intimidate the opposition. Cabinet Ministers do not dislike being seen in public with notorious Mafia leaders or *pezzi da novanta*.[1] The Mafia needs friends in Rome to displace unfriendly police officials or hostile judges, friends in the Regional Government to interpret the laws governing the awards of public contracts and the construction of buildings in new city districts. It must infiltrate all important government bureaus because one of the sources of its power is the sure knowledge of what is going on and what will happen tomorrow. For these reasons it collaborated wholeheartedly with the Bourbons, the *Liberali* of the Right, the *Liberali* of the Left, and, for a time at least, with the Fascists. It is therefore conceivable that, in the event of a Communist victory in Sicily, the Mafia will try to place its own men (or men easily blackmailed by it) in key Party positions, and will offer its precious aid to keep the people obedient and resigned to their fate.

Pantaleone describes the help given by the Mafia to the landowners of the past, which allowed them, the Sicilian barons, to defend their property from the bandits and to keep the starving peasantry in a docile frame of mind. He does not attach much importance to the fact that now, when these estates are mostly owned or controlled by the Regional Government, the

---

[1] The *pezzo da novanta* is literally and figuratively a big shot; it is the last and loudest explosion in a display of fireworks.

Mafia has successfully gained access to the organizations administering or distributing the land to the same starving peasants. Centralization and political control has, in fact, facilitated its task in many fields. It is not interested in land, poverty, or money as such. It is after power. Long ago it developed a natural technique to conquer and wield power, whatever form power may take at different times and places.

The phenomenon has always been too complex and elusive to be entirely enclosed within the limits of any theoretical scheme. The Mafia is notoriously two things, one of which, common to all Sicily, a subtle art of promoting one's interests without killing anybody, should be written with a lower-case m; the other—the Mafia with a capital M, the fluid organization, the secret, far-reaching elite which governs everything legal and illegal, visible and invisible—is to be found exclusively in the Western provinces of the island. (Marxists never manage to explain why, economic and social conditions in both parts of Sicily being virtually identical, one end of the island should have developed the Mafia while the other has always been free from it. They are also embarrassed by the fact that some characteristics and techniques of the Mafia were successfully transplanted to the United States, thousands of miles away in a law-abiding, democratic, industrialized society, but never took roots in Messina or Catania, a few hours distant from Palermo.) The two *mafie* are obscurely related. Surely one could be *mafioso* without being *Mafioso*, but a real *Mafioso* cannot acquire prestige and authority, and rise in the hierarchy of the organization, without being, at the same time, thoroughly *mafioso*.

\*     \*     \*

THERE ARE NUMEROUS and improbable theories concerning the origin of the word. Giuseppe Pitrè (1841–1916), the greatest authority on Sicilian folklore, simply believed that it came from a dialect term common in the Palermo district of Il Borgo expressing beauty and excellence. Palermitani, however, have a peculiar conception of beauty and excellence. You will hear the word used more frequently to describe a fiery and impatient

stallion, a vigorous, multi-colored rooster, a proud, overbearing
girl with flashing eyes and stamping feet. People will say:
"*Mizzica!* What a *mafioso* horse (or cock or woman)!" They
admire the kind of beauty that is flaunted as a challenge, that is
one of the visible aspects of power, the fatal beauty that will
damn timid people who try to conquer it. The word first appeared
in the criminal sense, with a capital *M*, in the title of a dialect
play, *I Mafiusi della Vicaria*, by Giuseppe Rizzotto, which enjoyed
great popularity in 1863. (La Vicaria is Palermo's jail.) The
approximate translation, at the time, would have been: "The
handsome and daring men of La Vicaria". The name stuck. It
has been commonly used by non-Mafia men ever since, but the
*Mafiosi* themselves never use it. They prefer to call themselves
*amici*, "friends" or "friends of friends", and their organization
"*l'onorata societa*", "the honored society" or "the society of
friends".

There is nothing complicated about the spirit inspiring the old
Mafia. A man who wants to preserve his self-respect must personally defend his dignity and honor without turning to the
authorities and the law, especially when the affront to be
punished is an open challenge or an unacceptable insult to his
family. To turn to the authorities and the law for aid is considered dishonorable, and it is more than dishonorable to inform
the police about the activities of anyone forced to defend his
prestige or punished an outrage in the only way open to him.
This imperative, known as *omertà*, is a sacred duty, made even
more sacred by the knowledge that people who talk to the police
sooner or later are found riddled with bullets behind a dusty
hedge of prickly pear. The code is similar to that of many isolated archaic societies, probably influenced by vague memories of
the code of chivalry, whose oral tradition is very much alive in
Sicily. It has been perpetuated by the puppet theater, a popular
form of entertainment, dedicated to the gallant adventures of
the noble knights at the court of Charlemagne. The code therefore has points in common with customs that prevailed until not
long ago among gentlemen everywhere, Southern plantation
owners, members of the Paris Jockey Club, Prussian cavalry

officers, or Monte Carlo gamblers. It was particularly useful in Sicily, where the distances were vast, the roads few, the public institutions practically non-existent, the police and courts impotent, all governments discredited as having been for a long time instruments of foreign oppression, and a man had to look out for himself. He could expect aid only from his relatives. The family was the source of his strength. His duty was to protect it, make it prosper, enlarge it by producing vigorous male children, widen its sphere of influence by allying it to other families, and cultivating influential friends.

There is one means by which a man assures the security and prosperity of his family in a country like Sicily. He must make himself respected, *farsi rispettare*. People must know that he has the power to retaliate for any offense done to him. He must be able to threaten a rival's reputation, his job, his income, and, as a last resort, his life. A man's position in society ultimately depends on the fear he casts in the hearts of envious people. To be sure, an able man does not resort to murder. The mere fact that he can order another man's death (and the suspicion that he might have done so in the past) is enough to ensure all the respect he needs. Here, of course, runs the blurred borderline between the mafia and the Mafia, between a code of primitive behavior and a criminal conspiracy. There is a point where a man becomes powerful enough to command the loyalty of thieves and killers, and to live entirely without the law, obeying only his own primitive idea of justice. He is a Mafia leader. In lonely villages such men, propelled by their own qualities, come out on top, above all rivals. They learn the art of frightening everybody into submission. Their families steal cattle, kidnap stubborn landowners, cut the vines or set fire to the hay of all the farmers who refuse to collaborate and pay a tribute, kill rivals and traitors. Everybody around has to come to terms with them or leave. Other people have to do what favors are requested, hide stolen sheep for one night, shelter a fugitive from justice, in exchange for tranquility. Favors done give a man the right to request favors from the Mafia in turn, or protection from rival Mafia families, and this is why it is almost impossible to tell whether or not a man is a bona fide member of the Society. Franchetti shrewdly noted that many Sicilians who did not belong boasted of being *Mafiosi* while real *Mafiosi* very often emphatically denied the fact.

The recognized chief of the family [Pantaleone writes] is its most authoritative member, even if, as sometimes happens, he is the youngest. The power of a family depends not only on the number of its members but also on the highly placed friendships made by its chief outside the village. The higher and more qualified these connections the higher his reputation and the respect given him by his followers. More than one family can exist on good terms in the same center only if their activities do not compete: for instance, one family might concern itself with the sale of agricultural and horticultural products while the other dealt with the slaughtering of animals; or one with the letting of arable or pasture land and another with robbery and the kidnapping of people.

*          *          *

A NUMBER OF FAMILIES often formed a loose coalition called *cosca*. *Cosca* is the heart of an artichoke. "A *cosca*", Pantaleone explains, "consists of a number of families . . . concerned with the same activity which must never clash with the interest of other *cosche*, or an armed conflict is bound to take place. In the days of huge *latifundia* and feudal lords, the various *cosche* agreed on the limits of each one's area of activity, and if the agreement was infringed, a feud began which led to a series of murders spread over many years." City *cosche* are slightly different. They are the degenerate forms of ancient guilds: they regulate the functions of particular markets, flowers, meats, fruit and vegetables, flour and bread, fix prices, prevent competition, exact a tribute on all transactions, and enforce their decrees first by threats, random shots, kidnappings, and finally, in extreme cases, murder. In the country and in the cities, the power of the *cosche* is such that they constitute states within the state, and control everything. No contract for public works is awarded, no farm is sold, no pasture land rented, no girl is married, no official is elected without the local *cosca*'s consent. There are no hard and fast rules. Pantaleone notes that:

the hierarchy, if such a term can be used, is established through the respect that each individual member can gain for himself. A real Mafia chief must be daring, cool-headed, astute, and violent at the same time; he must be quick-witted, and, if the occasion arises, even quicker-handed . . . Above all he must have connections in all levels of society. If he is isolated he cannot be strong; even if he is the most feared and violent man in the family or *cosca*, and the most experienced killer, he will never become a chief and will never carry any weight in the *consorteria*.

*Consorteria* is the alliance of various *cosche*. All this forms a fine network which encloses every activity in Sicily. Whatever a man does, water his garden, buy a book, take a ride in his automobile, he pays an invisible tribute to some Mafia or other.

The Bourbons considered the Mafia merely as an obstinate form of banditry, and tried to exterminate it with brutality. Entire families suspected of illegal activities were arrested, deported, or killed; villages were evacuated and destroyed, sometimes burned with all their inhabitants; property was indiscriminately confiscated on the strength of hearsay in formation without the pretense of legal forms. The *Mafiosi* were often forced to find shelter in wooded mountains and to behave with extreme caution. But the activities of the forces of order were sporadic, communications were slow and bad, roads almost nonexistent, and the government men scarce and isolated. The temptation to come to terms with the bandits was strong: they could assure a semblance of social peace and avoid disorders in exchange for almost insignificant favors. After the unification of Italy, General Giuseppe Govone, a Piedmontese, was sent in to pacify the island with twenty battalions of *bersaglieri*. He considered the *Mafiosi* reactionary armed rebels against the government of the new unified Liberal Italy. He treated them accordingly. Like his predecessors he killed thousands of people in the hope that among them were members of the Society, burned crops and villages, spreading terror everywhere. The problem was only partially solved, but the general's ways provoked cries of indignation from the press and Parliament. The *Liberali* governments adopted more humane methods that accorded with the prevalent ideas of the nineteenth century, and were based on a Parliamentary investigation and Baron Franchetti's report.

*       *       *

THE MAFIA, according to the view current at the time, was the product of the general backwardness of Sicilian life and of the bad governments which had ruled the island for many centuries. The *Liberali* slowly and parsimoniously started building roads and railways, schools, ports, bridges, promoted commerce and industry as well as they could, disseminated *carabinieri* posts in the villages, and set up courts to defend private property, and tried to govern Sicily as if it were an ordinary Italian region. Once again the Mafia prospered. The mildness of the new ways was mistaken for weakness. The Mafia not only resumed its old activities, but boldly enlarged upon them, exploiting the modest wealth produced by new investments, subsidies, and public works. Ambitious politicians who wanted to be elected *deputati* discovered how convenient it was to be on not too unfriendly terms with the local chief and treated him with some complaisance if not outright amiability: in troubled times, times of famine and social unrest, he kept the district peaceful and avoided all sorts of complications. He was always tactful, reliable, discreet, and kept in the background, dressed in his inconspicuous peasant velvet clothes. He was rarely associated with any crime. Eventually the *Liberali* had to admit that centuries-old social conditions could not be changed in a matter of decades.

The Fascists were helped to power by the Mafia. The "friends" well understood their use of paternalistic protection for the docile, and ruthless persecution for the rebellious. In the Mafia style also was the vigorous and manly appearance of the young blackshirts and their flashy uniforms. But Mussolini was too much like a Mafia leader himself to tolerate the secret existence of a parallel and rival organization. He decided to break its power and sent to Palermo a resolute high police official, Cesare Mori, with orders to do whatever was necessary within or without the law. Mori was successful for a time, arresting and deporting a number of Mafia leaders. Pantaleone admits: "Only a dictatorship can adopt such methods and achieve such results, because only a dictatorship can operate in the silence afforded by the suppression of information and criticism . . . After Mori's repressive measures people were able to go into the country without fear of attack . . . and they praised the new régime." The society lost prestige and authority. But the big *Mafiosi* did not panic. They waited, as they had waited before under the Bourbons and General Govone. Their day came in 1943, when, as Pantaleone points out, the newly landed Americans named most of the Mafia leaders mayors of their towns and villages: they were all officially classified as political victims of the Fascist tyranny.

*          *          *

AFTER THE WAR, the new democratic Republic attacked the problem on all fronts. All the past remedies were applied with new energy and new ones tried for the first time. The island acquired home rule, *autonomia regionale*, so that nobody could again say that the government and the laws represented the will of foreign oppressors. Land reform laws broke up the *latifundia* and destroyed what was left of the power of the barons. A flood of billions of lire, including American grants and loans from the World Bank, promoted public works, the creation of new industries, schools, roads, land reclamation, and irrigation projects on an unprecedented scale. The cities swelled out of their old boundaries, modern quarters were constructed for the new and affluent middle class. (The absence of a middle class was considered by Franchetti one of the factors determining the growth of the Mafia.) Meanwhile, sociologists, historians, economists, and political experts probed the deep causes of the phenomenon. The press played up Mafia crimes. A Parliamentary committee was formed with the broad powers necessary to investigate, provoke government action, and promote *ad hoc* legislation. The police forces and the *carabinieri* in Sicily were almost as numerous as the soldiers of General Govone; they acted within the law most of the time, and were furnished with modern equipment, automobiles, radios, radar, walkie-talkies.

The result of all this was somewhat discouraging, surely out of proportion to the money spent and the efforts made. The number of Mafia murders has steadily increased. The *Mafiosi* have infiltrated or control indirectly the nerve centers of the regional government, have a stranglehold on public contracts (they built most of the roads which were supposedly to spell their doom), and eventually exacted a tribute from the new activities of modern, industrialized, democratic Sicily. Their collaboration is still considered indispensable at election time and some candidates, the more successful ones, will do anything to secure it. As a result, if the Mafia now has more enemies in Rome than ever before, it also has more powerful friends. Some illegal activities, like dope smuggling to the United States and the introduction into Italy of contraband cigarettes, have opened opportunities for vast and regular gain in comparison with which the profits from stealing mangy sheep and kidnapping insolvent barons are insignificant. The old peasant *Mafiosi* are disappearing. There is now an urban, well-dressed, well-traveled, well-educated, slick, middle-class Mafia, which knows how to muscle in on big legitimate business deals, organize "protective societies", and rake in billions of lire in cuts and kickbacks. Many of them, the best and most powerful, have no visible connection with the Mafia. Their legal past is without a blemish. They are however more unscrupulous and ruthless than the older *Mafiosi*. They literally stop at nothing.

\* \* \*

ALL THIS is known to the police, the authorities, the members of the Parliamentary committee. Obviously most remedies tried were once again only partial. Some turned out to be no remedies at all, but incentives. Obviously the Mafia can exist even without poverty, illiteracy, social injustice, feudalism, *latifundia*, and foreign rulers. Like all other activities, it prospered, in fact, when backward social and economic conditions were removed. Probably too much emphasis was put on its criminal activities, which are the main subject of Pantaleone's book. This is not to say they are not important. But the killers are the last men in a long chain of command, the expendable foot soldiers, whose sergeants are the *cosca* chiefs, and whose captains are the *pezzi da novanta*. They all take orders from above and, as in all well-regulated empires, are employed when everything else has been tried in vain. For every man killed in Sicily there are thousands of cases in which violence was not used because it was not necessary. Obviously it is the silent intimidation of the multitudes that makes the Mafia what it is.

The men responsible are the great policy-makers, the generals and statesmen, the apparently respectable businessmen, the corrupt politicians who control entire sections of Sicilian legitimate activities. The best (as Mafia men have always done) do not employ force. They do not have to. But everybody knows that their power springs from the old Mafia roots. They can still condemn any man to death and can count on *omertà* to keep their secrets from the police. Pantaleone suggests that a vast press campaign should change the moral climate of the island. He is right, of course, but only partially right. A vast press campaign is going on, not only in Sicily but in the rest of Italy, Europe, and the world, which eventually may produce results. But press campaigns are seldom enough. The government should continue to do what it has been doing, encourage investments in industry and agriculture, disseminate schools, courts, police stations, along a network of roads. It will take time, but all this will eventually produce a more prosperous and modern society, in which younger men may consider Mafia murders and *omertà* intolerable anachronisms.

Results are slow because several factors are still hindering the process of transformation. To begin with, some of the best Sicilians, the resolute ones who refuse to play the Mafia game, have for decades been leaving the island for more tranquil surroundings in continental Italy and the rest of the world. Then, too, the Rome government is not so efficient and free from corruption as it should be to set things right in Palermo. Finally, in recently industrialized areas, where the economy is largely

influenced by politics, the power struggle characteristically produces methods for the intimidation and defeat of rivals that are
similar to the modern elusive Mafia techniques. Here the new
middle-class *Mafiosi* find themselves at home.

Will the Mafia ever be eradicated? The old, illiterate,
peasant, criminal Mafia is already doomed. How much longer
will the new Mafia endure? It will be destroyed only by time,
if at all. Italy is more and more becoming a Southern province
of a uniform, homogenized Europe, and Sicily a tiny island
adjunct to it. Palermo is no longer a far-away exotic city. It can
be reached in only a few hours from Rome, Paris, or London.
The ways of the Mafia may slowly, very slowly, go the way of all
primitive and quaint folk habits, curious traditions to be recounted to tourists and evoked by decrepit old men. Or they may
not.